US Foreign Policy and the Iran Hostage Crisis

Why did a handful of Iranian students seize the American Embassy in Tehran in November 1979? Why did most members of the US government initially believe that the incident would be over quickly? Why did the Carter administration then decide to launch a rescue mission, and why did it fail so spectacularly? *US Foreign Policy and the Iran Hostage Crisis* examines these puzzles and others, using an analogical reasoning approach to decision-making, a theoretical perspective which highlights the role played by historical analogies in the genesis of foreign policy decisions. Twenty years after the failure of the hostage rescue operation, Houghton uses interviews with key decision-makers on both sides to reconsider these events – events which continue to poison relations between the two states. The book will be of interest to students and scholars of foreign policy analysis and international relations.

DAVID PATRICK HOUGHTON is Lecturer in Government at the University of Essex. He has published widely in the fields of foreign policy decision-making, American foreign policy and International Relations, with articles in journals such as *British Journal of Political Science*, *Political Psychology*, *Policy Sciences* and *Security Studies*.

CAMBRIDGE STUDIES IN INTERNATIONAL RELATIONS: 75

US Foreign Policy and the Iran Hostage Crisis

CAMBRIDGE STUDIES IN INTERNATIONAL RELATIONS

Series list continues after the Index

US Foreign Policy
and the Iran Hostage Crisis

David Patrick Houghton

CAMBRIDGE
UNIVERSITY PRESS

PUBLISHED BY THE PRESS SYNDICATE OF THE UNIVERSITY OF CAMBRIDGE
The Pitt Building, Trumpington Street, Cambridge, United Kingdom

CAMBRIDGE UNIVERSITY PRESS
The Edinburgh Building, Cambridge CB2 2RU, UK
40 West 20th Street, New York NY10011–4211, USA
10 Stamford Road, Oakleigh, VIC 3166, Australia
Ruiz de Alarcón 13, 28014 Madrid, Spain
Dock House, The Waterfront, Cape Town 8001, South Africa

http://www.cambridge.org

First published 2001

Printed in the United Kingdom at the University Press, Cambridge

Typeface 10/12.5pt Palatino   *System* Poltype® [VN]

A catalogue record for this book is available from the British Library

Library of Congress cataloguing in publication data

Houghton, David Patrick.
U.S. foreign policy and the Iran hostage crisis/David Patrick Houghton.
    p.   cm. – (Cambridge studies in international relations; 75)
Includes bibliographical references and index.
ISBN 0 521 80116 8 – ISBN 0 521 80509 0 (pb)
1. Iran Hostage Crisis, 1979–1981.   2. United States – Foreign
relations – 1977–1981 – Decision making.   3. United States – Foreign
relations – Iran.   4. Iran – Foreign relations – United States.   I. Title:
United States foreign policy and the Iran hostage crisis.   II. Series.

E183.8.I55 H68 2001
955.05'42 – dc21   00-045453

ISBN 0 521 80116 8 hardback
ISBN 0 521 80509 0 paperback

Contents

Preface

Like most books, this one owes several profound debts of gratitude. The argument presented here – and my interest in analogical reasoning in foreign policy analysis generally, the subject of this book – owes a great deal to the work of Yuen Foong Khong. Reading Khong's *Analogies at War*, which is a study of how the Vietnam decision-makers reasoned analogically about whether to escalate America's involvement in that disasterous war, got me thinking about other areas of American foreign policy to which Khong's theoretical insights might be applied, and the book proved a constant source of guidance and inspiration. A similarly formative influence was Richard Neustadt and Ernest May's *Thinking in Time*, whose title, I learned later on joining the faculty of the Department of Government at Essex, was provided by Anthony King. This work also obviously owes an intellectual debt to a great many people whose prior research in this and related areas has inspired my own efforts. Apart from those already mentioned, Alexander George, Robert Jervis, Ole Holsti and Yaacov Vertzberger in particular have all contributed powerful insights to the study of foreign policy decision-making and/or the investigation of the role that analogizing plays in the policy-making process, and without their sterling work in these fields this book would almost certainly never have been written.

I would also like to extend particular thanks to the individuals who agreed to be interviewed in relation to this project, and to the staff of the Jimmy Carter Library in Atlanta, who were invariably friendly and helped me find my way around the initially daunting presidential library system. Former Secretary of State Cyrus Vance was particularly generous with his time, and talking to him in his law office in New York City was a special honour since this, so he assured me, was the first interview he had ever granted to an academic in relation to the Iran hostage crisis. We chatted for almost two hours about the hostage situation, and our discussion ranged over many other foreign policy topics as well, including his recent role in the attempt to reach a negotiated settlement to the recent war in Bosnia. Former Director of Central Intelligence Stansfield Turner was also especially helpful, as was ex-National Security Council Adviser Gary Sick. The author would also like to extend warmest thanks to Zbigniew Brzezinski, who also graciously agreed to be interviewed and gave generously of his time. Efforts were also made to contact former President Jimmy Carter, former Defence Secretary Harold Brown, former White House Chief of Staff Hamilton Jordan and former Assistant Secretary of State Harold Saunders, all of whom either declined to be interviewed or failed to respond to my request.

Three anonymous reviewers suggested numerous helpful changes to the text of this book, and I owe them another debt of gratitude. I am especially grateful to the reviewer who suggested that I contact Michael Csaky of the British film company Antelope Productions, for instance, since this turned out to have a major impact upon the development of the argument which appears in Chapter 3. This was excellent advice. Mr Csaky made a superlative documentary about the Iran hostage crisis during the course of 1997 and 1998, and in doing so had accumulated a large stock of interview transcripts with Iranian and American figures who played a major role in that crisis. Mr Csaky and his assistant Katrina Chaloner kindly made many of these transcripts available to me, and their help has undoubtedly made this a much better book than it would otherwise be. At Cambridge University Press, Steve Smith and John Haslam were always helpful, and Sheila Kane's first-rate copyediting greatly improved the book's style and language.

The argument presented in Chapters 4 and 5 draws on an article I published in the *British Journal of Political Science* in October 1996, entitled 'The Role of Analogical Reasoning in Novel Foreign Policy Situations'. The anonymous reviewers of this piece were immensely helpful in strengthening the argument set forward there, and many of their insights have naturally been incorporated into this larger work. Funding for the interview expenses associated with this project was generously provided by Bert Rockman's Colloquium on American Politics and Society (CAPS) and by the Department of Political Science, both at the University of Pittsburgh, where I was based as a Teaching Fellow and Ph.D. student during most of the research I conducted for this book. Another debt of gratitude is owed in particular to Brian

Ripley, who taught me practically all I know about cognition and foreign policy while I was a student at Pittsburgh, and to Guy Peters, who was kind enough to read some of the material included here in its original form as part of a Ph.D. dissertation, as were Morris Ogul and Phil Williams. My graduate student colleagues at Pittsburgh – notably Paul Taggart and Tony Zito, who now teach at Sussex and Newcastle respectively – were also invariably helpful.

Special thanks is also due of course to my numerous colleagues at the University of Essex, where I am now based. The author would especially like to thank Anthony King, Hugh Ward, Neil Robinson and Joe Foweraker for their incisive comments on an earlier version of Chapter 3 when it was presented at Essex's Department of Government seminar series. Joe was also kind enough to reduce my teaching duties during the 1998 Autumn term, allowing me the time I needed to write much of the text for this book. Albert Weale, who took over from Joe as Department Chair, did a similar thing in Autumn 1999 and was a constant source of encouragement in the writing of this book.

One of my greatest regrets is that I never got the chance to interview Richard Cottam in relation to this project. His office at Pittsburgh, where he taught since the 1960s, was just down the corridor from the carrel I occupied as a graduate student, but since he was suffering from cancer at the time I was never able to talk to him. That was unfortunate for me in several ways: Professor Cottam was not only an expert on Iran and foreign policy decision-making, but was also – as discussed in Chapter 4 – one of the American government's main negotiating channels to Iran at one stage during the hostage crisis. He was also stationed in the American embassy during the CIA's 1953 coup. This book is almost certainly all the poorer without the help and input he gave to others throughout his career.

My greatest debt of gratitude, however, is owed to my wife Annabelle Conroy, my daughter Isabelle and my parents. While I was writing much of this book, Annabelle was lecturing in the Government Department at the London School of Economics, but had to bear a very disproportionate share of the child minding duties while I wrote the text of this book, cloistered in our study. There is a sense in which Annabelle, Isabelle and Carlos were 'hostages' during the writing of this book; I am glad to finally set them all free.

1 Jimmy Carter and the tragedy of foreign policy

When an American president has been defeated at the November election held to determine who will sit in the Oval Office for the next four years, he usually spends the last days and hours of his presidency preparing for the handover of power which takes place the following January. He contemplates, usually with much regret, the change which has come over his life, undoubtedly mulling over the unpleasant and sometimes icy task of escorting the winning candidate to his inauguration. He begins to plan what will come next, perhaps thinking about the arrangements for the presidential library which will carry his name.

The end of Jimmy Carter's presidency was different. His last two days were spent cloistered in the Oval Office with his closest advisers, enmeshed until the very last minutes in an issue which had come to obsess him personally and which helped destroy any prospect he might have had of achieving re-election in 1980: the release of the American hostages who had been held in Tehran for almost 444 days. That issue was about to become another man's problem. But Jimmy Carter was not a man to leave loose ends. There was unfinished business to do.

The president and his closest advisers worked around the clock, eating their meals in the Oval Office, their only sleep an occasional cat nap on one of the sofas which now adorn the Jimmy Carter Library in Atlanta. The black and white photographs of these last hours tell the story more vividly than any words can. The photos – reminiscent of the vivid portraits of Lyndon Johnson during the last days of his struggle over Vietnam – show a haggard, sleep-deprived president, surrounded by similarly exhausted advisers doing what they can to reach a deal before time runs out. The photographs, and the ABC News film shot on the day Carter left the presidency, paint a compelling and tragic picture. Even in the car on the way to the inauguration ceremony that

1

would see Ronald Reagan become America's 40th president, Carter was still receiving last minute reports from his adviser Hamilton Jordan on the hostage situation.

The pressure on Carter to act decisively, to do something which would bring the crisis to its resolution and bring the hostages home, had been immense. From the very beginning, the hostage crisis had exerted a striking effect on ordinary Americans, who gradually became as obsessed as Carter with the fate of their countrymen.[1] On ABC television, Ted Koppel began hosting a nightly programme – which later became *Nightline* – endlessly detailing the latest developments in the crisis, while on CBS Walter Cronkite, a man implicitly trusted by most Americans, kept up the continual pressure on Carter by signing off his newscast each night with the number of days the hostages had been held in captivity. Americans bought yellow ribbons and Iranian flags in record numbers (the ribbons for tying to oak trees, the flags for public burning). Stunned by the hatred they saw broadcast daily from Iran on the nightly news but found well-nigh incomprehensible, Americans had responded with a nationalism, and often a jingoism, of their own. Archival television footage captures the vivid colours of the times: the yellow of the ribbons, the red, white and blue of Old Glory and effigies of Uncle Sam, the green and rusty brown of Iran's standard, and, perhaps most of all, the symbol-laden red and orange of fire.

By the spring of 1980 Carter had tried every peaceful means he could think of to obtain the release of the hostages. He had stopped importing Iranian oil, broken off diplomatic relations, asked the United Nations to intercede, sent a variety of third parties and intermediaries to Tehran, brainstormed America's Iranian experts in the universities, and more besides. Nothing he tried had produced the desired result. Five months into the crisis he had then, on 24 April 1980, resorted to a military rescue mission, an option initially considered so difficult to implement that it had been more or less rejected by military planners early on.

The mission was the greatest disaster of Carter's presidency. Eight servicemen died in the rescue attempt, all as a result of a collision between aircraft which occurred following the cancellation of the operation midway through. To make matters worse, the remaining members of the rescue force chose or were compelled to leave behind the bodies of their colleagues – together with sensitive government documents – in the Iranian desert. Both the bodies and the documents were

[1] Gary Sick, *October Surprise: America's Hostages in Iran and the Election of Ronald Reagan* (New York: Times Books/Random House, 1991), pp. 17–18.

soon publicly and triumphally paraded by Iran's Ayatollah Khomeini, much to President Carter's disgust. At 1.15 on the morning of 25 April the events of the previous day were made public in a statement issued from the White House; then, at 7 o'clock that same morning, a devastated and ashen-faced Jimmy Carter appeared live on national television and radio to announce that America had tried to free the hostages militarily but had failed. Speaking from the Oval Office, Carter made a frank statement:

> I ordered this rescue mission prepared in order to safeguard American lives, to protect America's national interests, and to reduce the tensions in the world that have been caused among many nations as this crisis has continued. It was my decision to attempt the rescue operation. It was my decision to cancel it when problems developed in the placement of our rescue team for a future rescue operation. The responsibility is fully my own . . . The United States remains determined to bring about their safe release at the earliest date possible.

Perhaps surprisingly, the immediate public reaction to the announcement of the failed mission was favourable to the president. On 4 November 1979 – the day the hostages were seized – Carter's approval rating was a meagre 32 per cent, but it rose dramatically to 61 per cent shortly thereafter. As Kenneth Morris explains, 'although the effect was not immediate, in the way that Americans rally behind the president in times of international crisis Carter soon saw his approval ratings rising. By the end of November they had once again crossed the 50 percent mark; by January they approached 60 percent.'[2] While these ratings began to fall again thereafter, there was also a rather more modest 'rally around the flag' effect after Carter announced that he had tried to rescue the hostages. Carter's approval rating rose from 39 per cent before the announcement to 43 per cent shortly after. Some members of America's foreign policy establishment also lauded Carter's attempt, seeing the move as a brave, well-intentioned and perhaps unavoidable effort to restore American pride. James Schlesinger, for instance, called it a 'courageous decision', which had 'drawn the public support deservedly given to Presidents during times of trouble'. The global dangers of not acting in the face of such an unforgivable provocation were too great and were outweighed by the disadvantages, he argued.[3] Former Secretary of State Henry Kissinger and future CIA Director James

---

[2] Kenneth Morris, *Jimmy Carter: American Moralist* (Athens, Georgia: University of Georgia Press, 1996), pp. 277–8.
[3] James Schlesinger, 'Some Lessons of Iran', *New York Times*, 6 May 1980.

Woolsey also voiced their support in the days after the failed raid.[4]

In the longer term, however, the effects were deeply negative. By the middle of Summer 1980, the proportion of Americans saying that they approved of Carter's overall performance had fallen to a low of 21 per cent.[5] For many in the American and international media, the failed mission was emblematic of the Carter administration as a whole, providing yet further evidence of the foreign policy incompetence with which they had long charged James Earl Carter as a president.[6] The campaign of Ronald Reagan consciously fed upon the atmosphere of disillusionment, frustration and national impotence which the failed rescue mission had helped to instil. While foreign policy was certainly not the only or decisive factor which led to Carter's defeat in the presidential election of 1980 – the state of the economy, as is so often the case at national US elections, had a decisive effect upon the incumbent's fortunes – seemingly insoluble foreign and economic policy difficulties meshed together to create the inevitable appearance of a well-intentioned but ultimately failed presidency.

This book is about the crisis which brought Jimmy Carter to this point. It is about a tragedy in American and Iranian foreign policy which continues to affect relations between the two nations today, memories of which continue to engender distrust and dislike. Before embarking upon the narrative which follows, however, some disclaimers are in order. This book is not intended as a full history of US–Iranian relations. This task has already been undertaken with consummate skill by others. Nor is it even intended as a full history of the Iranian hostage crisis, or an attempt to document the twists and turns which beset the process of negotiating the release of the hostages (interesting though these may be to students of diplomacy or bargaining technique).[7] Some phases in the hostage crisis are deliberately given

---

[4] See 'US Patience Not Endless, Kissinger Says of Effort', *Los Angeles Times*, 26 April 1980; R. James Woolsey, 'Sometimes The Long Shots Pay Off', *Washington Post*, 28 April 1980.

[5] The polling data are taken from James Q. Wilson, *American Government: Institutions and Policies*, 5th edn (Lexington, Massachusetts: DC Heath, 1992), p. 557 and Charles Kegley and Eugene Wittkopf, *American Foreign Policy: Pattern and Process* (New York: St. Martin's Press, 1996), p. 280.

[6] See, for instance, *Newsweek*, 5 May 1980; *Time*, 5 May 1980; Richard Barnet, 'The Failure of a Raid – and of a Policy', *Los Angeles Times*, 29 April 1980; *The Economist*, 'Shrunken America', 3 May 1980.

[7] See for instance, James Bill, *The Eagle and the Lion: The Tragedy of American–Iranian Relations* (London: Yale University Press, 1988), which is probably the best introduction to the subject in print. For a detailed analysis of the negotiations, see Russell Moses, *Freeing the Hostages: Re-Examining the US–Iranian Negotiations and Soviet Policy, 1979–1981* (Pittsburgh, Pennsylvania: University of Pittsburgh Press, 1985).

more attention than others in this book, and the bulk of the narrative focuses by necessity on the American side rather than the Iranian one, not least because we know so much more about the former than we do the latter. Rather than attempting to be any of these things, this book represents an effort to understand the positions taken by the major actors in the conflict over the hostages. It seeks to explain, in broad brush strokes, why they came to the decisions they did at key moments of decision.

The puzzles to be explained

Any thoughtful reader of historical accounts of the Iran hostage crisis is confronted by numerous puzzles which seem to demand one's attention. Not least of these – from a Western commentator's perspective at least – is why the crisis occurred at all. On 4 November 1979 several hundred Iranian students managed to storm the American embassy in Tehran and take the embassy staff hostage, thus precipitating one of the longest and most diplomatically damaging crises in both American and Iranian history. And yet our understanding of why the students acted as they did is still incomplete. Many of Carter's former advisers to this day dismiss the action as a politically inspired if ingenious ruse constructed by the Ayatollah Khomeini to drum up support for his own faction in the power struggle which accompanied the Iranian revolution of 1979. Others – notably Carter himself – suggest that it was simply an act of madness, so irrational that it cannot be explained in terms reasonable people might comprehend. Neither of these explanations seems to accord with the facts now available, however. This study is motivated in part by the conviction that there has to be some more 'human' reason why the students seized the embassy building in the first place. In the United States particularly, it has been difficult for even the most sober commentators not to get swept up in the emotions which the hostage crisis inevitably evoked. Rather than seeking to condemn or condone the students' actions, however, this book simply attempts to explain why these actions occurred.

The puzzles multiply on the American side of the equation. Initially, the Carter administration tried to resolve the crisis by peaceful means. Spearheaded by Secretary of State Cyrus Vance, the United States tried numerous attempts to open up negotiation channels with the Khomeini regime in Tehran. This track was abandoned in April 1980 when President Carter tried to free the hostages using military force. Why, though, did Carter and Vance – two individuals strikingly similar in world-view and overall philosophy – come by the early part of that year to such different conclusions about the prospects for a negotiated solution, the latter to the point where he felt he could no longer in good conscience serve the former?

Vance had always opposed the rescue bid, and he resigned soon after its failure, having already tendered his resignation in private before the mission was launched.[8] Whereas Carter felt that the mission should go ahead because 'our people would be far safer in the hands of the American rescue team', Vance was convinced that negotiations had to be given more time, that even a successful mission would backfire on the United States, and that it probably would not succeed in any case. Why, though, was Vance so persuaded that this was likely to be so, and on what basis did he continue to predict that the hostages would eventually be released unharmed in the absence of military action, even after practically everyone else in the government – ardent doves included – had concluded that enough was enough? Clearly, simple belief system approaches will not suffice to account for such variability, so some explanation is needed as to why the secretary of state disagreed so strongly with the President's other advisers and with Carter himself.

A third puzzle addressed here concerns the Iran rescue mission itself and the reasons why a president like Jimmy Carter would undertake such an operation. The greatest puzzle of all in the Iran hostage crisis, and arguably the hardest to understand, is why a president as *moralistic*, idealistic and committed to non-military means of conflict resolution as this one would launch an operation which he had been warned would almost certainly result in at least some loss of life. As numerous commentators on his administration have pointed out, Jimmy Carter advocated an intensely moralistic vision of foreign policy in which human rights were to be given overall priority, and government was to engage in a 'humane mission' or crusade to convert the rest of the world to American ideals. William Morris, for instance, has argued that Carter is 'propelled by powerful moral passions', which he traces to his evangelical Christian faith, Southern populism and the influence of the 1960s civil rights movement.[9] Erwin Hargrove similarly notes that for Carter 'religious faith was central to his life. Faith shaped his understanding of himself and others, his belief about the political purposes of

---

[8] He was the first holder of that office to resign on a matter of principle since William Jennings Bryan in 1915, and the only one in the years since.
[9] Morris, *Jimmy Carter*, pp. 7–8.

government and his style of authority . . . he saw politics as a moral activity.'[10] Stephen Skowronek also sees a strong moral strain in Carter, arguing that he set himself leadership standards so high that they were well-nigh impossible to meet,[11] Charles Jones notes that Carter 'is a moralizer . . . motivated to do what is right'[12] and Gary Sick says that Carter 'was the personification of small-town middle-American values', with religious beliefs 'that were so deep as to be instinctive'.[13]

In the Iranian case, this general concern with morality and rights translated into a particular concern for the lives of the hostages, and led to a determination to give the matter absolute priority. As Carter himself points out in his memoirs, 'the safety and well-being of the American hostages became a constant concern for me, no matter what other duties I was performing as President . . . I was restrained from a preemptive military strike by the realization that the Iranian fanatics would almost certainly kill the hostages in response.'[14] And yet, as president, Carter embarked upon a course of action which – since even successful rescue operations invariably lead to some loss of human life – seemed irretrievably bound to violate his own canonistic ideals. According to one estimate provided in a memorandum sent to CIA Director Stansfield Turner on 16 March 1980 – a little over a month before the mission was launched – no less than 60 per cent of the hostages were likely to lose their lives if the raid went ahead: 20 per cent during the initial assault on the embassy, 25 per cent during the location and identification of the hostages and 15 per cent during their evacuation to the waiting American C-130 aircraft. 'It is presumed to be equally as likely that the Amembassy (*sic*) rescue attempt would be a complete success (100% of the Amembassy hostages rescued), as it would be a complete failure (0% of the Amembassy hostages rescued)', the report concluded.[15]

Of course, such estimates can only be conjecture, since the operation

---

[10] Erwin Hargrove, *Jimmy Carter as President: Leadership and the Politics of the Public Good* (Baton Rouge, Lousiana: Louisiana State University Press, 1988), p. 8.

[11] Stephen Skowronek, *The Politics Presidents Make: Leadership from John Adams to Bill Clinton* (Cambridge, Massachusetts: Belknap Press, 1997).

[12] Charles Jones, *The Trusteeship Presidency: Jimmy Carter and the United States Congress* (Baton Rouge, Louisiana: Louisiana State University Press, 1988), p. 217.

[13] Gary Sick, *All Fall Down: America's Tragic Encounter With Iran* (New York: Random House, 1985), p. 257. See also David Kucharsky, *The Man From Plains* (London: Collins, 1977).

[14] Jimmy Carter, *Keeping Faith: Memoirs of a President* (Fayetteville, Arkansas: University of Arkansas Press, 1995), p. 468.

[15] Cited in Pierre Salinger, *America Held Hostage: The Secret Negotiations* (Garden City, New York: Doubleday, 1981), pp. 237–8.

never actually reached the stages alluded to. Moreover, the significance of the above report has subsequently been discounted by Stansfield Turner as playing no meaningful role in the decision-making. 'There was such a report', Turner admits, but he argues that its message and significance have been 'greatly exaggerated'. The report began, he said, 'with a description of a social scientific theory which purported to predict the likelihood of events occurring'. Written by someone lower down in the echelons of the CIA, 'I received this report which said that there was about a 35% probability of success', but it also concluded that 'this is not something on which you should make a decision'.[16]

It is unclear whether the president himself ever saw this report. Nevertheless, what is clear is that Carter knew that there would almost certainly be at least *some* casualties if the mission went ahead. According to Benjamin Schemmer, Carter was explicitly told that 'there could be casualties on both sides if something went awry' in a meeting with military briefers on 16 April 1980, a week before the mission went ahead.[17] James Vaught, one of the mission's commanders, estimated at the meeting that 'six or seven members of Delta and two or three hostages' would likely be killed in the operation.[18] As Carter's press secretary Jody Powell puts it, 'no one doubted that there would be American casualties, even in a successful operation. One Israeli soldier and three hostages had been killed at Entebbe, and the problems that faced our planners, and would face the strike force, were many times more difficult than anything the Israelis had confronted.'[19] And most critically, according to Admiral James Holloway – author of an official but limited post-mortem which examined the military conduct of the operation – the Joint Chiefs had estimated that the mission had a 60–70 per cent chance of success, but as Paul Ryan notes, this estimate 'meant also that it had a 30 to 40 percent chance of failure. These were not good odds when the lives of fifty-three American hostages were hanging in the balance.'[20] Chairman of the Joint Chiefs David Jones and his colleagues were telling Carter, in other words, that the chance of failure was one in three.

[16] Stansfield Turner, interview with the author, McLean, Virginia, 28 October 1994.
[17] See Benjamin Schemmer, 'Presidential Courage – And the April 1980 Iranian Rescue Mission', *Armed Forces Journal International*, May 1981, p. 61.
[18] Quoted in David Martin and John Walcott, *Best Laid Plans: The Inside Story of America's War Against Terrorism* (New York: Harper & Row, 1988), p. 4.
[19] Jody Powell, *The Other Side of the Story* (New York: William Morrow, 1984), p. 226.
[20] Paul Ryan, *The Iran Hostage Rescue Mission: Why it Failed* (Annapolis, Maryland: Naval Institute Press, 1985), p. 125. See also Special Operations Review Group, Rescue Mission Report, August 1980, Jimmy Carter Library.

As well as the danger to the hostages and to American agents on the ground, Holloway argued, there would have been significant casualties and loss of life among their Iranian captors had the mission gone ahead. As Ryan puts it, once the American servicemen were inside the embassy 'it was certain that the Iranian guards would have been met by a stream of bullets', and in the words of 'Chargin' Charlie' Beckwith – another commander of the operation – the Iranians would simply have been 'blown away'.[21] When asked by Deputy Secretary of State Warren Christopher at the 16 April briefing what would happen to the Iranian captors, Beckwith reportedly replied 'we're going to shoot each of them twice, right between the eyes'.[22] We know that any resistance encountered outside the embassy – for instance, from an Iranian mob – would also have been quelled using military force. In the words of Major Logan Fitch, who would have led the assault on the embassy had it gone ahead as planned, 'we were going to kill a lot of people'.[23]

Although Carter states in his memoirs that the rescuers were under strict orders 'to avoid bloodshed whenever possible' and claimed in a message to Congress that the rescue operation 'was a humanitarian mission',[24] it is virtually inconceivable that this particular president – immersed as ever in the details – was unaware of the uncomfortable facts stated above.[25] As Martin and Walcott note, 'no one who listened to Charlie Beckwith could mistake the fact that the President was sending men to their deaths'.[26] For Carter to give the go-ahead for any sort of military operation was deeply uncharacteristic. During his whole four years in office, this was in fact the only such operation for which the president gave his approval. How, then, did Carter and his advisers (bar Secretary Vance) convince themselves that the considerable risks inherent in the mission were manageable ones?

Like the conflict with Vance, the fact that Carter went ahead with the rescue mission presents a genuine puzzle for those who would argue that beliefs or ideas are what motivate human behaviour. There is a long tradition in the study of foreign policy decision-making (FPDM) which views belief systems as the central determinants of

---

[21] Ryan, *Iran Hostage*, pp. 125, 102. According to Ryan, Beckwith had a sign on his desk which read 'Kill 'Em All. Let God Sort 'Em Out.'
[22] Martin and Walcott, *Best Laid Plans*, p. 4.   [23] Ibid.
[24] See President Carter's 26 April communication to the House and Senate, reproduced in *Congressional Quarterly Almanac*, 96th Congress Second Session 1980, volume XXXVI (Washington DC: Congressional Quarterly, 1981).
[25] Carter, *Keeping Faith*, p. 520. Indeed, the phrase 'whenever possible' indicates a recognition that it would not always be possible to avoid bloodshed, and that casualties were perhaps inevitable.   [26] Martin and Walcott, *Best Laid Plans*, p. 5.

decisions.[27] It has never been satisfactorily explained, however, why someone so obviously wedded to idealism as a public philosophy should have been so seemingly seduced by the notion of a rescue operation which, even if successful, would have inevitably led to the loss of life. At the time there was no indication that any of the hostages had been killed or tortured or that immediate harm was about to come to them. As Rose McDermott notes, 'Carter's action was not only completely contrary to his humanitarian emphasis in world politics but was a highly risky prospect from a military standpoint as well.'[28]

Our fourth and final puzzle is actually a set of puzzles, which can be grouped together under the general heading of why the mission was implemented in the way it was and not in any other way. This was to become an important question during the post-mortems on the rescue mission, many of which were critical of the manner in which the rescue planners had proceeded. Why, in particular, were so few – in fact, only eight – helicopters used in the operation? Why was there such an effort initially to employ an even smaller number? In accounts of Jimmy Carter's management style, one tendency has been widely and repeatedly attributed to his presidency – that of 'micromanagement'. Carter had a well-known habit of immersing himself in details, a trait which has been traced to his technical frame of mind. And yet, when the Iran hostage operation was mounted, the president essentially left the key operational details to the on-site commanders, James Vaught, James Kyle and Charles Beckwith.[29]

This presented a notable contrast with the practice of previous executive level officials. As defence secretary under Gerald Ford during the evacuation of American personnel from Lebanon in 1976, Donald Rumsfeld was apparently in constant telephone contact with – and giving direct orders to – the military rescuers. According to Edward Luttwak, during the *Mayaguez* rescue operation of 1975 'President Ford spoke directly with Navy pilots actually over the target, to make tactical

27 For some classic discussions representative of this approach, see for instance Ole Holsti, 'The Belief System and National Images: A Case Study', *Journal of Conflict Resolution*, 6: 244–52, 1962; Alexander George, 'The "Operational Code": A Neglected Approach to the Study of Political Leaders and Decision-Making', *International Studies Quarterly*, 23: 190–222, 1969; Alexander George, 'The Causal Nexus between Cognitive Beliefs and Decision-Making Behavior: The "Operational Code" Belief System', in Lawrence Falkowski (ed.), *Psychological Models and International Politics* (Epping: Bowker, 1979).
28 Rose McDermott, 'Prospect Theory in International Relations: The Iranian Hostage Rescue Mission', *Political Psychology*, 13: 237–63, 1992, p. 237. In the existing literature, only McDermott has attempted to resolve this conundrum.
29 Schemmer, 'Presidential Courage', p. 61.

decisions in minute detail,'[30] and John Kennedy famously interfered in the operational details of the Bay of Pigs invasion. Given his known predilections, why did Carter not adopt a more characteristic interventionist approach, as others had done in the past?

This book sets out to provide answers as to why the embassy was seized in the first place, why the Carter administration's decisions to negotiate and then to proceed with the rescue operation might have been made, and why these decisions were then implemented in the manner that they were. It is not the only conceivable such set of answers – foreign policy decisions are rarely the result of single causal linkages – but it does seek to throw light upon questions which have hitherto been only partially answered. The argument will be set out in the following section. In order to set the theoretical claims to be made in context, however, a preliminary sketch of the existing published work on the Iran hostage crisis is in order.

The existing literature

The secondary literature examining the questions posed above is considerable, and still increasing steadily: domestic politics, groupthink, bureaucratic politics, prospect theory and personality based accounts have all been offered to explain American decision-making during the hostage crisis.[31] We shall defer a discussion of the existing work on the

[30] Edward Luttwak, *The Pentagon and the Art of War: The Question of Military Reform* (New York: Simon and Schuster, 1984), p. 86.

[31] A substantial secondary literature exists on American decision-making during the hostage crisis: see, for example, Ryan, *The Iran Hostage Rescue Mission*; Steve Smith, 'Policy Preferences and Bureaucratic Position: The Case of the American Hostage Rescue Mission', *International Affairs* 61: 9–25, 1984/1985; Steve Smith, 'Groupthink and the Hostage Rescue Mission', *British Journal of Political Science* 15: 117–23, 1985; James David Barber, *The Presidential Character: Predicting Performance in the White House*, 3rd edn (Englewood Cliffs, New Jersey: Prentice-Hall, 1985), pp. 452–6; Martin Hollis and Steve Smith, 'Roles and Reasons in Foreign Policy Decision Making', *British Journal of Political Science* 16: 269–86, 1986; Betty Glad, 'Personality, Political and Group Process Variables in Foreign Policy Decision-Making: Jimmy Carter's Handling of the Iranian Hostage Crisis', *International Political Science Review* 10: 35–61, 1989; Irving Janis, *Crucial Decisions* (New York: Free Press, 1989), pp. 193–6; Rose McDermott, 'Prospect Theory in International Relations'; Michael Link and Charles Kegley, 'Is Access Influence? Measuring Adviser–Presidential Interactions in the Light of the Iranian Hostage Crisis', *International Interactions* 18: 343–64, 1993; Scott Gartner, 'Predicting the Timing of Carter's Decision to Initiate a Hostage Rescue Attempt: Modelling a Dynamic Information Environment', *International Interactions* 18: 365–86, 1993; David Patrick Houghton, 'The Role of Analogical Reasoning in Novel Foreign Policy Situations', *British Journal of Political Science*, 26: 523–52, 1996. Of these, only the accounts of McDermott and Houghton detail the historical precedents employed by the key participants in the crisis.

Iranian side until chapter 3. A detailed discussion of the American decision-making literature is also deferred until chapter 6, when it will be examined in order to compare the findings of this book with previous research. Nevertheless, one or two general observations about the existing work as a whole seem in order at this point. One of its most notable features is that the hostage crisis has so far not been subjected to a full-length, political science analysis in book form. All of the existing accounts have been published as academic articles, and those book treatments which exist – excellent though they are as historical accounts – do not apply established theories of foreign policy decision-making to the case.[32] There is also no book length study of the psychological perceptions of the decision-makers involved in the Iran hostage case. Interestingly, an internal CIA report does exist which examined the reasons why the CIA failed to predict the Iranian revolution, and its author is Robert Jervis, one of the pioneers of the analysis of psychological perceptions in international relations. The report apparently does not probe the decision-making surrounding the hostage taking, however, and it remains classified.[33] While earlier notable events in the history of American foreign policy – particularly the Cuban missile crisis – have been analysed extensively and exhaustively, we still possess no full-length political science account of the hostage crisis as a whole. There are, no doubt, good reasons for this: while the deliberations of the ExComm during the Cuban missile crisis, for instance, were tape recorded by a pre-Watergate president using hidden microphones – and transcripts of its key meetings are now therefore available to researchers – it seems most unlikely that President Carter ever recorded the discussions of the National Security Council (or of the much smaller, four-man rescue planning group) during the Iran crisis.[34] We also lack official documentary records of the key meetings on Iran, since these have still not been declassified over two decades later.

[32] Gary Sick's excellent *All Fall Down*, for instance, is a broad-ranging account by the note taker at many of the key policy meetings, but it is primarily the work of a practitioner rather than a piece of foreign policy theorizing. Russell Moses's book *Freeing the Hostages* is a little more theoretical, but focuses almost exclusively on the negotiation phase of the decision-making.

[33] The existence and main findings of the report – entitled 'Iran Postmortem' – are described in Bob Woodward, *Veil: The Secret Wars of the CIA 1981–1987* (New York: Simon and Schuster, 1987), pp. 108–11.

[34] As Michael Beschloss notes, 'since the uproar over the Nixon tapes in 1973, Presidents have shrunk from that kind of comprehensive secret recording'; see Beschloss (ed.), *Taking Charge: The Johnson White House Tapes, 1963–1964* (New York: Simon and Schuster, 1997), p. 552.

12

For all of his claims of openness in government, former President Carter has largely failed to grant researchers access to the relevant materials. Anyone seeking to reconstruct these meetings, then, must do so from memoir accounts, personal interviews and secondary sources.[35]

Much of the existing literature on the American side also treats the decision to mount the rescue operation in a relatively isolated way, examining only the March–April 1980 decision-making process and omitting discussion of the previous decisions made during the crisis. This is rather problematic, in the sense that it leaves out an account of the early reasoning processes of the decision-makers as they grappled with the question of how to get the hostages out of Tehran and leaves the reader without a sense of the context in which the eventual decision to launch a rescue operation was made. What follows represents an effort to remedy this problem by examining puzzles derived from several stages of the hostage crisis.

Why the hostage crisis?

Much of this book, as noted already, deals with the American side of the decision-making, and there are a number of analytical reasons – beside the aforementioned incompleteness of the existing literature – for look-ing at the Carter administration's decision-making during the hostage crisis rather than some other case study. Principal among these is its status as a 'hardest case to prove' for the analogical reasoning argument to be elaborated on below. There are a number of reasons why this might be the case.

---

[35] We are blessed with an already substantial biographical literature on Jimmy Carter and the Carter presidency in general. See, for example, Glenn Abernathy (ed.), *The Carter Years: The President and Policy Making* (London: Pinter, 1994); Douglas Brinkley, *The Unfinished Presidency: Jimmy Carter's Journey Beyond the White House* (New York: Viking, 1998); Peter Bourne, *Jimmy Carter: A Comprehensive Biography from Plains to Post-Presidency* (New York: Scribner, 1997); John Dumbrell, *The Carter Presidency* (Manches-ter: Manchester University Press, 1995); Betty Glad, *Jimmy Carter: In Search of the Great White House* (New York: W.W. Norton, 1980); Garland Haas, *Jimmy Carter and the Politics of Frustration* (Jefferson, North Carolina: McFarland, 1992); Hargrove, *Jimmy Carter as President*; Jones, *The Trusteeship Presidency*; Maddox, *Preacher at the White House*; Morris, *Jimmy Carter: American Moralist*; Jerel Rosati, *The Carter Administration's Quest for Global Community: Beliefs and their Impact on Behavior* (Columbia, South Carolina: University of South Carolina Press, 1987); Herbert Rosenbaum and Alexej Ugrinsky (eds.), *Jimmy Carter: Foreign Policy and the Post-Presidential Years* (Westport, Connecticut: Greenwood Press, 1994) and *The Presidency and Domestic Policies of Jimmy Carter* (Westport, Connecticut: Greenwood Press, 1994); and Donald Spencer, *The Carter Implosion: Jimmy Carter and the Amateur Style of Diplomacy* (New York: Praeger, 1988).

First of all, Jimmy Carter provides us with a quite striking example of a president who has a reputation for a 'non-historical style' (in other words, someone who was not in the habit of thinking in historical terms). If President John F. Kennedy and former academics like McGeorge Bundy and Dean Rusk were predisposed to use the lessons of history by virtue of their backgrounds and experiences, the Carter administration offers us an instance of the opposite tendency, according to former Carter speechwriter James Fallows. Carter himself 'would blithely forego the lessons of experience and insist on rediscovering fire, the level, the wheel', Fallows says. 'In two years the only historical allusions I heard Carter use with any frequency were Harry Truman's rise from the depths of the polls and the effect of Roosevelt's New Deal on the southern farm', he recalls. He traces this defect to the president's 'cast of mind', arguing that it stemmed from Carter's engineering and problem-solving background, from 'his view of problems as technical, not historical, his lack of curiosity about how the story turned out before'.[36] Elsewhere Fallows has spoken of Carter thus: 'He viewed problems as cube roots . . . if you find the right answer and use your powers of logical deduction that was it.'[37] Neustadt and May strongly agree with Fallows' analysis, and suggest that 'the staff work inspired by Carter was markedly ahistorical'.[38] Indeed, so widespread was this reputation for ahistoricity among those who had worked in the administration that in the immediate aftermath of the failure of the Iran hostage rescue mission, Carter's former secretary of energy surmised that the mission had probably only been attempted because the Carter officials lacked the 'institutional memory' to recall episodes like the 1970 Son Tay raid, a mostly well executed rescue operation conducted behind enemy lines in Vietnam which went awry when the rescuers discovered that the hostages had been moved to another location.[39] If there is such a thing as an 'ahistorical' thinker – and there seems little room for doubt that some are more taken to the use of historical analogies than others – it is possible that analogizing generally occurs where those confronting a problem are simply inclined to treat it historically, and not because of the cognitive dynamics of the situation or some other factor.

[36] James Fallows, 'The Passionless Presidency', *The Atlantic Monthly*, 243: 33–48, May 1979, p. 44.
[37] See James Fallows, Exit Interview, Jimmy Carter Library, 14 November 1978.
[38] Richard Neustadt and Ernest May, *Thinking in Time: The Uses of History for Decision-Makers* (New York: Free Press, 1986), p. xiv.   [39] Schlesinger, 'Some Lessons of Iran'.

A second reason for examining this case study – and for expecting the analogical reasoning perspective to garner only weak empirical support here – is the unique characteristics of the embassy seizure and its status as a seemingly 'unprecedented' act. In the eyes of many of the participants in the Carter decision-making, there simply was no directly analogous situation available to guide their deliberations. Most notably, a hostile power had never before – at least in the memory or knowledge of most of the Carter people – seized a US embassy abroad or taken its diplomats hostage. Jimmy Carter expressed this belief himself on a number of occasions both during his presidency and after he left office. In 1982, for example, Carter said 'I guess for six hundred years of recorded history as far as I know a host government has never endorsed or condoned the abuse or attack or kidnapping of a nation's emissaries and diplomats. This was a departure from all historical precedent.'[40] Similarly, Deputy Secretary of State Warren Christopher considered the seizure of the Tehran embassy 'an almost unprecedented act and one of extraordinary repugnance',[41] former National Security Adviser Zbigniew Brzezinski argues that 'there was no precedent for such an act, of such duration, to which to refer', while former CIA Director Stansfield Turner notes simply that 'it was such an outrageous thing, such an unprecedented thing'.[42] The thinking of the administration was well summarized by Roberts Owen in his oral argument before the International Court of Justice, where the president initially took his case:

> In diplomatic history and practice there is absolutely no precedent or justification for the seizure of a diplomat – let alone an entire diplomatic mission – and the imprisonment and trial of such persons for the purpose of coercing capitulation to certain demands. I respectfully suggest that it is difficult to think of a more obvious or more gross and flagrant violation of international law.[43]

A third reason for expecting the use of analogical reasoning to be thin on the ground in this case relates to the nature of the strategic circumstances surrounding any possible rescue mission. Many of the

---

[40] Interview with Jimmy Carter, Miller Center Interviews, Carter Presidency Project, 29 November 1982, p. 38, Jimmy Carter Library.

[41] Warren Christopher, 'Introduction', p. 1, in Christopher and Kreisberg, *American Hostages in Iran: The Conduct of a Crisis* (New Haven, Connecticut: Yale University Press, 1985).

[42] Zbigniew Brzezinski, interview with the author, Washington DC, 3 February 1995; Stansfield Turner, interview with the author.

[43] Roberts Owen, 'Oral Argument', pp. 7–8, Box 88, 'Iran–International Court of Justice', Jimmy Carter Library.

decision-makers clearly viewed the mission as hampered by a number of almost unique difficulties, including the location of the hostages and the distances that any rescue team would have to travel in order to make a rescue attempt. According to W. Graham Claytor, for example, 'the entire problem was that the hostages were in Tehran, which is way inland. If it had been on or near the coast, we could have got them out . . . that was a big, unprecedented problem.'[44] According to a still classified CIA report of the time, '*no* analogous large-scale rescue attempts have been mounted in heavily populated urban areas within hostile territory during the past 15 years. The only roughly similar attempts (Son Tay Nov. 1970; *Mayaguez* May 1975; Entebbe July 1976) were all made in lightly populated areas of hostile territory.'[45] Paul Ryan makes a similar point, arguing that 'such an operation had never before been attempted. There was a limited amount of useful information that could be drawn from the raids on Entebbe and Mogadishu, as they were so unlike the Iranian rescue plan.' No helicopters were used in the former missions, Ryan notes, and the rescuers spent relatively little time in enemy territory. 'In the absence of any precedent, how was the decision reached to go ahead?', he asks.[46] Exacerbating these immediate problems was the fact that US forces were unaccustomed to dealing with this kind of threat. Mired as it had been in the Cold War and preoccupied with the Soviet threat, the United States had focused on building up its nuclear armaments in preparation for a possible superpower confrontation, but nuclear resources were next to useless in this case.

For all of these reasons, we have good cause to expect the situation which confronted the Carter people to be treated *sui generis*, as a one-off event to be dealt with in a special and particularized manner. As we shall see in the next chapter, however, analogizing played an especially prominent role in the decision-making, even among a group of people with a reputation for being historically averse. The novel features of the Iranian situation produced deep uncertainty as to how the situation ought to be defined and what the consequent policy response should be, and possibly helped to produce confusion and drift in the decision-making process. The degree of uncertainty was exceptionally high due

---

[44] Quoted in Scott Armstrong, George Wilson and Bob Woodward, 'Debate Rekindles on Failed Iran Raid', *Washington Post*, 25 April 1982, p. A15.
[45] CIA Report to Stansfield Turner dated 16 March 1980, quoted in Salinger, *America Held Hostage*, p. 238.
[46] Ryan, *The Iran Hostage Rescue Mission*, pp. 25–6.

to the decision-makers' general lack of familiarity with the region, the unexpected nature of Iran's actions and so on. The Iran hostage case, then, gives us an excellent opportunity to examine what allegedly technical or non-historical thinkers do when confronted with a highly uncertain, discrete, foreign policy-making task where few direct precedents are available to make sense of the situation. What do decision-makers do when confronted with such an unusual, decidedly non-routine problem?

The argument summarized

The argument as it emerges will be threefold: first, we shall propose that the decisions taken during the crisis – including the decision by the Iranian students to seize the embassy and Carter's fateful decision to mount the rescue operation – were critically affected by a barrage of historical analogies. In order to understand why a group of fanatical Iranian students would suddenly decide to occupy what was then one of the world's best fortified embassies and take its inhabitants hostage, a knowledge of recent events in Iran is essential, as is an appreciation of how previous hostage crises affected consideration of this one on the American side. Despite the fact that many members of the Carter administration viewed the hostage crisis as unique in some significant respects, there is a good deal of evidence to suggest that most of the decision-makers drew upon their own stock of analogies in order to make sense of the crisis. In turn, the choice of analogy, we shall contend, critically affected each actor's 'definition of the situation'. This study, like some earlier decision-making analyses, draws on the findings of cognitive psychological research to understand why this might have been so.

Secondly, it is further proposed that what psychologists have termed the *availability* and *representativeness* of the historical analogies drawn upon by both sides had a crucial effect. For instance, the recency and vividness of the successful Entebbe and Mogadishu rescue missions made them especially available cognitively to the American decision-makers, and the Entebbe analogy, in particular, played a notable role in persuading them that the risks inherent in the rescue operation were ones worth taking. This is suggested by its effect upon the leading advocate of the Tehran mission – National Security Adviser Zbigniew Brzezinski – by the consultations which went on at the outset of the crisis between the Carter administration and the Israelis, by the

attempts the rescue planners made to 'overcome' the differences between Tehran and Entebbe and by the even more explicit effect of
Entebbe upon plans for a second rescue mission. Again, this finding is
bolstered by psychological research which suggests that analogies
which are most cognitively available are most likely to be utilized by
decision-makers in real life cases (we will examine this point in more
detail in chapter 2).

Finally, the analogies used, we shall contend, were not mere rhetorical flourishes designed to convince others of the desirability of various
options after the fact. This is suggested by the fact that the vast majority
of the analogies drawn were done so by individuals with *personal
experience* of the event cited, and were not simply 'grabbed' indiscrimi-
nately from the history books for advocacy purposes alone. This
reinforces the conclusion of an earlier study of analogical reasoning and
its role in foreign policy decision-making – *Analogies at War* by Yuen
Foong Khong – that analogies are genuine cognitive mechanisms used
to make sense of, and impart some kind of order to, the complexities of
political life under conditions of uncertainty. As Khong puts it, 'what is
needed is a perspective that allows an independent cognitive role for
analogies in decision-making without denying that they may also play
an instrumental role in persuading and convincing others in the policy
process'.[47] This study's findings complement those of Khong, and are
highly compatible with what he terms the AE (Analogical Explanation)
framework. As Khong puts it, 'analogies . . . can be viewed as intellectual devices often called upon by policymakers to perform a set of
diagnostic tasks relevant to political decision-making'.[48] We shall return to the debate about the purposes analogies serve in chapter 6, but
we shall proceed from the initial assumption that Khong is correct, and
then compare this cognitive explanation with the rival *ex post* view in
that later chapter.

The major difference between Khong's analysis and this one is that,
while Khong is investigating the question of whether analogies are
truly cognitive mechanisms used for making sense of reality, as opposed to ex-post justifications, I am primarily interested in seeking
answers to two (related) questions. First of all, does the 'style' of
individual decision-makers make a difference to the use of analogical
reasoning? Previous case studies of analogizing in policy-making have

---

[47] Yuen Foong Khong, *Analogies At War: Korea, Munich, Dien Bien Phu and the Vietnam
Decisions of 1965* (Princeton, New Jersey: Princeton University Press, 1992) p. 16.
[48] Ibid., p. 20.

tended to focus on the Kennedy and Johnson administrations – broadly speaking, the same set of individuals – but one could make the argument that a group of individuals less prone to 'think historically' might well not have analogized to the extent that the Kennedy and Johnson people appear to have done during the Bay of Pigs, the Cuban missile crisis, Vietnam, the Dominican crisis and other case studies. The choice of the Carter administration is intended to represent the closest example we have towards a tendency to think in 'non-historical' ways.

A second question also motivates this study: how do decision-makers reason when confronted by a problem which seems almost entirely 'novel' in character and therefore without precedent? Again, many previous case studies have examined the confrontation of problems which – while obviously not identical – bore a superficial similarity to the case in hand. During the Bay of Pigs planning, the plan to overthrow Fidel Castro was frequently compared with, and modelled upon, the overthrow of Arbenz in Guatemala in 1954, and the Dominican Republic was often compared to Cuba in 1965, but in both instances analogies were relatively 'easy' to draw because of the superficial similarities between the cases. Similarly, the Vietnam case bore a superficial similarity to Korea, as Khong notes. In all three of these examples, the geographical proximity between the countries being compared is readily apparent, for instance. A rather more demanding test for the analogical perspective, then, is to ask what happens when no case seems remotely 'like' that at hand. As argued above, when viewed from the Carter administration perspective the Iran case presents us with an especially intriguing opportunity to find out.

The plan of the book

The plan of the book is as follows. Chapter 2 roots the arguments to be made in the findings of cognitive psychologists who have worked in the area of analogical reasoning, and examines what this literature may tell us about the conditions under which such frameworks and approaches may be useful in the study of foreign policy decision-making. Chapter 3 looks at an often pondered question: why did the Iranian radicals seize the embassy in the first place? This is a critical issue, for there could obviously have been no Iran hostage crisis without this simple but politically earth shattering action. Nevertheless, one sees competing explanations for this event in the existing literature, and it is worth considering whether the overarching theoretical approach adopted in this book – derived almost exclusively from the work of American scholars, looking mostly at American case materials – has anything to say about the behaviour of ordinary Iranians.

Chapter 4 looks in depth at the first few months of the Iran hostage crisis and how the American decision-makers dealt with it, setting the context for the hostage rescue mission by examining the negotiations and deliberations which preceded it. Chapter 5 examines the immediate run-up to the rescue mission and the decision to proceed with the operation itself. It also goes on to examine the aftermath of the failed operation and the plans for a second raid, ending with the release of the hostages in January 1981. Chapter 6 analyses what this tells us about the applicability of the analogical reasoning approach to the case, and it is argued that the 'heuristics' perspective proposed by cognitive psychologists such as Daniel Kahneman and Amos Tversky has much to tell us about the appeal of one analogy over another. We shall also consider to what extent the Carter decision-makers used their analogies purely as *ex-post* justifications for policy preferences already arrived at via some non-analogical route.

There are some well-known problems with single case studies – not least the danger that a researcher may present hypothesis-confirming data and suppress non-hypothesis confirming material – but chapter 7 attempts an element of control by re-examining the case in the light of some of the major existing explanations for the rescue operation and the decision-making in general. Ultimately, the strength of the analogical approach here should be judged by the degree to which it 'explains more' than other theoretical accounts, and chapter 7 assesses to what degree this is the case in this instance. Chapter 8 concludes the analysis by relating the analogical reasoning form of explanation to two other approaches to foreign policy decision-making often considered rivals to it: the domestic politics perspective and the bureaucratic politics approach. We examine here the question of what makes a historical analogy persuasive in policy-making contexts, and the broad conclusion is that persuasiveness is as much a political and bureaucratic process as it is a cognitive one. We begin in chapter 2 by locating the argument within the burgeoning literature of cognitive psychology.

2 Locating the argument: a review of the existing literature

The philosopher and psychologist William James believed that 'humans can understand things, events and experiences only from and through the viewpoint of other things, events and experiences'.[1] Although James was writing in the 1890s, many modern cognitive psychologists have picked up his mantle in recent years, proposing that under certain conditions human beings are apt to rely heavily on analogizing as a mode of comprehension and perception; experience of past situations in which the options and alternatives under consideration were tried – either successfully or unsuccessfully – may help guide the decision-maker as he or she deals with a current problem. In recent years we have seen the emergence of a much discussed 'cognitive revolution' in the study of psychology, a shift away from the older behaviourist tradition typified by B. F. Skinner and towards an information processing approach.[2]

Taking this shift in world-view or metatheory as inspiration, a growing number of scholars in political science have sought to probe the role which cognitive processes, including analogical reasoning, play in the formation of foreign policy decisions, thus helping to initiate a nascent research programme to which this book aims to contribute. In this chapter we first outline the underlying assumptions of the framework to be adopted. Like any such framework, the approach adopted in this thesis is nested in a broader theoretical orientation and tradition, and it

[1] Quoted in David Leary, 'William James and the Art of Human Understanding', *American Psychologist*, 47: 152–60, 1992, p. 152.
[2] Bernard Baars, *The Cognitive Revolution in Psychology* (New York: Guilford Press, 1986). For a good general introduction to the information processing approach to studying foreign policy, see Yaacov Vertzberger, *The World in Their Minds: Information Processing, Cognition and Perception in Foreign Policy Decisionmaking* (Stanford, California: Stanford University Press, 1990).

rests upon certain assumptions which are best made explicit at the outset. We then sketch the major research conducted in the field of analogical reasoning within cognitive psychology. There is a vast and growing literature which examines human problem solving, a considerable portion of which deals with reasoning by analogy. We then compare this with the growing literature in political science connected with, and mostly inspired by, this cognitive literature. Finally, we conclude the chapter by outlining the methodological approach to be employed and some of the limitations of the present enquiry.

The purpose of this chapter is to illustrate the interesting overlap in the work which political scientists and psychologists have been conducting in recent years, and is intended to provide the argument to be made in later chapters with a measure of independent verification derived from experimental research. However, since the remainder of this chapter represents a necessary precursor to the argument rather than the argument itself, the reader should note that he or she may skip this section and move on to chapter 3 without impairing comprehension of the book as a whole.

Underlying assumptions of the framework

The most important assumption we shall adopt at the outset is that analogies are cognitive tools which are most often employed in the effort to make sense of a complex reality. In other words, we shall assume that analogies can be treated as the independent variable in some kinds of decision-making situation, while always remaining mindful of how well this assumption and its related propositions performs in the empirical case study to be examined. Historical analogies are viewed as essential models for thought and action in what follows. The nature of policy responses, we shall assume, is determined principally by the 'cognitive structuring of the problem'. How a problem is cognitively structured by a given policy-making group depends on the composition of the group, on the nature of the experiences to which they have each been exposed and also to some extent on the recency of these experiences. By cognitive structuring, we mean the collective pattern of thought processes which go into the policy-making process at the uppermost levels of government, and which depend primarily upon the nature of the events that each member has been exposed to and on the lessons which he or she draws from these, as well as on the extent to which one group of analogizers is able to convince (or otherwise effectively overcome) another group which defines the situation differently.

This book follows a tradition or approach recently popular in both cognitive psychology and the study of FPDM in assuming that policy-makers are cognitive actors, as opposed to purely rational actors, and that policy-making can best be viewed as a form of human problem solving. Decision-making in politics involves what one analyst has termed 'fuzzy, ill-structured tasks', problems in which the criteria for determining whether one's goal has actually been reached, the information needed to solve the problem and its boundaries, and the range of alternative options or possibilities for solving it are all unclear.[3] Policy-makers can be described as both 'intuitive scientists' and 'cognitive misers', in the sense that they both try to make sense intuitively of the events around them and often attempt to deal with uncertainty about the future by using the past as a cognitive guide or yardstick. Requiring methods for both problem definition and prediction but compelled to operate under conditions of uncertainty, human beings have typically been found to exhibit a pronounced tendency to utilize cognitive biases or heuristics. Conventionally bypassing the rigorous criteria employed by laboratory scientists, their inferential processes reflect certain pro-cedures which distort the processes usually associated with 'hard' scientific methodologies, such as those employed to assess the likeli-hood or probability of a particular event occurring.[4]

These assumptions rest principally upon the findings of psychologi-cal researchers working in the laboratory, and they are associated principally with attribution theory and schema theory.[5] It is to this literature – and, more specifically, to the literature on analogical reason-ing – that we now turn. What follows is not intended as a full or comprehensive account of the intricacies of this complex literature, which has already been ably reviewed by others.[6] Nevertheless, some

---

[3] See Herbert Simon, 'The Information-Processing Theory of Human Problem Solving', in William Estes (ed.), *Handbook of Learning and Cognitive Processes*, vol. V (Hillsdale, New Jersey: Lawrence Erlbaum, 1978), pp. 286–7.

[4] This argument is associated in particular with two major works: Richard Nisbett and Lee Ross, *Human Inference: Strategies and Shortcomings of Social Judgment* (Englewood Cliffs, New Jersey: Prentice Hall, 1980) and Daniel Kahneman, Paul Slovic and Amos Tversky (eds.), *Judgment Under Uncertainty: Heuristics and Biases* (London: Cambridge University Press, 1982).

[5] For an excellent review of both these literatures designed for the political scientist, see Deborah Welch Larson, *Origins of Containment: A Psychological Explanation* (Princeton, New Jersey: Princeton University Press, 1985), pp. 24–65.

[6] See for instance Khong, *Analogies at War, passim.*

effort to sketch out the major findings which have some relevance to the current enterprise is in order before we proceed to analyse the Iranian case.

What cognitive psychologists have said

Much recent research in cognitive psychology has supported the 'Jamesian' approach referred to at the beginning of this chapter, finding (among many other things) that case law, science teaching, mathematical problem solving, learning to read and the process of acquiring a foreign language all rely heavily upon analogical reasoning.[7] Although this body of literature – the vast majority of it generated only over the past twenty years – is now too vast to be summarized in its entirety, a number of key findings stick out by virtue of their replication by a number of researchers.

One major finding in the growing literature on human problem solving is the fact that analogical reasoning is a cognitive mechanism that tends to be used when an individual is confronted by novel or unusual circumstances. As Michael Eysenck and Mark Keane note,

[7] The literature is vast, but see, for instance, Roy Dreistadt, 'The Use of Analogies and Incubation in Obtaining Insights in Creative Problem Solving', *Journal of Psychology*, 71: 159–75, 1969; David Rumelhart and A. A. Abrahamson, 'A Model for Analogical Reasoning', *Cognitive Psychology*, 5: 1–28, 1973; Andrew Ortony, *Metaphor and Thought* (New York: Cambridge University Press, 1979); Kurt VanLehn and J. S. Brown, 'Planning Nets: A Representation for Formalizing Analogies and Semantic Models of Procedural Skills', in R. E. Snow *et al.* (eds.), *Aptitude, Learning and Instruction* (Hillsdale, New Jersey: Lawrence Erlbaum, 1980); Mary Gick and Keith Holyoak, 'Analogical Problem Solving', *Cognitive Psychology*, 12: 306–55, 1980; Thomas Gilovich, 'Seeing the Past in the Present: The Effect of Associations to Familiar Events on Judgements and Decisions', *Journal of Personality and Social Psychology*, 40: 797–808, 1981; Mary Gick and Keith Holyoak, 'Schema Induction and Analogical Transfer', *Cognitive Psychology*, 115: 1–38, 1983; Dedre Gentner, 'Structure Mapping: A Theoretical Framework for Analogy', *Cognitive Science*, 7: 155–70, 1983; Keith Holyoak, 'The Pragmatics of Analogical Transfer', in Gordon Bower (ed.), *The Psychology of Learning and Motivation*, vol. I (New York: Academic Press, 1985); Dedre Gentner and Cecile Toupin, 'Systematicity and Surface Similarity in the Development of Analogy', *Cognitive Science*, 10: 277–300, 1986; Robert Haskell, *Cognitive and Symbolic Structures: The Psychology of Metaphoric Transformation* (Norwood, New Jersey: Ablex, 1987); David Helman, *Analogical Reasoning: Perspectives on Artificial Intelligence, Cognitive Science and Philosophy* (Boston, Massachusetts: Kluwer Books, 1988); Mark Keane, *Analogical Problem-Solving* (New York: Wiley, 1988); Stella Vosniadou and Andrew Ortony, *Similarity and Analogical Reasoning* (Cambridge: Cambridge University Press, 1989); Diane Halpern, Carol Hansen and David Riefer, 'Analogies as an Aid to Understanding and Memory', *Journal of Educational Psychology*, 82: 298–305, 1990; Barbara Spellman and Keith Holyoak, 'If Saddam is Hitler then Who Is George Bush? Analogical Mapping Between Systems of Social Roles', *Journal of Personality and Social Psychology*, 62: 913–33, 1992; Bipin Indurkhya, *Metaphor and Cognition* (Boston, Massachusetts: Kluwer Books, 1992).

much of the existing research on human problem solving examines how people deal with familiar, routine and recurring problems. 'But people can also solve unfamiliar or novel problems. Sometimes we can produce creative solutions when we have no directly applicable knowledge about the problem situation.'[8] One mechanism through which we do this is analogical reasoning. By extension, any situation which provokes a high degree of uncertainty or ambiguity – either through lack of information or too much of it – may provoke the use of analogizing.

A second central finding – which relates primarily to the processes through which analogical reasoning occurs – is that analogizing involves what several authors have referred to as a 'mapping' process. As Eysenck and Keane put it, 'various theorists have characterized this analogical thinking as being the result of processes that map the conceptal structure of one set of ideas (called the base domain) into another set of ideas (called a target domain)'.[9] The innovators in developing this mapping theory have been Dedre Gentner, Mary Gick and Keith Holyoak. According to Gick and Holyoak, for instance, 'the essence of analogical thinking is the transfer of knowledge from one situation to another by a process of *mapping* – finding a set of one-on-one correspondences (often incomplete) between aspects of one body of information and aspects of another'.[10] In analogizing, 'isomorphic' relationships are discovered between one event, situation or object and another.

This point can be illustrated by the following simplified example.[11] Suppose that we have two situations – situation 1 and situation 2 – the first of which precedes the second in time or is currently occurring at that time (say, in some other organization or country). Suppose also that we observe that situation 2 has property a in common with situation 1. Perceiving that situation 1 and situation 2 have property a in common, we also notice that situation 1 has property b as well. We then surmise that it is likely that situation 2, since it clearly has property a, also has property b (though the number of common, or apparently common, properties in real-life situations will almost always exceed two). Here we have 'mapped' the relations between the two situations, where property a in situation 1 is assumed to correspond to property a in situation 2 and property b in situation 1 is assumed to correspond to property b in situation 2. Analogical reasoning thus involves a process

---

[8] Michael Eysenck and Mark Keane, *Cognitive Psychology: A Student's Handbook* (Hove: Lawrence Erlbaum, 1990), p. 399.   [9] Ibid., p. 401.
[10] Gick and Holyoak, 'Schema Induction and Analogical Transfer', p. 2.
[11] This example is drawn from Indurkhya, *Metaphor and Cognition*, pp. 315–56.

of inference, whereby the likely properties of one situation are deduced from knowing the actual properties of another.

A third, closely related point to note is that analogical reasoning is a *structural* process. An analogy, Dedre Gentner finds, is not simply a statement that something is like something else; rather, it is a comparison in which the subject assumes that the perceived similarities are 'structural' (or causally significant) as opposed to merely 'superficial'.[12] She distinguishes analogies from 'mere appearance matches' and things which are literally similar.[13] This distinction may best be appreciated by noting that policy-makers – and human beings generally – quite often do not draw analogies between things which are very similar if the similarities do not seem causally important. For instance, the fact that both Saddam Hussein and Adolf Hitler have moustaches does not strengthen the appeal of an analogy between the two, while factors such as expansionist tendencies or the use of secret police do. One can also appreciate the structural nature of analogies by recognizing that just as not all similarities count in favour of an analogy, not all differences necessarily *weaken* a comparison. For instance, to stick with the Persian Gulf War example just alluded to, for most analysts the appeal of the Munich analogy is probably not weakened by the fact that Kuwait is in the Middle East and Poland in Eastern Europe.

The analogical reasoning approach is intimately connected to a larger body of theorizing in psychology usually referred to as schema theory. The notion of a schema has been used in different ways, but in essence a schema 'refers to a general cognitive structure into which data or events can be entered, typically with more attention to broad brush strokes than to specific details'.[14] A fourth prominent finding is that analogical reasoning appears to play a key role in schema formation. Analogizing aids, in other words, the construction of general rules for solving a particular category of problem, and analogical reasoning is seen by most psychologists as closely related to schematic processing in general. According to Gick and Holyoak, when the individual has solved a problem successfully in the same way on two or more occasions, he or she will eventually form a general 'problem schema', a set of abstract principles for dealing with that problem type which derives from particular analogical cases but which acquires an

---

[12] Gentner, 'Structure Mapping'.
[13] Dedre Gentner, 'The Mechanism of Analogical Learning', in Vosniadou and Ortony (eds.), *Similarity and Analogical Reasoning*.
[14] Henry Gleitman, *Psychology*, 4th edn (London: W. W. Norton, 1995), p. 268.

independent identity of its own. In this way, general rules may be formed which derive from – and yet go beyond – any particular case, abstract beliefs for which analogies supply examples and provide concrete support.[15] Similarly, as Kurt VanLehn notes, 'if one gives subjects the same set of problems many times, they may learn how to solve them and cease to labor through . . . understanding and search processes'. Under such circumstances, individuals 'seem to recognize the stimulus as a familiar problem, retrieve a solution procedure for that problem, and follow it', and they develop a schema which can be repeatedly applied to a series of similar problems.[16] As VanLehn notes, this sort of schema-driven problem solving 'seems to characterize experts who are solving problems in knowledge-rich domains' (in other words, where solving a given task requires a relatively high degree of specialized knowledge).[17] Notably, he includes public policy formation as one such knowledge-rich domain.[18]

Cognitive psychologists have long debated the issue of whether underlying mental processes are fundamentally rule or instance-based; Arthur Reber and his associates, for instance, have argued that much human reasoning is rule-based or abstract in nature, while others like Lloyd Brooks have suggested that it is fundamentally analogical or case-based.[19] Whatever the respective merits of these contentions, however, it is probably true to say that the greater the number of similar events or experiences a decision-maker has gone through, the greater the tendency for a lesson to become disassociated from any one event in particular. In this case, the individual will derive a generalized lesson, and will often feel no compulsion to 'explain' his or her choice of policy option A by reference to a situation where option A worked in the past. As Roy D'Andrade notes, 'an important part in the construction of schemas of all types . . . is the use of analogy and metaphor', but once

---

[15] Gick and Holyoak, 'Schema Induction and Analogical Transfer', p. 32.
[16] Kurt VanLehn, 'Problem Solving and Cognitive Skill Acquisition', in Michael Posner (ed.), *Foundations of Cognitive Science* (Cambridge, Massachusetts: MIT Press, 1989), p. 545.   [17] Ibid.   [18] Ibid., p. 528.
[19] Lloyd Brooks, 'Non-Analytic Concept Formation and Memory for Instances', in E. Rosch and B. Lloyd (eds.), *Cognition and Categorization* (Hillsdale, New Jersey: Lawrence Erlbaum, 1978); Brooks, 'Decentralized Control of Categorization: The Role of Prior Processing Episodes', in U. Neisser (ed.), *Concepts and Conceptual Development* (New York: Cambridge University Press, 1987); Arthur Reber, 'Transfer of Syntactic Structure in Synthetic Languages', *Journal of Experimental Psychology*, 81: 115–19, 1969; Reber, 'Implicit Learning and Tacit Knowledge', *Journal of Experimental Psychology*, 118: 219–35, 1989.

formed these schemas seem to go beyond any particular instance that may have formed them.[20]

Conversely, it appears that decision-makers rely on analogies under highly novel situations because the number of 'like' experiences under such situations is too few to have led to generalized problem schemas or rule-based formations. Where this is so, there are no generalized rules or standard operating procedures available to deal with the problem, and thus the reasoning employed will be case- rather than rule-based. This also means that under such circumstances belief systems will provide little or no guidance to the policy-maker, and that he or she will hence be forced to rely upon one or two analogies in order to make sense of what is going on. VanLehn makes a similar distinction between two types of problem solving: routine and non-routine. Routine problems are ones for which schemas already exist, whereas solving a non-routine task requires a complex search and comprehension process.[21] Similarly, P. N. Johnson-Laird argues that individuals use analogies 'when a causal model fails to explain some phenomenon',[22] while Keith Holyoak and his colleagues have offered the view that the key inducement is failure to solve a problem.[23] Hence, analogizing appears to form a kind of 'default' mechanism where no other kind of cognitive guidance is available.

These findings are arguably consistent with what one observes in everyday life. Individuals do not *always* use analogies, and whether they do or not appears to vary with the situation. What is being suggested here is that decision-makers 'resort' to the use of analogy when other (presumably more reliable) cognitive mechanisms – such as standard operating procedures or other decision rules – are unavailable. The relevance of this research should be apparent in the analysis of the Iran hostage crisis case. Here the US decision-makers are confronted with a problem which is so novel that it appears entirely without precedent, at least to most of them, which would seem to rule out analogizing on purely logical grounds. However, it is plausible that they will nevertheless draw on analogies in some way, since the novelty

[20] Roy D'Andrade, 'Cultural Cognition', in Posner (ed.), *Foundations of Cognitive Science*, p. 810.   [21] VanLehn, 'Problem Solving and Cognitive Skill Acquisition', p. 545.
[22] P. N. Johnson-Laird, 'Mental Models', in Posner (ed.), *Foundations of Cognitive Science*, p. 487.
[23] Gick and Holyoak, 'Schema Induction and Analogical Transfer'; Holyoak, 'The Pragmatics of Analogical Transfer', in Bower (ed.), *The Psychology of Learning and Motivation*; Holyoak, and Paul Thagard, 'Rule-Based Spreading Activation and Analogical Transfer', in Vosniadou and Ortony (eds.), *Similarity and Analogical Reasoning*.

and unfamiliarity of the circumstances place a premium upon 'anchoring' what they are doing in some sort of historical model.[24]

A fifth finding is that individuals often draw analogies between things or events which exhibit only a superficial surface similarity. As Clement and Gentner succinctly put it, 'suppose we know three facts: *It rains in San Francisco, There is a mime troop in San Francisco* and *It rains in Urbana.* Clearly we do not want our theory of analogy to tell us that *There is a mime troop in Urbana.*'[25] Unfortunately, in the complex world of foreign policy decision-making things are rarely so clear cut. If Kosovo looks sufficiently like Vietnam in terms of its terrain or the kind of military commitment necessary to win the conflict, then it is easy to conclude that escalated American involvement in the former Yugoslavia would meet with the same result encountered in Southeast Asia. In policy-making, surface similarities are usually easy to confuse with underlying structural ones. Plausible causal or higher order relations must be mapped between base and target in order for the analogy to be useful for predictive purposes, but this is relatively easy to do in political decision-making. This emphasis on surface similarity, of course, renders analogical reasoning inherently flawed as a method of comprehension. Looking at the invasion of Kuwait in 1990 or the expansion of North Vietnam into the South during the 1960s without the benefit of hindsight, it was relatively easy to see both events as comparable to Hitler's invasion of Poland in 1938. Mistakes, biases and errors are thus an inherent part of the analogical process, not least because analogical reasoning usually involves reasoning from an *n* of one, a practice which any good student of political methodology knows to be fraught with potential error.

During the 1970s Amos Tversky and Daniel Kahneman conducted a number of classic surveys which examined how people depart from statistical rules or 'pure rationality' in order to overcome uncertainty, and their findings have had strong implications for research on analogical reasoning.[26] They highlight two main categories of error or misperception that frequently occur when humans make judgements, which they term the *availability* and *representativeness* heuristics.[27] An event may reasonably be judged as likely to occur if it happens more

---

[24] We will of course have more to say on this point in subsequent chapters.
[25] Catherine Clement and Dedre Gentner, 'Systematicity as a Selection Constraint in Analogical Mapping', *Cognitive Science*, 15: 89–132, 1991, p. 90.
[26] Amos Tversky and Daniel Kahneman, 'Judgment under Uncertainty: Heuristics and Biases', *Science*, 185: 1124–31, 1974.   [27] Ibid.

frequently than other events, since the more often the event occurs the greater the statistical likelihood that it will occur in the future; and yet the availability of an event in memory can be influenced by factors which are totally unrelated to the objective frequency with which it occurs. It may be accessed because it is especially salient, or simply because it has occurred recently. The perceived importance of an event in history, for instance, may lead to an overconcentration on that event and a consequent predilection to exaggerate the likelihood that it will re-occur. US policy-makers have overwhelmingly tended to use the Munich and Vietnam analogies when comparing current military conflicts to the past, for example, even though many of these conflicts may arguably bear a greater similarity to other (lesser known) situations. Equally, the recency of an event may make policy-makers more likely to draw an analogy with that event simply because it is more available or accessible in memory.

One especially vivid example of the availability heuristic at work was provided by Combs and Slovic.[28] They showed that when asked to judge the frequency of 'spectacular' forms of death such as dying in a terrorist incident, plane crash or earthquake as opposed to more 'normal' forms such as cancer or heart disease, people have a tendency to overestimate the occurrence of the former at the expense of the latter. The reason, Combs and Slovic find, is that the former are more available in memory, due to the fact that the mass media tend to report spectacular or newsworthy deaths and usually ignore more routine forms (unless, of course, the victim happens to be a celebrity of some sort). Other studies have found that 'vivid' (and therefore more easily recallable) evidence tends to exert a disproportionate effect upon the judgements of jurors in court cases.[29]

Like the availability heuristic, the representativeness heuristic leads to cognitive bias and error, but it is error of another sort. The representativeness heuristic, Kahneman and Tversky argue, leads an individual to estimate the likelihood of an event according to the extent to which it appears to fit some archetypical category.[30] For instance, when asked to judge the likelihood that Saddam Hussein or Colonel Ghaddafi is 'another Hitler', most people will ask themselves to what extent Hus-

---

[28] Barbara Combs and Paul Slovic, 'Causes of Death: Biased Newspaper Coverage and Biased Judgments', *Journalism Quarterly*, 56: 837–43, 1979.
[29] R. M. Reyes, W. C. Thompson and G. H. Bower, 'Judgmental Biases Resulting from Differing Availabilities of Arguments', *Journal of Personality and Social Psychology*, 39: 2–12, 1980.   [30] Tversky and Kahneman, 'Judgment under Uncertainty'.

30

sein or Ghaddafi fit the typical characteristics which one would associate with Adolf Hitler. What they do not generally do, however, is to
examine the *statistical* odds that Hussein, for instance, is a Hitler. We
know that in the wider population or universe of world leaders most –
in fact, the great majority – are not Hitlers, so the statistical odds that
Hussein is a Hitler are fairly low. However, in the real world people
usually ignore such odds. In the same way, most individuals judge the
likelihood of an event occurring by assessing how far the known
characteristics of the event fit some established mental category or
archetype. Thus the relevance of the Vietnam analogy to any given
conflict is not assessed by reference to the fact that there has only ever
been one major war in which the United States did not prevail and
numerous others in which it did – the statistical measure – but by
examining how far the current situation seems to fit the characteristics
associated with Vietnam.

The relevance of both heuristics should become clear in chapters 3, 4
and 5. Lastly, and most importantly for our purposes, there is general
agreement on the proposition that the underlying analogical processes
observed by testing individuals in the laboratory are probably little
different from analogizing in real world contexts. Before considering
the extent to which this is true in the Iran case, however, we must first
turn our attention to what has been written about analogical reasoning
in political contexts.

What historians and political scientists have said

The use of analogical reasoning in foreign and domestic policy-making
has long been commented upon, although it has only recently been
viewed as an explicitly psychological process.[31] In the main, this

---

[31] Ernest May, *Lessons of the Past* (New York: Oxford University Press, 1973); Robert
Jervis, *Perception and Misperception in International Politics* (Princeton, New Jersey:
Princeton University Press, 1976), pp. 217–87; Glenn Snyder and Paul Diesing, *Conflict
Among Nations: Bargaining, Decision Making and System Structure in International Crises*
(Princeton, New Jersey: Princeton University Press, 1977), pp. 313–21; Larson, *Origins
of Containment*, pp. 50–7; Neustadt and May, *Thinking in Time*; Dwain Mefford, 'Ana-
logical Reasoning and the Definition of the Situation: Back to Snyder for Concepts and
Forward to Artificial Intelligence for Method', in Charles Hermann, Charles Kegley
and James Rosenau, *New Directions in the Study of Foreign Policy* (Boston, Massa-
chusetts: Allen and Unwin, 1987); Vertzberger, *The World in Their Minds*, pp. 296–341;
Alex Hybel, *How Leaders Reason: US Intervention in the Caribbean Basin and Latin America*
(Cambridge, Massachusetts: Basil Blackwell, 1990); Hybel, 'Learning and Reasoning by
Analogy', in Michael Fry (ed.), *History, the White House and the Kremlin: Statesmen as
Historians* (New York: Pinter, 1991); Dwain Mefford, 'The Power of Historical Ana-

literature has sought to provide answers to two sets of questions. First of all, many authors have pondered the time-honoured question of whether the past is generally a useful or misleading guide to the present and future. Neustadt and May's *Thinking in Time*, for instance, is intended as a kind of 'how-to-do-it' manual for policy-making, being primarily concerned with the question of how decision-makers can make better use of historical lessons. Their collaboration builds upon May's earlier *Lessons of the Past*, which offers the now commonplace view that decision-makers usually employ history poorly and in inappropriate ways. Their major purpose is to help policy-makers use history better, and they catalogue a variety of US cases – drawn from both foreign and domestic policy – in which analogies are used well, poorly or not at all. They find that analogical reasoning played a prominent role in decision-making with regard to Vietnam, the Cuban missile crisis, social security reform in 1983, Korea, the swine flu episode of 1976, the *Mayaguez* affair, President Carter's first year in office, the Bay of Pigs fiasco and a number of other instances.[32]

The second set of questions has to do with the status of analogizing as a cause, rather than an effect, of decision-making. Given that analogizing undoubtedly takes place, what role do analogies generally play? Are they cognitive tools used for making sense of a complex world, or simply *ex-post* mechanisms which decision-makers employ with the sole intention of convincing their colleagues of the appropriateness of a pre-set course of action? The first political science author to reflect upon analogizing as an explicitly *psychological* process was Robert Jervis, who devotes a chapter of his *Perception and Misperception in International Politics* to the use of history by decision-makers, and almost all recent work in the field of analogizing has taken its inspiration from him.

logies: Soviet Interventions in Eastern Europe and US Interventions in Central America', in Fry, *History, the White House and the Kremlin*; Yuen Foong Khong, 'The Lessons of Korea and the Vietnam Decisions of 1965', in George Breslauer and Philip Tetlock (eds.), *Learning in US and Soviet Foreign Policy* (Boulder, Colorado: Westview Press, 1991); Khong, *Analogies at War*; Khong, 'Vietnam, the Gulf, and US Choices: A Comparison', *Security Studies*, 2: 74–95, 1992; Houghton, 'The Role of Analogical Reasoning'; Gary Williams, 'Analogical Reasoning and Foreign Policy Decisionmaking: US Intervention in the Caribbean Basin with Particular Reference to Grenada 1983', unpublished dissertation, University of Hull, England, 1996; M. J. Peterson, 'The Use of Analogies in Outer Space Law', *International Organization*, 51: 245–74, 1997; David Patrick Houghton, 'Historical Analogies and the Cognitive Dimension of Domestic Policymaking', *Political Psychology*, 19: 279–303, 1998; Houghton, 'Analogical Reasoning and Policymaking: Where and When Is it Used?', *Policy Sciences*, 31: 151–76, 1998; Christopher Hemmer, 'Historical Analogies and the Definition of Interests: The Iran Hostage Crisis and Ronald Reagan's Policy Toward the Hostages in Lebanon', *Political Psychology*, 20: 267–89, 1999.   [32] Neustadt and May, *Thinking in Time*.

Jervis's analysis stresses the origin of analogical reasoning in the past personal experiences of decision-makers, showing how analogies can lead the policy-maker to misdefine the character of situations and/or to arrive at policy choices poorly suited to the task at hand.

Jervis's account of how decision-makers learn from history seems remarkably prescient and insightful when read in the context of the analogical reasoning literature within psychology, much of which was published several years after he wrote. For instance, he notes that individuals tend to learn most from their own firsthand or personal experiences and that 'the amount one learns from another's experience is slight even when the incentives for learning are high', so that leaders of one state tend not to learn much from the experiences of another.[33] Jervis also contends that 'the only thing as important for a nation as its revolution is its last major war . . . What was believed to have caused the last war will be considered likely to cause the next one.'[34] Jervis was by no means the first to make this point; there is, for instance, an old adage that 'generals are always fighting the last war'. Nevertheless, his arguments about drawing on personal experiences and on recent events are both highly consistent with Kahneman and Tversky's availability heuristic framework.

While illustrated by a number of examples, Jervis's thoughts on analogical reasoning mostly took the form of theoretical observations on the psychological character of the phenomenon and its general effects on international relations, so much later work by supporters of the cognitive approach to decision-making has sought to apply these observations to actual case studies. Alex Hybel, for instance, found that analogical reasoning played a significant role in seven major post-war episodes of US intervention in the Caribbean and South America, Dwain Mefford finds that analogies played a prominent role in President Eisenhower's decision to overthrow the Arbenz regime in Guatemala in 1954 and Houghton argues that the Johnson and Carter administrations' choices were heavily conditioned by a range of analogies during the Detroit riots of 1967 and the Iran hostage crisis respectively.[35] Khong's book *Analogies at War*, however, is by far the most sustained and in-depth analysis of analogizing in foreign policy to appear to date. Examining the decisions by the Johnson administration

---

[33] Jervis, *Perception and Misperception in International Politics*, p. 242.
[34] Ibid., pp. 266–7.
[35] Hybel, *How Leaders Reason*; Mefford, 'The Power of Historical Analogies'; Houghton, 'The Role of Analogical Reasoning' and 'Historical Analogies'.

to escalate US involvement in the Vietnam War in 1965, he finds that analogies played a prominent part in the reasoning processes of both those who opposed the escalation and those who supported it. Under Secretary of State George Ball, for instance, argued that increased American involvement there would soon lead to 'another Dien Bien Phu', to a repeat of the disastrous French experience in Indochina. However, for President Johnson and many of his other advisers (such as Dean Rusk), Korea was the analogy of choice. Khong argues:

> To be sure, Johnson was informed by many lessons of many pasts, but Korea preoccupied him . . . Whatever it was that attracted Johnson to the Korean precedent, a major lesson he drew from it was that the United States made a mistake in leaving Korea in June 1949; the withdrawal emboldened the communists, forcing the United States to return to Korea one year later to save the South. Johnson was not predisposed toward repeating the same mistake in Vietnam.[36]

Others, like McGeorge Bundy and Henry Cabot Lodge, drew on the perceived lessons of the Munich–World War II experience in predicting the scenarios they believed would occur if the United States did not intervene.[37]

Khong argues that we can think of analogies as 'diagnostic devices' which assist policy-makers in performing six crucial functions: they '(1) help define the nature of the situation confronting the policy-maker, (2) help assess the stakes, and (3) provide prescriptions. They help evaluate alternative options by (4) predicting the chances of success, (5) evaluating their moral rightness, and (6) warning about dangers associated with the options.'[38] He develops what he calls the 'AE Framework', essentially a short-hand term for the belief that analogies are genuine cognitive devices which perform the tasks specified above.

The primary research purpose of Khong's book is to argue against the view proposed by Arthur Schlesinger and others that analogies are used solely to 'prop up one's prejudices' or to justify decisions which have already been decided upon using some other rationale. Unlike Jervis, he explicitly draws on both schema theory and the Kahneman and Tversky heuristics approach, finding that the Johnson people tended to use historical analogies which drew upon then recent events such as the missile crisis, the Berlin crises, Korea, Pearl Harbor and Munich.[39] Consistent with the findings of Dedre Gentner and other psychologists working in this area, Khong shows that in choosing a

[36] Khong, *Analogies at War*, pp. 110–11.   [37] Ibid., p. 134.   [38] Ibid., p. 10.
[39] Ibid., p. 214.

historical analogy which seemed to 'make sense' of Vietnam, Johnson's advisers picked a historical example on the basis of its superficial similarities to the case in hand.[40]

The 'fit' between psychology and FPDM

Unfortunately for analysts of policy-making, psychologists are only just beginning to study the processes of non-routine problem solving, for instance 'when more than one schema is applicable to a given situation' or 'when no schema will cover the whole problem, but two or more schemas each cover some part of the problem'.[41] Much experimental research has also focused on careful delineated, structured tasks rather than non-structured or ill-defined ones, most have been examined in the laboratory as opposed to naturalistic settings, and the majority of experiments have required subjects to perform 'knowledge-lean' tasks where no special expertise is required. Clearly, one must not lose sight of the limitations of laboratory work as a grounding for our present endeavour. These limitations are several. First, the nature of what cognitive psychologists are testing differs in one important respect from political problem solving. In the typical experiment which psychologists have employed in this area, the subjects are usually presented with a mental puzzle or problem of some sort, and are then offered one or two analogies which can potentially be used to solve the problem.[42]

This kind of experimental design, while perfectly satisfactory for some purposes, presents some potential difficulties for us. The chief problem relates to the fact that in the vast majority of these experiments the subjects lack any vested interest or 'stake' in the outcome, one way or another. Stated differently, the context of politics is absent from the situations in which we are interested, and hence the choice of analogy is presumably determined by purely cognitive (as opposed to affective) factors. For instance, in Gick and Holyoak's classic experiments, subjects were asked to solve a vexing medical problem: how to destroy a harmful tumour using powerful radioactive rays, without destroying the healthy tissue surrounding it. The subjects were offered a military analogy which would help them solve the problem if they thought about it, and Gick and Holyoak found that around 80 per cent of the

---

[40] Ibid., pp. 217–18.
[41] VanLehn, 'Problem Solving and Cognitive Skill Acquisition', pp. 549–50.
[42] For some examples, see the works cited in footnote 75.

subjects were able to solve the medical problem using the military analogy once the fact that it would be helpful was brought to their attention.[43] While the choice of the Munich or the Vietnam analogy, for instance, makes a key difference to the policy-makers involved and to ordinary members of the American public, whether the radiation problem is solved using a military or engineering analogy makes little difference to the participants in this sort of test. Put another way, the subjects are not systematically 'biased' one way or another by any predisposing element, while we could plausibly assume that policy-makers manifestly are. The *reception* of analogies is clearly distorted in certain ways in policy-making contexts, for the goals and objectives associated with particular governmental roles ensure that policy-makers will tend to exhibit different value hierarchies, and the reception of a given analogy will be determined in part by what it implies about the fate of the policy-maker's most treasured goals and values.

Secondly, experimenters who use this design often ask their subjects to draw analogies between things which lie within very different semantic domains. When policy-makers search for analogies, however, the prima facie evidence suggests that they overwhelmingly draw analogies from the same domain as the target problem (that is, from politics and policy-making, and often from the same policy area they happen to be working in). Thirdly, most of the experiments test a subject's ability to solve novel problems by *presenting* him or her with a single analogy, which then – if employed correctly – provides the subject with the entire solution to the novel problem, while in the real world of policy-making, the actors are more usually *spontaneously* recalling an analogy from the recent or distant past. They are not usually being presented with some ready-made analogy to it, unless one decision-maker is attempting to persuade another of the utility of a given analogy. A fourth difference to note is that the task of the subjects in these experiments is typically to apply the lessons of a single analogous situation to a novel problem, immediately after that potential analogy has been suggested to them. The experimenter then measures the success of the subject in doing this. In real world policy-making, however, decision-makers will rarely be confronted with a single relevant analogue; there will almost always be *several* competing analogies on offer, all of which have some appeal to the decision-maker by virtue of possessing a degree of resemblance to the problem at hand. Furthermore, in the real

---

[43] Gick and Holyoak, 'Analogical Problem Solving' and 'Schema Induction and Analogical Transfer'.

world few analogies will be fully comprehensive – that is, will match the novel problem closely and provide all the elements of the solution – but will most likely be 'partial' in nature.

Unfortunately, few of the existing experiments faithfully mimic the specific contextual conditions under which political decision-makers work. Consequently, considerable uncertainty remains as to what happens when the subject is confronted with a whole range of potential analogies, all of which seem relevant to solving the policy problem at hand but which push the decision-maker in diametrically different directions if followed and adhered to. Nor can we tell from these experiments with much certainty what happens in such a situation where the subjects – for whatever reason – are predisposed to favour one analogy over another. It is here, however, that policy analysts and psychologists may have something interesting to say to one another, since the former *are* primarily concerned with how individuals react when addressing non-structured, non-routine problems. Viewed from a cognitive perspective, all policy-making involves a process of reasoning about 'ill-structured problems'.[44]

As Eysenck and Keane say of the cognitive psychological literature in general, 'most of the research on the use of expertise deals with how people solve relatively familiar problems'.[45] Some policy-making tasks certainly do involve the solving of familiar problems, but many do not, and it is into this latter category that the Iran hostage crisis falls. As we shall see in chapter 3, most if not all of the decision-makers would see the seizure of the Tehran embassy – and the search for a means of getting the hostages out – as anything but routine. For the Carter people, it might be said, decision-making on the hostage issue took the form of an 'ill-structured task' in which the motivations of the hostage takers, their future behaviour, the fate of the hostages and the outcomes of various policy options available to the American decision-makers were all highly uncertain.

And yet despite the obvious limitations of this body of research for our own purposes, it nevertheless presents us with an intriguing and suggestive starting point. True enough, the precise contextual conditions of politics are not replicated in the laboratory, nor can they ever be. Nevertheless, what all of this indicates is that in the real world the

---

[44] James Voss and Ellen Dorsey, 'Perception and International Relations: An Overview', in Eric Singer and Valerie Hudson (eds.), *Political Psychology and Foreign Policy* (Boulder, Colorado: Westview Press, 1990), p. 3.
[45] Eysenck and Keane, *Cognitive Psychology*, p. 399.

analogical process is more complex, and is subject to various 'distorting' processes. One should not automatically assume that the cognitive processes used by humans in everyday political situations are necessarily *fundamentally* different from those employed by subjects in the laboratory. Indeed, Herbert Simon's research over several decades strongly suggests that the processes employed in these two domains are not different in their basic respects, and experimentally obtained results have often been observed in the real world in this and other domains of psychology.[46] What systematic cognitive research there is on analogical processes *outside* the laboratory has in fact supported the larger, more conventional body of work. Barbara Spellman and Keith Holyoak, for example, conducted what they called a 'naturalistic investigation of analogical reasoning' in the public debate preceding America's role in the Persian Gulf War. Their key substantive conclusion was that the Munich analogy allowed many ordinary Americans to impose sense and meaning upon a highly novel and uncertain situation about which they had little knowledge. An important product of their investigation was that laboratory experimentation probably does not distort or misrepresent 'natural' or real world analogical processes.[47]

Moreover, what laboratory research exists on the role of analogizing in politics has reached the same kind of conclusion. Thomas Gilovich conducted a laboratory experiment in which forty-two subjects – all of them international relations students at Stanford University – were each presented with one of three scenarios involving possible military intervention. Two of these were designed to mimic some of the features of an actual historical situation, but without explicitly referring to it by name. The first called to mind Munich and the events leading up to World War II, the second resembled Vietnam and the third (control) story was designed to evoke no particular analogy. As expected, students presented with the Munich version advocated military intervention, while those who read the Vietnam version urged a peaceful solution. Interestingly, those who heard the control story showed a predilection towards seeing the event described as another Vietnam, probably demonstrating the greater generational availability of this episode to the students being tested.[48]

---

[46] Simon, 'The Information-Processing Theory of Human Problem Solving'. One of the more famous 'matches' between real world and laboratory findings was conducted by Stanley Milgram.
[47] Spellman and Holyoak, 'If Saddam is Hitler then Who is George Bush?'
[48] Gilovich, 'Seeing the Past in the Present'.

As a political scientist, it is tempting to borrow concepts from psychology under the pretense that in doing so one is providing 'scientific' justification for one's arguments in a way that closes off debate, as if the study of psychology were not also a paradigmatic struggle between competing attempts to impose meaning upon a complex social reality. Although there is fundamental agreement on the notion that decision-makers do analogize under certain conditions, there is nevertheless a still-raging debate among psychologists as to how, precisely, the analogical process works in the human mind. The claim of scientific certainty, then, is not being invoked in this analysis. For one thing, we still do not know enough about analogizing as a cognitive process. Nevertheless, the reader is being asked to notice the interesting match between results gleaned from the laboratory and what we observe every day in the political world. When the findings of psychologists using the experimental method in the laboratory 'gel' with those of political scientists using the case study method, those common findings acquire a powerful measure of plausibility, especially where the two are working independently of one another.

Methodological considerations and limits of the enquiry

Having laid out the core assumptions upon which this study will proceed, it is probably just as important to make clear at the outset what is *not* being assumed here, as well as what this study is not designed to do. First, this study is not designed to address any of the other questions which typically arise when the topic of analogical reasoning is broached. We shall be concerned in what follows primarily with the question of what decision-makers do when confronted by a highly novel situation, rather than with the issue of how reliable analogies are as a guide to the future, whether the analogies could have been better used in the case studied, and so on. Judgements such as these can be inferred from the Iran hostage case with a fair amount of ease, but it is largely left to the reader to draw his or her own conclusions about which historical analogy was more appropriate or useful (or indeed, whether it was wise to rely upon an analogy at all).

Secondly, in arguing that analogizing is probably a prevalent decision-making aid in some instances but not in others – for instance, where established decision rules and/or standard operating procedures exist – we are explicitly recognizing the fact that human beings are infinitely complex and varied creatures subject to an array of often conflicting pressures. It would be absurd, of course, to assume that analogical reasoning is the only mental tool humans ever employ in order to make sense of situations. At various points in the narrative which follows, the decision-makers do not appear to decide analogically, and nor should we expect them to. As Gary Sick has suggested, all policy-making events are to some extent treated *sui generis*.[49] Rather than seeing the future as a carbon copy re-run of the past, decision-makers usually employ history as a predictive *guide* to what may or may not happen. Moreover, a single analogy will rarely dictate a given policy decision, and decision-makers will often be confronted with a range of subjectively 'similar' analogues, usually suggesting markedly different scenarios. Any decision will usually represent the product of a careful weighing up of different values and goals, so that in highlighting the importance of analogical reasoning we assume that this phenomenon is often the key motivating factor or influence in some situations, but not that it is the only influence.

Thirdly, it should be noted that whatever propositions and statements we derive from our analysis here are likely to represent matters of *tendency* rather than Newtonian law. As Herbert Simon has noted, the predictions we can make about the kind of problem-solving strategy likely to be employed simply by knowing the type of problem being confronted will by necessity be incomplete.[50] Any propositions we derive from our analysis, in other words, are likely to be of a probabalistic, rather than a deterministic, character. The Iran hostage crisis is also a single case study, and therefore may not be in any sense 'typical' of a wider population of cases which could be characterized as novel situations. Nevertheless, the findings which emerge may at the very least generate hypotheses which may subsequently be subject to further testing by other researchers.

Investigating the presence of analogical reasoning during the Iran decision making naturally requires intensive and qualitative assessment of data, of the kind which the case study technique embodies. This method constitutes a venerable and well-established tradition within public policy research, and as Neil Smelser points out, case studies 'have proved to be of great value in generating hypotheses, refining

---

[49] Gary Sick, interview with the author, New York City, 14 December 1994.
[50] Simon, 'The Information Processing Theory of Human Problem Solving', p. 273.

relations among variables, and the like'.[51] Like the device of counterfactual reasoning, the case study method is intended to overcome as far as possible the central limitation of politics as a 'hard' science; namely, the fact that we cannot re-run history in the manner in which (in a sense) scientists working in the laboratory can. Those who employ the case study methodology for the purpose of verifying their theories empirically are typically faced with a choice between two alternatives, neither of which is ideal from a social scientific viewpoint. First of all, one can engage in an intensive analysis of one (or perhaps two) empirical cases. Alternatively, one can undertake a less in-depth (but much wider) analysis of numerous cases studied in tandem with one another. Obviously, what one gains in depth from the first choice, one loses in width, and vice versa if the second alternative is selected. Why is the former strategy selected here? In essence, for the simple reason that depth is what we are seeking here. We are attempting to understand why the Iranian militants, the Ayatollah Khomeini and key members of the Carter administration made the choices they did, and this obviously necessitates an in-depth examination of the reasoning processes employed by the actors, so far as these can be discerned after the fact.

Methodologically speaking, any research strategy from the very outset needs to arrive at decisions regarding how best to 'get at' the data offered by the case study selected. Unfortunately, many of the relevant US documents are still not available for the Iran hostage crisis case, since most remain classified as of the year 2000, and on the Iran side written documentation of the decision-making probably does not exist. Given the absence of declassified archival records, the methodology adopted here involves a multiple indicator approach, consisting of an analysis of those archival records and oral history interviews which are available in the Jimmy Carter Library, analysis of the available memoirs, examination of second-hand accounts and media resources, transcripts of interviews conducted with the Iranian students who seized the American embassy and a number of face-to-face interviews with key members of groups which made the decisions in the Iran case.

The absence of official, declassified records of the decision-makers' deliberations is in one sense a barrier to understanding. We still know relatively little, for instance, about the decision-making processes of the small, secretive group which planned the hostage rescue mission. When declassified, the US archival sources will undoubtedly provide

---

[51] Neil Smelser, *Comparative Methods in the Social Sciences* (Englewood Cliffs, New Jersey: Prentice Hall, 1976), p. 199.

data of a more objective sort, which may reveal information that has not already been uncovered in face-to-face interviews or the extensive leaks to the press that were especially characteristic of the Carter administration. Given that our chief concern is with the private use of analogies behind the scenes, a search of archival records would appear to be the most appropriate methodology under the circumstances, since it would allow us to analyse the statements and arguments of those involved *directly*, as they were made at the time.

Nevertheless, the absence of such records as data need not represent an insurmountable problem in this case. First, the key positions adopted and the policy preferences expressed by the main participants in the Iran decision-making process are fairly well established and are not in dispute. With the notable exception of former President Carter, several of the key participants in the US decision-making process made themselves available for interview in the current study, and we are able to piece together a fairly comprehensive account of the decision-making thereby. We also have a wealth of memoirs, interview transcripts and secondary accounts with which to flesh out the case. There are certainly gaps in our existing knowledge which later researchers will be able to fill, but the overall picture seems clear two decades after the events themselves.

Secondly, while it is obviously preferable to have verbatim, contemporaneous documentary records through which to trace the course of a decision-making episode, in this instance we are unlikely to have the kind of detailed transcripts of the meetings available in the Cuban missile crisis case. According to Gary Sick – the note taker at many of the critical Iran meetings – the records of the meetings which will one day be declassified mostly just summarize the positions taken by the key players and do not mention the detailed arguments each used to justify his or her case.[52] This is by no means something peculiar to the Iran case study. However, even when declassified and made available to researchers, official documents sometimes fail to reveal – and almost always do not *wholly* reveal – the underlying thinking of those involved. Transcripts or descriptive accounts of meetings, even where available, are usually incomplete, for as Robert Axelrod found in a major study of foreign policy decisions, 'assertions are infrequently supported by specific evidence' in policy debates. Policy-makers very often 'do not footnote their arguments as if they were conducting an

---

[52] Sick, interview with the author.

academic debate', as Zbigniew Brzezinski has put it, even though such unstated notes are strongly associated with their underlying beliefs and knowledge structures.[53] These structures are rarely placed on view in such settings, either because these are too well known to other decision-makers to require elaboration or because such broader accounts do not lend themselves to incisive and persuasive argumentation, so one should not expect documentary evidence to reveal the full incidence of analogizing in a particular case. Even if we had access to Sick's notes in the Iran case, then, it would arguably still be necessary to conduct supporting personal interviews which probe the *reasoning* behind the advocacy of particular positions.

Equally, there are certain well-known problems associated with the use of the interview technique as a source of qualitative or quantitative data. Decision-makers may embellish, exaggerate or otherwise distort their positions after the event for personal or political reasons, or they may simply forget what they said, especially where the researcher is investigating events which occurred some years ago. Both problems might conceivably hamper the case study in question. Since the rescue mission (to take one prominent puzzle examined in this book) was ultimately a failure, those decision-makers who favoured it have a ready made incentive to downplay their involvement, or even to deny that they approved of Carter's decision to go ahead with the operation. Secondly, since many of the interviews upon which this book draws were conducted between 1994 and 1998 – a number of years after the hostage crisis ended – some problems in recollecting detail might be expected.

Interestingly, the accounts given of 'who said what' are remarkably consistent with one another. Although there were obvious differences on both sides of the crisis in the ways which the decision-makers viewed the crisis, no major disagreements were encountered in the interview data among the interviewees regarding what positions and preferences were expressed in the key meetings on the American side, for instance, and no discrepancies were observed between the published accounts of the decision-making and the information offered by those interviewed. Moreover, those who could be expected to minimize their role in the planning of the mission made no observable effort to do so. Zbigniew Brzezinski, for instance, was intimately involved in the

---

[53] Robert Axelrod, 'Argumentation in Foreign Policy Settings: Britain in 1918, Munich in 1938 and Japan in 1970', *Journal of Conflict Resolution*, 21: 727–56, 1977, p. 743; Zbigniew Brzezinski, interview with the author, Washington DC, 3 February 1995.

genesis of the rescue operation and was a leading advocate of this option from the first days of the hostage crisis, but he freely and openly admitted to being a strong mover and shaker behind the decision to go ahead. This is not very surprising, since the broad policy positions adopted by Brzezinski, Vance and others during the crisis have been known some years prior to the interviews taking place, thus minimizing the room for the interviewees to make self-serving or distorted statements (assuming that they wished to do so). On the Iranian side, the recollections of the students who seized the embassy have been remarkably similar also.

The second potential problem, on the other hand, was present to some degree. Unsurprisingly, some of the interviewees encountered in face-to-face interviews with the author stated that they could not recall some of the reasoning adopted or statements made by themselves or others. For instance, Stansfield Turner stated that he could not remember Secretary of State Vance referring to the Iran case as being similar to the *Pueblo* hostage crisis, an analogy which Vance himself vividly recalls drawing to the other decision-makers' attention (Vance's claim, as we shall see in later chapters, is also supported by the recollections of other participants, such as Brzezinski and Hamilton Jordan). In the face-to-face interviews conducted by the author, the memory problem was generally remedied by asking each interviewee a reasonably standardized set of questions in order to fill in gaps in one decision-maker's recollections with the memories of others. In general, moreover, the events of the hostage crisis formed such a vivid and memorable part of the decision-makers' careers that on the whole they showed little difficulty in recalling their own arguments and preferences. Again, these recollections proved remarkably consistent with what is already known about the positions taken in debates about how best to get the hostages out.

Obviously, no one method utilized here is ideal for our purposes. Arguably, however, the limitations of the data to be employed here are not prohibitive so long as: (a) the researcher is aware of them; (b) he or she makes sure that the reader is aware of them; and (c) the data derived from the use of one method are bolstered by supporting evidence drawn from other methodologies appropriate to the case. This, of course, is the angle adopted here. As Philip Tetlock advises, 'whenever possible, investigators should seek methodological cross-validation of their findings . . . experimenters should try to determine whether empirical relationships observed under laboratory conditions hold up in the real world via content analysis, expert ratings, or case studies'.[54] The tandem methods or 'multimethod convergence' approach, as Tetlock calls it – drawing on a variety of published and interview transcript sources – is designed to minimize the risk of the findings arrived at being attributable to the peculiarities of the methodological line of attack adopted by the researcher, and the conclusions we arrive at in our chosen cases ought to acquire a strong measure of reliability thereby.

[54] See Philip Tetlock, 'Psychological Research on Foreign Policy: A Methodological Overview', in Ladd Wheeler (ed.), *Review of Personality and Social Psychology* (vol. IV), (Beverly Hills, California: Sage, 1983), p. 54. Implicitly, both Yuen Foong Khong and Deborah Welch Larson – as well as a host of other researchers – have employed this kind of technique, since the appeal of their work rests partly upon the overlap between their case study findings and those observed in the laboratory. Tetlock cites a number of works which utilize this methodological perspective.

3 The origins of the crisis

We had no feeling for the view of the vast majority of the Iranian people at the time. Because they believed as an article of faith that if the Shah came to the United States, it would usher in a series of events similar to those that had happened in 1953, when the CIA . . . assisted the pro-Shah demonstrators in overthrowing Mohammed Mossadegh and putting the Shah back on the Peacock throne. They believed that as an article of faith. Whether it was true or not is irrelevant.

Former American hostage Charles Scott[1]

Iran is an island of stability in one of the more troubled areas of the world

President Jimmy Carter, speaking on 31 December 1977

Implicit in chapter 2 is the assumption that the psychological approach to foreign policy analysis popularized by scholars like Robert Jervis, Ole Holsti and Alexander George explains the behaviour of *human beings* in a decision-making context, not merely that of decision-makers in the United States.[2] Yet most case study analyses which employ a foreign policy decision-making approach have examined their case materials as they were viewed from the American perspective and as the issues were confronted by American decision-makers. The Cuban missile crisis has been exhaustively analysed from the perspective of John Kennedy and the ExComm, for example. The decisions of Third World states, on the other hand, are rarely viewed through cognitive psychological lenses, and there is even a paucity of theoretically driven studies of British foreign policy. One looks in vain for studies of

[1] Interview with Charles Scott, Iranian Project, Antelope Productions.
[2] See Vertzberger, *The World in Their Minds*, for an analysis that makes this assumption explicit.

Anthony Eden's ill-fated adventure in Suez or Thatcher's decision-making during the Falklands War which apply concepts and theories drawn from the huge literature on FPDM (as opposed to narrowly historical accounts of these events, which are relatively plentiful). There are, of course, some examples of attempts to study non-US decision-making from such an angle – sections of Graham Allison and Philip Zelikow's classic *Essence of Decision*, for instance, are devoted to an analysis of why the Soviet Union might have acted as it did during the missile crisis, and both Indian and Israeli decision-making have also been examined from an FPDM perspective – but such efforts have been few and far between.[3]

There are doubtless at least *some* good reasons for this concentration on American cases. Archival documents and personal interviews are often easiest to come by in the United States, and since that country has always been the home of the decision-making perspective, it is a relatively straightforward matter to apply theoretical frameworks to empirical materials one is already familiar with (and relatively difficult to go to the trouble of acquainting oneself with the political arrangements of other countries). Another reason may relate to training, philosophy and style. International relations programmes in Europe have traditionally been dominated by classical realist, Marxist or 'historical' approaches, none of which is especially hospitable to the FPDM approach, with its focus on individual psychology, bounded rationality and the like.

And yet it is difficult to believe that British scholars, say, have largely overlooked the importance of approaches like groupthink, bureaucratic politics or cognitive models simply because most have not been trained in the use of such perspectives. In fact, scholars like Christopher Hill and Steve Smith have long taught these approaches in Britain. It is tempting to conclude, then, that what really accounts for the paucity of

[3] Graham Allison and Philip Zelikow, *Essence of Decision: Explaining the Cuban Missile Crisis*, 2nd edn (New York: Longman, 1999). For some studies of Israeli decision-making from an FPDM perspective, see Janice Gross Stein and Raymond Tanter, *Rational Decision-Making: Israel's Security Choices, 1967* (Columbus, Ohio: Ohio University Press, 1980) and Zeev Maoz, 'The Decision To Raid Entebbe: Decision Analysis Applied to Crisis Behavior', *Journal of Conflict Resolution*, 25: 677–707, 1981, and for India see Yaacov Vertzberger, 'Bureaucratic-Organizational Politics and Information Processing in a Developing State', *International Studies Quarterly*, 28: 69–95, 1984. For rare examples using British cases, see John Henderson, 'Leadership Personality and War: The Case of Richard Nixon and Anthony Eden', *Political Science*, 28: 141–64, 1976 and Richard Ned Lebow, 'Miscalculation in the South Atlantic: The Origins of the Falklands War', in Robert Jervis *et al.*, *Psychology and Deterrence* (London: Johns Hopkins University Press, 1985).

non-US case studies in the FPDM field is the non-applicability of this body of research outside the United States. This criticism seems to have particular force in relation to Third World states like Iran.

The applicability of psychological approaches to Third World states has been particularly questioned. Early work on comparative foreign policy – notably by James Rosenau – emphasized the role of leader characteristics in determining the foreign policies of underdeveloped states. Yet many of the classic discussions of this subject dismiss the primacy of psychological factors. Franklin Weinstein, for instance, doubts the relevance of the original statement of FPDM theory – Richard Snyder *et al.*'s *Foreign Policy Decision-Making* – to the study of foreign policy in the Third World, although he bases that conclusion on Indonesia alone. 'The applicability of the decision-making approach in a less developed country like Indonesia is questionable. Rarely are issues confronted in a clear-cut fashion in terms of alternative policy choices.' Methodologically speaking, he also casts doubt on our ability to verify such theories empirically. 'In less developed countries, limitations on freedom of the press make it very hard to get detailed contemporary "insider" accounts of decisions, a deficiency which is aggravated by the passage of time because of the scantiness of documentary materials and the inadequacy of archival facilities.'[4] Similarly, Bahgat Korany berates what he terms the 'conceptual blinkers of psychological reductionism', the result, he argues, of 'a general bias that has dominated the field all along'.[5]

Theorists of international relations have also generally given psychological accounts of Third World behaviour short shrift. World Systems theorists and Waltzian neo-realists – though they agree on little else – concur that the study of individual decision-making in Third World states is effectively a wasted effort, since both hold that overlying structures account for the most important aspects of state behaviour. In both perspectives, the psychological attitudes and cognitions of decision-makers constitute epiphenomena, in that they allegedly add little of interest to a causal explanation of why events occur. In World Systems and dependency theory, for instance, it matters little who leads the exploited state and what his or her beliefs happen to be, since the Third World is said to be entrapped within an all-encompassing struc-

---

[4] Franklin Weinstein, 'The Uses of Foreign Policy in Indonesia: An Approach to the Analysis of Foreign Policy in the Less Developed Countries', *World Politics*, 24: 356–81, 1972, p. 359.

[5] Bahgat Korany, 'The Take-Off of Third World Studies? The Case of Foreign Policy', *World Politics*, 35: 464–87, 1983, p. 480 and pp. 468–9.

ture. In virtually all versions of realism, on the other hand, analysts reach this same conclusion by assuming that states which possess 'more power' will inevitably triumph over those with 'less', leading inexorably to the same assumption, that individual decision-makers in the less powerful state need not be studied.

In order for structural or system level forces to drive outcomes, states must recognize the existence of the pressures and constraints. And yet, as Robert Jervis suggests, even the most powerful states in the system may fail to recognize the existence of such constraints.[6] Despite the popularity of structural models in recent years, there are many examples of instances where less powerful states conflicting with more powerful ones nevertheless manage to 'win' the conflict and to impose their preferences upon the more powerful adversary; cases, in other words, where the structure or distribution of power fails to predict the outcome accurately. In Africa and the Middle East, for instance, the Cold War often effectively empowered dependent states by conferring bargaining advantages upon them relative to one or both of the superpowers. In other cases, the weaker state simply prevailed over the stronger. The Vietnam War – where a tiny, economically weak nation was able to impose its will upon that of the world's foremost economic and political superpower – is a particularly obvious case in point.[7] The Iran hostage crisis, where for 444 days an American president was apparently powerless to release the hostages by his own actions, presents us with another especially stunning example. As Rose McDermott notes, 'structuralism would predict that the power discrepancy in the international system [between the United States and Iran] would play to the advantage of the United States'.[8] This is a critical observation, for it suggests that sub-systemic analysis is essential in order to explain why Iran decided to act in ways which a realist would regard as contrary to its position in the international system, why the United States did not bring its enormous military superiority to bear upon the situation and why the power imbalance between the two countries failed to produce the expected outcome.

The temptation to dismiss the relevance of FPDM approaches to Third World or even Western European states should be resisted. Whatever the reasons why the approach has yet to take firm hold

[6] Robert Jervis, *System Effects: Complexity in Social and Political Life* (Princeton, New Jersey: Princeton University Press, 1997), p. 104.
[7] David Baldwin, 'Power Analysis and World Politics: New Trends Versus Old Tendencies', *World Politics*, 31: 161–94, 1979.
[8] McDermott, 'Prospect Theory in International Relations', p. 238.

amongst scholars of foreign policy in nations other than the United States, for instance – and those reasons are undoubtedly complex – it is not accurate to conclude that decision-making theories developed originally within that country have no empirical relevance outside it. Chapter 4 attempts to build upon the few existing non-US case studies in the field by examining Iranian decision-making during the early stages of the Iran hostage crisis. More specifically, we shall attempt to explain why a handful of Iranian students should have seized the American embassy in Tehran in November 1979, asking ourselves whether the analogical reasoning approach might have any role to play in resolving this puzzle.

While obtaining reliable information about the deliberations of the Iranian decision-makers is admittedly difficult – indeed, this is one of Weinstein's grounds for altogether dismissing the applicability of decision-making theory to Third World states – more and more information about the Ayatollah Khomeini's reasoning and that of the students who seized the American embassy has become available over the past few years. This chapter draws in particular on interviews conducted during November and December 1997 in Iran and the United States by the British film company Antelope Productions. These interviews – which formed the basis of the BBC documentary *444 Days*, broadcast in the United Kingdom in November 1998 – were kindly made available to the author and provide a wealth of information about the motives and intentions of the hostage takers, some of whom were interviewed directly, as well as detailing the thinking and reactions of American decision-makers and many of the hostages themselves. The argument offered here also draws upon the large number of interviews with the hostages reproduced in Tim Wells's *444 Days: The Hostages Remember*, on the memoirs of former members of the Carter administration, oral history interviews contained in the Jimmy Carter Library in Atlanta, Georgia, and other secondary accounts of the hostage crisis.

Seizing the embassy

The 4th of November 1979, a Sunday, began as a routine working day for many in America's embassy in Tehran.[9] What happened in mid-morning was decidedly not routine, however, and it took almost everyone – in Tehran, Washington DC and even in the moderate Iranian

---

[9] Friday is the holy day in Iran, so the US embassy used Sunday as the beginning of the working week.

government – by surprise. At around nine o'clock in the morning a group of Iranian students, making their way to Tehran University as part of a larger demonstration being held to commemorate the death of students killed by the shah's forces the previous year, broke away from the larger body and began to congregate outside the walls of the embassy. 'Death to America!' and 'Death to the Shah!', they shouted, by now familiar slogans which the embassy staff were accustomed to hearing in the streets since the fall of the shah's regime. Although the noise level was apparently greater than usual, no one suspected that anything unusual was going on. Lee Schatz, an agricultural attaché at the embassy whose recollections are typical in this respect, notes that 'whenever there was a demonstration in Tehran, it was the norm for people to pass the embassy in groups', and since the university was in the western part of the city, it was both normal and expected for those going to a demonstration there from the eastern section to pass directly in front of the embassy building.[10] As former hostage Tom Schaefer, recalls:

> it looked like a bunch of students this time were coming by. I was not even concerned that students were going by, until someone said 'They're getting through the gate.' I honestly felt that's all it was, it was a bunch of students. They probably just want to talk to us. And eventually we found that there was more than this because they were taking other American workers out of the outbuildings, blindfolding them, with guns to their heads, and that was my first indication really that this is more than just a student visit to our embassy, that this is serious.[11]

Early that Sunday morning, about 300 Iranian students had gathered at a secret location to hear details of a plan to seize the embassy building. At around 2 a.m. Washington time and 10.30 a.m. Tehran time, a large (and probably even more substantial) group of students poured through the main gate of the compound and clambered over the walls of the embassy.[12] Despite the best efforts of the embassy staff to

[10] Lee Schatz, quoted in Tim Wells, *444 Days: The Hostages Remember* (San Diego, California: Harcourt Brace, 1985), p. 37.
[11] Quoted in CIA, 'Moving Targets', BBC, Broadcast in Britain, July 1992. Schaefer was the Defence Intelligence Agency's chief in Tehran between 1978 and 1979.
[12] Tehran is eight and a half hours ahead of Washington DC. A host of US commentators has poured scorn upon the notion that those who conducted the hostage taking were genuine 'students' in the sense in which we understand that term in the West. However, the evidence we now have suggests that this scorn was misplaced. Many of the hostage takers were in fact science students. See Christos Ioannides, 'The Hostages of Iran: A Discussion with the Militants', *Washington Quarterly*, 3: 12–35, 1980.

prevent the takeover, within a couple of hours the students had control of the building and took the sixty-five Americans inside hostage. They quickly blindfolded their hostages and were soon parading them before the television cameras of the world.

The seizure of the embassy was not a spontaneous action. It had been planned in advance during the last week of October by the students who undertook it, following the entry of the shah to the United States. And yet the motives and intentions of the hostage takers remain something of a mystery to Westerners, and analysts have puzzled for years as to why the Iranian students might have acted as they did. One theory proposes that the hostages were taken as a 'bargaining chip' to try to compel the return of the shah, who had fled the country in January 1979, to Iran. A second explanation simply posits an ideological fanaticism to the students, stemming from their radical Islamic beliefs. Jimmy Carter claimed in his memoirs that 'Khomeini was acting insanely,' although he also says that 'we always behaved *as if* we were dealing with a rational person' (my italics).[13] According to this account, the embassy was taken mainly because the students – 'extremists' and 'fanatics' caught up in the midst of a revolution – took out their irrational rage and frustration upon an obvious target. And thirdly, some inside the Carter administration have long argued that the embassy was taken for mostly instrumental, political reasons. Needing to stamp his authority upon a political landscape in chaos after the departure of the shah, Ayatollah Khomeini engineered the takeover of the embassy in order to establish his radical credentials, according to this interpretation. The leading advocate of the instrumental-political view has been former NSC staff aide Gary Sick. Sick argues that 'the Ayatollah was at least generally aware of the plans for an attack on the embassy and consciously exploited it for his own domestic political purposes . . . the fate of the shah was never the real issue. The real issue was Khomeini's constitution and the realization of his vision of an Iranian republic.'[14] Similarly, Zbigniew Brzezinski suggests that 'the issue of the shah as a person and his wealth was thus a conventional tool . . . for radicalizing Iranian politics. The hostage crisis was an externalization of this internal Iranian turmoil,'[15] while Lloyd Cutler believes that 'if we had not admitted the shah, within a month the embassy would have been seized and the hostages taken

[13] Carter, *Keeping Faith*, p. 468.   [14] Sick, *All Fall Down*, p. 251.
[15] Zbigniew Brzezinski, *Power and Principle: Memoirs of the National Security Adviser, 1977–1981* (New York: Farrar, Strauss and Giroux, 1983), p. 471.

anyway. The whole thing was done for internal political reasons to galvanize and unify the country against the Americans, and if they hadn't had that immediate opportunity they would have found another one.'[16]

All three explanations contain obvious but varying grains of truth, and each tells a part of the story. However, there are also notable problems with each. First, while the students did indeed call for the return of the shah to Iran, the bargaining chip hypothesis suffers from the major defect that Ayatollah Khomeini – far from attempting to negotiate with the Americans – actually refused to talk to Carter's representatives. Repeated attempts by the Carter administration to establish negotiation channels to Khomeini came to naught. If the students' objective was to force the Americans to return the shah, why was no *quid pro quo* offered? According to former Iranian Foreign Minister Sadegh Ghotbzadeh, Khomeini 'understood very well that Jimmy Carter could not extradite the shah to Iran as demanded and therefore that this was not a real condition for the release of the hostages'.[17]

The second and third explanations, on the other hand, seem to have more to recommend them. It seems self-evidently true that the students were radical Muslims who were ideologically opposed to the United States. Nevertheless, this account suffers from more than a hint of Western bias. Given the conventional Western equation of Islam with extremism, it is easy to view the students as a bunch of immature young hotheads caught up in the fervour of their times and to dismiss their actions as simply 'irrational', as former President Carter has. No doubt some of them could be described as politically immature, and some of the hostages themselves later described their captors as exceptionally naive. Nevertheless, this account robs any real assumption of considered purpose from the explanation, denying that the students might have had some more basic human reason (other than simple revenge or hatred) for doing what they did. This account is also historically anaemic, for it disregards the whole context of US–Iranian relations which provided the backdrop for the students' actions, beyond simply noting that the years of shah's rule as an American proxy had left the students eager for revenge.

The instrumental argument – Sick's notion that 'the embassy seizure

[16] Lloyd Cutler, Exit interview, 2 March 1981, Jimmy Carter Library, p. 16.
[17] Paraphrased in Richard Cottam, *Iran and the United States: A Cold War Case Study* (Pittsburgh, Pennsylvania: University of Pittsburgh Press, 1988), pp. 211–12.

was almost entirely a function of Iranian internal politics'[18] – clearly has much to recommend it. However, it too suffers from a central flaw: there is little or no evidence that the ayatollah himself planned the embassy takeover, that this was somehow a premeditated act on his part or that he was even aware of what the students were planning to do before they actually did it. Close associates insist that he had no knowledge of the students' plans until the takeover had actually taken place. According to Ayatollah Musavi Khoieniha, an associate of Khomeini who did have prior knowledge of these plans, 'the students wanted to tell their plans to Iman Khomeini and to get his backing for their action. I prevented this and convinced them to proceed with their plans without the knowledge of the Iman.'[19] Similarly, Baqer Moin, author of the best English-speaking biography of Khomeini, argues that his subject was 'taken by surprise by the affair of the embassy'. For some days, he said nothing about the hostage incident publicly since he 'needed time to gather his thoughts and assess the potential advantages and disadvantages of any pronouncement by him for or against the move'. It was only when it became clear that the advantages outweighed the disadvantages that he publicly backed the students.[20]

The evidence we now have suggests that three students – Ibrahim Asgharzadeh, Abbas Abdi and Mohsen Mirdammadi – played an especially central role in the planning.[21] Others – notably Massoumeh Ebtekar, who acted as an interpreter inside the embassy – played a major role both during the invasion and after it had taken place. The available evidence suggests that the students did not intend to occupy the embassy for very long. It was designed to last anywhere between three and seven days, although recollections vary slightly on this point (three days, according to Asgharzadeh, five to seven according to Abdi). The original idea seems to have been Asgharzadeh's. Initially, pulling the feat off must have seemed quite remote, not least because the students knew that the embassy had been additionally fortified

[18] Sick, *All Fall Down*, p. 241.
[19] Interview with Musavi Khoieniha, Iran Project, Antelope Productions. Quoted in *Storyline: 444 Days*, broadcast on British television, BBC 2, 14 November 1998.
[20] Baqer Moin, *Khomeini: Life of the Ayatollah* (London: I. B. Tauris, 1999), pp. 226–7. William Shawcross, *The Shah's Last Ride* (London: Chatto and Windus, 1989), pp. 260–2, suggests that Khomeini's support for the students' actions was instantaneous, but this claim is probably incorrect.
[21] Scott Macleod, 'Radicals Reborn', *Time*, 15 November 1999; John Daniszewski, 'Twenty Years After Revolution, Iran Has Hope', *Los Angeles Times*, 11 February 1999; Daniszewski, 'Twenty Years After Hostages, Iran Reflects on Costs', *Los Angeles Times*, 4 November 1979.

against external attacks during the course of that year.[22] In late October, Asgharzadeh had sent fellow students sympathetic to the occupation idea to find out the habits and routines of the US Marines who guarded the embassy. Having done this, the students knew that some means would have to be found to get large numbers of their forces inside the embassy compound, without all of them having to scale the walls, and they thus came prepared on 4 November. As Scott Macleod (who interviewed Asgharzadeh in depth) relates, 'to break the chains locking the embassy's gates, a female student was given a pair of metal cutters that she could hide beneath her chador'.[23]

Most significantly for the instrumental approach, all three of the central figures have repeatedly denied in interviews given since the hostage crisis ended that the ayatollah knew anything about their plans before they were actually implemented.[24] Moreover, their stories have not changed over time. At the beginning of March 1980 – before the failed American rescue mission, but with the hostage crisis still in full swing – Ebtekar and another student radical (identified only as 'Shapoor') were interviewed by a Greek academic called Christos Ioannides. In a remarkable scoop, Ioannides was able to talk frankly to the two hostage takers inside the American embassy itself. Both radicals adamantly denied that the embassy seizure was ordered by Khomeini.[25]

This claim is further supported by others in Khomeini's immediate circle. The ayatollah, Ibrahim Yazdi insists, had no foreknowledge of the embassy takeover, although the students 'informed him afterward'.[26] According to another observer, Khomeini was actually 'very angry' at the students during the first three days of the takeover, probably because he may have felt initially that this action would actually provoke American intervention rather than forestall it, thus jeopardizing the revolution.[27] Yazdi backs this up to some extent, claiming that Khomeini was one of those who initially asked him to get the students out, since he 'told me in private, who are these gangs, go

---

[22] The US embassy in Tehran was dubbed 'Fort Apache' for this reason.
[23] Macleod, 'Radicals Reborn'. One wonders whether the female student in question was Massoumeh Ebtekar.   [24] See, for instance, ibid.
[25] Ioannides, 'The Hostages of Iran', p. 30.
[26] Interview with Ibrahim Yazdi, Iranian Project, Antelope Productions. Yazdi was a close associate of Khomeini during his exile in Paris and served as foreign minister of Iran for much of 1979.
[27] Interview with Mansour Rouhani, Iranian Project, Antelope Productions. Rouhani is a former Iranian minister.

and see if you can keep them out'.[28] If this is true, however, it is clear that at some point during the first few days of the crisis Khomeini changed his mind about the desirability of taking the American embassy, and began to perceive its utility to him as a domestic political device. As Cyrus Vance noted in his memoirs, 'probably, it was not until Khomeini saw the hysterical mob reaction and sensed the hostages' potential for uniting the warring factions against a hated foreign enemy that he decided to use them as a rallying point for bringing about a new Iranian state'.[29] According to Henry Precht, there may also have been emotional reasons why Khomeini changed his mind. As Precht puts it, 'when a group saying they were following the line of the Ayatollah [came along] . . . I think he felt obliged to stand with them. Especially to stand against the Shah, and against the United States, two of the fabled enemies of the revolution.'[30]

What is some way beyond doubt is that Khomeini utilized, and took political advantage of, the takeover once it had *already* occurred, and that the hostages soon became, in Vance's words, 'pawns in the Iranian power struggle'.[31] But while this is probably a valid explanation for Khomeini's behaviour in the days after the embassy takeover – indeed, the domestic political utility of the hostages to him within Iran accounts for his lack of interest in negotiation initially, and for the eventual release of the hostages once this utility had diminished – it is questionable as an explanation for the seizure itself, for it tells us nothing about the original motivations of the students who planned and executed the takeover.

We are admittedly on somewhat shaky ground in attempting to adjudicate between the rival theories outlined above, since we lack 'impartial' accounts of the decision-making on the Iranian side. The very insider status that endows Iranians in a position to know what went on within the student planning group also makes them untrustworthy in the eyes of many Westerners. There is, however, a fourth explanation which has been suggested forcefully by Christos Ioannides, Barry Rubin and a number of others, but has not yet been expressed in the language of the foreign policy decision-making literature. According to Rubin, the students based their actions 'on a desire to block an

---

[28] Yazdi interview, Antelope Productions. See also Bill, *The Eagle and the Lion*, p. 295.
[29] Cyrus Vance, *Hard Choices: Four Critical Years in Managing America's Foreign Policy* (New York: Simon and Schuster, 1983), p. 376.
[30] Interview with Henry Precht, Iranian Project, Antelope Productions. Precht was the State Department's director of Iranian affairs during the Carter administration.
[31] Vance, *Hard Choices*, p. 377.

alleged American-sponsored counter-revolution and to destroy the moderate regime'.[32] The ayatollah himself, in endorsing the takeover, suggested that the embassy was critical since it would be the base for this supposed counterrevolution. 'America expects to take the shah there, engage in plots, create a base in Iran for these plots, and our young people are expected simply to remain idle and witness these things',[33] Khomeini stated. Rubin argues that the hostages were essentially an insurance policy against a US intervention, since they were 'not fully convinced of their ability to prevent a dramatic reversal of the revolution and the restoration of the Shah to power – as, after all, had occurred in August, 1953'.[34] Similarly, for Ioannides 'the action of taking the American diplomats hostage was viewed as the only way to defend Islam and Iran from another defeat at the hands of the West. In the extremists' eyes, it was the only way to prevent a repetition of 1953.'[35] Fully expecting that the United States would try to repeat its actions of that year, the radicals sought to forestall such an attempt. In other words, they appear to have reasoned by historical analogy.

To dismiss the behaviour of the Iranian revolutionaries as simply 'irrational' misses the point that there was some objective basis to the popularity of conspiracy theorizing. During the previous two centuries, Iranians had lived almost continuously under the shadow of external powers. As James Bill notes, 'throughout the nineteenth century Britain and Russia intrigued in Iran, each state jealously seeking to draw Iran into its sphere of influence'.[36] After Reza Shah Pahlavi – who ruled Iran between 1925 and 1941 – began to display Nazi sympathies, Iran was invaded during World War II by Britain and the Soviet Union. Reza Shah was driven into exile, and the invading powers replaced him with his own son, Muhammed Reza Shah. Iran's strategic and economic position in the Middle East during World War II, and later during the Cold War, was not lost on the Americans, and the United States from 1942 onwards began to play an increasingly active role in the country. After World War II the Allies agreed to withdraw their forces from Iran, but the Middle East in general also became a vital Cold War battleground in the struggle between the superpowers.

In 1951 a perceived threat would emerge to US interests in the region, when Mohammed Mossadegh became prime minister of Iran.

---

[32] Barry Rubin, *Paved With Good Intentions: The American Experience and Iran* (New York: Penguin, 1981), p. 298.   [33] Ibid.   [34] Ibid., p. 303.
[35] Christos Ioannides, *America's Iran: Injury and Catharsis* (Lanham, Maryland: University Press of America, 1984), p. 97.   [36] Bill, *The Eagle and the Lion*, p. 16.

Mossadegh was in no sense a communist; in Bill's words, he was 'an old-fashioned liberal' who 'believed neither in ideological dogma nor in the use of coercion'.[37] He was, rather, a nationalist and a democrat, part of a political tide of opinion in Iran which valued its territorial sovereignty – and abhorred foreign intervention – above all else. A particular bone of contention amongst Iranian nationalists was the role played by foreign powers in its oil industry, especially that of the Anglo-Iranian Oil Company, which had been doing business in Iran for most of the twentieth century. While Mossadegh came to power on the back of these broad social forces, his own political position – and the diverse coalition which supported him – was precarious, and as the conservative and religious elements of this coalition deserted him, he was forced to rely more heavily upon the radical left. In August 1953 Mossadegh was overthrown in a *coup d'état*, originally proposed by the British but engineered and organized in large part by the Central Intelligence Agency.[38] The monarchy and Mohammed Reza Shah were reinstated, and would rule Iran until the revolutionary events of 1979.

In the years after 1953, the CIA's role in Mossadegh's overthrow would be much analysed and debated, becoming the stuff of legend. As Gary Sick puts it, 'the belief that the United States had single-handedly imposed a harsh tyrant on a reluctant populace became one of the central myths' in the relationship between the United States and Iran.[39] The CIA's manoeuvres, it has often been noted, could not have succeeded had Mossadegh's popularity not been declining and that of the shah ascending. Stansfield Turner, for instance, points out that 'covert actions to overthrow governments work best when the situation is unstable and only a small push is needed to change it, as was true with Mossadegh'.[40] Nevertheless, whatever the weight one attributes to American actions in the downfall of Mossadegh, it was viewed in Iran as yet another instance of interference in its domestic political and

---

[37] Ibid., p. 56.
[38] The coup was a joint British–American operation, but recently published portions of a still classified CIA report on the coup reveal how secondary the British role was. Athough the original idea to overthow Mossadegh was their own, Britain was forced to go along with the US candidate to replace Mossadegh – General Zahedi – even though they had grave doubts about his suitability, and the Americans also apparently lied to them about some details in the plan. The report also alludes to the contempt the CIA had for the shah as a leader. See James Risen, 'Secrets of History: The CIA in Iran', *New York Times*, 16 April 2000. See also Mark Gasiorowski, 'The 1953 Coup D'Etat in Iran', *International Journal of Middle East Studies*, 19: 261–86, 1987.
[39] Sick, *All Fall Down*, p. 7.
[40] Stansfield Turner, *Terrorism and Democracy* (Boston, Massachusetts: Houghton Mifflin, 1991), p. 77.

economic affairs by an outside party, and a clear violation of its political sovereignty. Whether it had succeeded or not, the United States, like Britain and the Soviet Union before it, had attempted to interfere in Iran's affairs, in a very visible and public way. As Charles Scott notes, it was people's perceptions of 1953 that mattered in 1979, regardless of whether or not these perceptions were accurate.[41]

In the United States, the events of 1953 were not well publicized until the congressional investigation years which followed Watergate in the 1970s. President Eisenhower, for instance, deliberately hid America's involvement in those events both at the time they occurred and when he subsequently came to write his memoirs. In places, his account of Mossadegh's fall is deliberately misleading, and the former president even reproduces a letter he wrote to Mossadegh – dated the same year as the coup – in which he affirmed that 'the government of Iran must determine for itself which foreign and domestic policies are likely to be most advantageous to Iran and the Iranian people'.[42] Until the late 1970s, American foreign policy textbooks and other scholarly works also very often failed to mention a coup in Iran that year.[43] In Iran itself, however, the story was different. Generations of Iranians were brought up in the shadow of 1953, and it became a defining experience and national rallying point – part myth perhaps, but also part historical fact – in their lives. Consequently, when another Iranian leader whose political priorities clashed markedly with Western interests appeared on the scene after the fall of the shah, it is easy to see why that historical experience should have become activated in such a striking way. John Kifner, observing events in Tehran for the *New York Times* as the shah was admitted to hospital in the United States, observed that the 'sense of plot' was so widespread in the city that it was 'almost impossible to find anyone who believes the Shah is actually sick'.[44] As Henry Precht recalls, 'the one constant theme that obsessed the movement against the Shah, both the leader of the revolution and the followers, was a fear that the United States would repeat 1953 (when the Shah was restored to his throne with US help) in destroying Iran's revolution'.[45] That ordinary

---

[41] Interview with Charles Scott, Iran Project, Antelope Productions.
[42] Dwight Eisenhower, *The White House Years: Mandate for Change, 1953–1956* (London: Heinemann, 1963), p. 162.   [43] Bill, *The Eagle and the Lion*, p. 87.
[44] John Kifner, 'Bitter Hatred – of the Shah and the US – Reunites Iran', *New York Times*, 18 November 1979. The shah had been diagnosed with cancer, and allowed into the United States by Jimmy Carter on humanitarian grounds.
[45] Quoted in Harold Saunders, 'The Crisis Begins', in Christopher (ed.), *American Hostages in Iran*, p. 43.

Iranians and their leaders should have been seduced by the 1953 analogy – and should have misjudged America's intentions under Jimmy Carter so markedly – should hardly be surprising, however, for America's people and leaders exhibited a similar lack of understanding and knowledge about Iran. One misperception, or set of misperceptions, essentially mirrored the other.

The students, as already noted, were living through highly uncertain and turbulent times. As the preceding discussion of the cognitive bases of analogical reasoning emphasized, the key inducement to think analogically appears to be a high degree of uncertainty. To draw upon what one knows – in particular, upon one's own recent history – is a classic pyschological coping mechanism. Many of the students appear to have believed that Carter and Vance would step in to crush the revolution and to re-establish the position of the shah in 1979, just as Eisenhower and Dulles had done in 1953. Moreover, they clearly misinterpreted American actions from the Spring of 1979 as a re-run of the events which led to the Mossadegh coup. From the early part of that year onwards, the Carter administration began trying to re-establish the American embassy in Tehran, whose membership had been much depleted by the onset of the revolution, and attempted to 'normalize' relations with the new political authorities in Iran. Yet as former hostage Michael Metrinko puts it, 'what we saw as normalization with the new provisional government, with the new revolutionary government, the students and a lot of clergy – a lot of the ultra-militant – would see as the destruction of revolution'.[46] Like Kifner, Metrinko recalls that many Iranians did not believe that the shah was sick 'until he actually died, and even then [they doubted it]'.[47]

When the Americans decided to allow the shah of Iran into the United States for medical treatment on 22 October, this only strengthened Iranian suspicions, causing radical Iranians to view this as 'a prelude to some imminent coup attempt'.[48] After fleeing Iran in January, the shah passed through a succession of countries looking for a safe haven. After it was learnt that he was suffering from cancer, the Carter administration reluctantly agreed to allow the shah to enter the United States. But as Ibrahim Asgharzadeh recalls, this provoked enormous suspicion amongst the Iranians: 'the decision to occupy the embassy began with our reaction to what America had done. We felt

---

[46] Interview with Michael Metrinko, Iran Project, Antelope Productions. Metrinko was a political officer at the Tehran embassy. [47] Ibid.
[48] Rubin, *Paved With Good Intentions*, p. 303.

that by allowing the Shah into America they were conspiring against the revolution.'[49] This is consistent with Hamilton Jordan's recollection. Jordan notes that many in Iran simply did not believe that the shah was being admitted for medical reasons. 'They were sceptical that it was true', he says, 'they thought it was part of some conspiracy to try to return the Shah to power.'[50]

This perception was also apparently shared by Khomeini himself. As Baqer Moin notes, Khomeini believed that the United States would not accept the new regime he intended to fashion, and that it was only a matter of time before it intervened. As Moin puts it, 'when the cancer-ridden Shah was allowed into the United States for medical treatment . . . Khomeini fumed at what he considered to be a provocative act. To him, this was evidence of American plotting. His statements became increasingly belligerent, and he railed against the machinations of the "Great Satan".'[51]

Another incident – just prior to the seizure of the embassy – also helped convince the students that the Americans were plotting another 1953. As William Daugherty – a hostage and CIA member who had only recently arrived in Iran just prior to the embassy seizure – points out:

> to the ever-suspicious Iranian radicals, the admission of the Shah for medical treatment was a sham designed to hide a conspiracy aimed at overthrowing their revolutionary government. To add more fuel to the fire, Prime Minister Mehdi Bazargan and Foreign Minister Ibrahim Yazdi (a graduate of a US medical school who had practiced his profession in the United States, and who held a Permanent Resident Alien green card) met briefly with National Security Adviser Brzezinski in Algiers on 1 November 1979, during the celebration of Algeria's independence day. In this meeting, which was not pub-licized in Algiers, the Shah and the future of US–Iranian relations were discussed.[52]

The meeting between the National Security Adviser and moderates within the provisional Iranian government undoubtedly enflamed the students and helped reinforce the historical analogy already in their heads. Henry Precht makes a similar point, arguing that 'when we brought the Shah to New York, it fuelled those suspicions, which were

---

[49] Interview with Ibrahim Asgharzadeh, Iran Project, Antelope Productions.
[50] Oral history interview with Hamilton Jordan, Miller Center Interviews, Carter Presidency Project, 6 November 1981, vol. VI, p. 81, Jimmy Carter Library.
[51] Moin, *Khomeini*, p. 220.
[52] William Daugherty, 'A First Tour Like No Other', *Studies in Intelligence*, 41: 1–45, 1998, p. 6.

further sparked by the Brzezinski-Yazdi-Bazargan meeting in Al-giers'.[53]

Upon entering the embassy, many of the students were under the impression that everyone in the embassy was engaged in intelligence activity, and that it was in effect what the Ayatollah Khomeini's son Ahmad called a 'nest of spies'.[54] An extensive search for these spies was immediately carried out. Interviews with the hostages themselves repeatedly confirm this, but the experiences of two of the hostages – press officer Barry Rosen and communications officer Charles Jones – may serve as typical examples. When Rosen was asked what his job was inside the embassy by an Iranian interrogator, he replied that he was a press officer. The interrogator, however, simply did not believe him. 'No, this is a lie. You are CIA!,' she said, and then 'went into a tirade about how the CIA had destroyed Iran'.[55] Similarly, Charles Jones relates that he 'tried to explain a little bit to them about international diplomacy and what the functions of an embassy were. But it was hopeless. They were absolutely convinced that everyone in the embassy was a spy.'[56]

Another indication of this belief in a plot to restore the shah to power can be found in the students' efforts to reconstruct embassy documents which American diplomats had begun to shred when the building was seized. Some time after the building had come under the control of the militants, English-speaking Iranians sympathetic to the revolutionary cause managed to painstakingly piece together many of the shredded documents, some of which were later published in Iran. The effort involved in undertaking such an enterprise can hardly be underestimated, and in the West this action was seen by many as evidence of sheer fanaticism and paranoia. However, the most likely reason the students did this is not simply that they were looking for general evidence of interference in Iranian affairs, though they were certainly hoping to come across this (and, in fact, they did uncover some evidence of CIA efforts to recruit agents within the moderate post-shah

---

[53] Quoted in Saunders, 'The Crisis Begins', p. 43. Representatives of the State Department are generally more willing to argue that Brzezinki's behaviour in Algiers may have contributed to Iranian conspiracy theorizing than are those who worked for Brzezinski, such as Gary Sick. Sick dismisses the Iranian reaction to the Algiers meeting as opportunism on Khomeini's part, arguing that it provided an 'excuse' to dismiss Yazdi and Bazargan from the government rather than contributing to genuine fear amongst the revolutionaries. See Sick, *All Fall Down*, p. 222.

[54] Quoted in John Stempel, *Inside the Iranian Revolution* (Bloomington, Indiana: University of Indiana Press, 1981), p. 225.   [55] Quoted in Wells, *444 Days*, p. 87.

[56] Ibid., p. 90.

regime). More particularly, they were probably searching for confirmation of what they had thought all along to be true: that the CIA was planning to topple a second revolutionary regime which it viewed as running counter to the interests of the United States.

While there were in fact several CIA operatives inside the embassy, the assumption that everyone was a spy was of course incorrect. Moreover, it was perhaps a supreme irony that all of this happened under the presidency of Jimmy Carter rather than that of, say, Richard Nixon or Lyndon Johnson. Nevertheless, the statements and attitudes of the radicals do throw considerable light upon their psychological perceptions. It is difficult to understand why the students – apparently well-educated and intelligent individuals – would be so 'absolutely convinced' that the embassy was being used as a base for counterrevolution, and the venom with which the American flags and effigies of Uncle Sam were hoisted and burnt, without appreciating that many of the students and clerics genuinely felt that another 1953 was afoot, and easy to dismiss the actions of the radicals as irrational unless one places oneself in their shoes. As William Daugherty recalls, 'CIA involvement in the overthrow of Prime Minister Mohammed Mossadeq in 1953 loomed extraordinarily large in the minds of Iranians', and this had a clear effect on the way the students reasoned. 'Always suspicious of US motives and sincerity', he notes, 'Iranians during this period were constantly looking for signs of US intentions to repeat the coup of 1953. These signs appeared with the admittance of the Shah to the United States and with the meeting in Algiers between Brzezinski and Bazargan.'[57]

The accounts of the hostage taking offered by Sick, Cutler and Brzezinski, on the one hand, and by Rubin, Ioannides, Daugherty and Precht on the other, disagree on the importance of ideas versus interests. For the first group, Khomeini's domestic political interests – and his Machiavellian manoeuvrings within various factional disputes – were the real motivators behind the embassy takeover. For the second group, on the other hand, it was the ideas and images of the United States that Iranians held and their deep insecurity about the possibility of another US intervention or counterrevolution which led them to act as they did. At its root, this is really a dispute about the sources of human motivation, the age-old debate about whether ideas matter, or whether these are simply rationalizations or ex-post justifications for

---

[57] Daugherty, 'A First Tour Like No Other', p. 13.

plain self-interest. The truth, of course, probably lies somewhere inbetween, but it is clear that the students did have firmly held beliefs, and so did Khomeini, so it is rather unconvincing to posit that their actions stemmed from self-interest alone. To claim that the conspiracy theories of which Khomeini talked incessantly were purely cynical inventions designed to mobilize naïve young radicals on his side neglects the point that he did have some obvious basis for these theories based upon Iran's own recent history. If America had stepped in to dispose of Mossadegh, why (from the radicals' perspective) would it hesitate to do the same with Khomeini?

To reiterate, the exact truth in all this may never be known, since the veracity of the existing sources is hard to establish. The evidence in favour of the argument that the 1953 analogy was a prime motivating force behind the embassy takeover is therefore strongly suggestive rather than definitive. Recently, however, a former hostage taker who helped plan the takeover has provided further evidence in support of this interpretation. In an interview conducted with *Time* magazine in Tehran in 1998, Abbas Abdi – one of the student leaders behind the embassy takeover – defended the decision by the militants as justified 'against a potential US-backed *coup d'état*'. As related by Scott Macleod, 'they genuinely feared, Abdi insists, that the Shah's arrival in New York City in 1979 for medical treatment was part of a US plot to restore him to power, as was done by a CIA-engineered *coup d'état* in 1953'.[58]

Abdi also backs up the assertion that the Ayatollah Khomeini had no prior knowledge of the planned takeover. 'The way we saw it, the Imam would either approve of the action afterward or disapprove of it, in which case we would have left the embassy', he said.[59] No doubt in years to come the evidence in favour of or against Abdi's claim will mount, but it is certainly entirely consistent with the evidence provided by Khoienha and Asgharzadeh, and the part played by visions of 1953 in the students' actions is attested to by those, like William Daugherty, who were actually interrogated by those students. What makes this interpretation even more compelling, however, is the congruence of these findings with those of Kahneman and Tversky regarding availability and representativeness of events and the roles these play in human reasoning.[60]

---

[58] Scott Macleod, 'Can Iran Be Forgiven?', *Time*, 3 August 1998, p. 27.   [59] Ibid.
[60] Amos Tversky and Daniel Kahneman, 'Judgment under Uncertainty: Heuristics and Biases', *Science*, 185: 1124–31, 1971.

The availability and representativeness of the 1953 analogy

There is considerable evidence that the 1953 analogy was *available* to ordinary Iranians due to its vividness. Clearly, it was not the recency of the Mossadegh overthrow which made it available cognitively. Intuitively, one might expect that the events of 1953 had happened so long ago that those who seized the embassy would be only dimly familiar with them. In November 1979, Asgharzadeh was 24, Abdi was 23, Mirdammadi 24 and Ebtekar 19, and the average age of the 400 or so students occupying the embassy in March 1980 was estimated at 22 by one reliable contemporary observer who visited the building.[61] Simple mathematics tells us that none of the major participants, then, was even born in 1953. Nevertheless, the events of that year had of course been the stuff of Iranian folklore in the years in which the students were growing up. Iranians had not forgotten their own history and the role played by external powers in it; they had taught it to their sons and daughters. As James Bill aptly puts it, 'this direct covert operation left a running wound that bled for twenty-five years . . . for years, Iranians harshly condemned the Central Intelligence Agency and Britain for coordinating the activities of royalist Iranians and distributing money to hired demonstrators. These actions were recalled in the anti-American chants and speeches of the 1978–79 revolution.'[62]

The potency of the 1953 experience, and its centrality to the force of Iranian nationalism, is something which decision-makers in the United States do not appear to have understood. As Metrinko notes, 'in Washington there was a failure to understand the vast degree of suppressed hatred that had been caused by our bringing about the collapse of the Mossadegh government. That was Iran's chance to become democratic. We screwed it up, and we bragged about it.'[63] Similarly, though he disputes the idea that the embassy seizure was motivated by fear of another 1953, Gary Sick readily concedes the point that Washington's decision-makers failed to understand the potency of this memory in Iran. In the United States, he notes, 1953 'had all the relevance of a pressed flower . . . in Iran, however, the memory (or mythology) of 1953 was as fresh as if it had happened only the week before'.[64]

---

[61] See Ioannides, 'The Hostages of Iran', p. 14.   [62] Bill, *The Eagle and the Lion*, p. 86.
[63] Metrinko, Iranian Project interview, Antelope Productions.
[64] Sick, *All Fall Down*, p. 8. Another event which may have made the events of 1953 particularly available to at least some Iranians was the publication in 1979 of Kermit Roosevelt's memoir of his central role in the 1953 coup, *Countercoup: The Struggle for the*

It is fairly clear, then, that 1953 was cognitively available to many Iranians. The frequency with which it is mentioned in interviews and other accounts is striking, and according to Ioannides the fear of another US coup 'was shared by the moderates of the Bazargan government and the middle and professional classes'.[65] Nevertheless, it is somewhat harder to establish exactly why many Iranians found the events of 1979 *representative* of those of 1953. We know that images of 1953 had been activated in the minds of many people in Tehran, but we cannot be absolutely sure why. After all, from a Western perspective there were numerous differences between the two episodes. Not least of these is the fact that the American president was Jimmy Carter in 1979 instance and Dwight Eisenhower in 1953, the first committed to an idealist foreign policy which put America's 'moral' beliefs first, the second to a more realist and covert war against radical communist forces.

Nevertheless, there are some significant clues as to why 1979 triggered the 1953 analogy in the minds of many Iranians. Some of these can be derived intuitively. One obvious clue – or aspect of similarity – is simply that Khomeini, like Mossadegh, was perceived as a threat to Western (and specifically American) interests, which were not unnaturally identified with the rule of the shah. Hence, returning to our discussion in chapter 2 of the psychological research which underpins analogical reasoning approaches to FPDM, Khomeini may readily be 'mapped' onto Mossadegh in the 1979 case. Secondly, as Bill notes, the movements upon which Mossadegh and Khomeini fed were both fiercely nationalistic. Both men, thirdly, were presented in the United States as irrational and even insane figures.[66] And lastly, another superficial similarity was the Zahedi connection. In 1953, General Zahedi had been installed as Mossadegh's replacement, largely at the behest of the United States. In 1979, his son Ardeshir Zahedi was the shah's ambassador to the United States during the last days of the regime. According to Marvin Zonis, few did as much as the younger Zahedi to try to preserve his monarch's place on the Peacock throne.[67]

And yet there is another rather less obvious reason for the activation

---

Control of Iran (New York: McGraw-Hill, 1979). It would be unrealistic to assume that the radical students had all read this book, but at least one of the hostages thinks that the publicity surrounding the book in Iran did have an effect upon them. See Metrinko interview, ibid.   [65] Ioannides, *America's Iran*, p. 107.

[66] Bill, *The Eagle and the Lion*, p. 96.

[67] Marvin Zonis, *Majestic Failure: The Fall of the Shah* (Chicago, Illinois: Chicago University Press, 1991), pp. 144–5.

of the analogy amongst ordinary Iranians. This relates to the shah's specific behaviour in the two instances. In 1953, the shah had fled Iran and took shelter in a third country; in 1979, he did the same, and once he was permitted to enter the United States, it looked to many radicals in Iran as if an identical train of events was being set in motion. Ibrahim Yazdi, Khomeini's foreign minister of the time, stresses this interpretation:

> You must keep in your mind . . . What happened in August 1953 in Iran. That the Americans and the British . . . made a military coup against the national government of Dr Mossadegh and the Shah . . . fled the country. They brought him back. The moment that they wanted to take the Shah to the United States, all these memories came to the mind of our people. They say 'oh no', that's again the same story.

Yazdi notes that at the time he and his colleagues requested that a team of Iranian doctors be allowed to come to the United States and examine the shah, so that ordinary Iranians would accept that the shah was indeed sick and not about to be restored to power. This request was refused.[68]

So potent were the recollections of 1953 inspired by those of 1979 that the shah himself seems to have placed his faith in that analogy. At times, Mohammed Reza Pahlevi appears to have blamed the United States for his departure from Iran.[69] Nevertheless, at other times he seems to have expected that the Americans – or at least *some* kind of third force – would again restore him to the Peacock throne. According to Hamilton Jordan, the Shah 'had the dream, totally unrealistic, that Khomeini might quickly fall on his face and that there might be a chance for him to return to Iran just as he had done in 1953 with the help of the CIA'.[70] Similarly, former ambassador to Iran William Sullivan records in his memoirs that the shah felt sure that 'he would be recalled to Tehran as he had been in 1953 and would be able to resume the throne as in that earlier experience'. Sullivan cites unnamed observers in Egypt as his source.[71] And Gary Sick notes that members of the Carter administration were perplexed when the shah suddenly decided

---

[68] Interview with Ibrahim Yazdi, Iran Project, Antelope Productions.
[69] On this point, see for instance, Amir Taheri, *The Unknown Life of the Shah* (London: Hutchison, 1991), p. 294.
[70] See Jordan, Miller Center interview, Jimmy Carter Library, p. 80.
[71] William Sullivan, *Mission to Iran* (New York: Morton, 1981), p. 241. Sullivan was rebuffed when he cabled Washington with his view that such thinking was 'pure moonshine'.

to spend two days in Aswan, Egypt, with then Egyptian President Anwar Sadat. Although he never explained why he had done this, 'there were persistent reports that the shah was persuaded by some of his advisers to remain as close as possible to Iran in case of a sudden turn of events'. Like Precht and Sullivan, Sick believes that in 1979 the Shah probably 'anticipated a similar reversal' to 1953.[72] 'Don't worry, I won't be away for long', the Shah is reported to have told members of the Imperial Guard who urged him not to leave Iran for a second time.[73]

For the shah himself, 1953 was as potent a historical image as it was for his former subjects. And the image became activated in 1979 because the shah, as before, had fled the country expecting to return in due course. But there are also deeper similarities, most notably the meandering way in which the shah flitted, almost birdlike, from country to country, after deciding to leave Iran. Henry Precht attributes the activation of images in 1953 to this aspect of the shah's behaviour. When the shah left Iran, the original intention was that he would stay in California, and Carter's staff fully expected him to do so. However, he rather puzzlingly decided to spend a couple of days in Egypt, and then went to Morocco. 'When he left though, someone, I'm not sure who, got to him and persuaded him to stop off in Morocco', Precht recalls. 'I think the thought was just as in 1953 . . . he went as far as Rome and then he was summoned back after a coup had taken place. I think he thought "I'll stop on Morocco, the coup will take place, I'll be called home in triumph".'[74]

CIA operative Kermit Roosevelt, the leader of the group which lobbied for and implemented the 1953 coup, describes a meeting he arranged that year with the shah to determine how the latter – who had foreknowledge of the events – would conduct himself while the 'uprising' was in progress. After discussing various options, it was agreed that the shah would go to the Caspian coast of Iran and wait there until the signal came to return. Accordingly, on 10 August the shah left Tehran and drove with his wife to Kelardasht, a village retreat on the Caspian coast where he often went in times of crisis. But when the CIA plan appeared to be about to fail – it initially did not seem to be working, and because of this was actually cancelled at one point by CIA chiefs in Washington – the shah and his entourage fled the country on

---

[72] Sick, *All Fall Down*, pp. 164–5.
[73] See Fereydoun Hoveyda, *The Fall of the Shah* (London: Weidenfeld and Nicolson, 1980), p. 145.   [74] Interview with Henry Precht, Iran Project, Antelope Productions.

16 August, flying to Baghdad.[75] After a short stay, they then flew on to Rome on 20 August. As one historical account relates, the shah and his wife were eating lunch at the Hotel Exclesior in the Italian capital when news arrived that Mossadegh had been toppled from power.[76] They returned to Tehran in triumph on 21 August.

There is some evidence to suggest that the shah's reasoning in leaving Tehran the first time was itself analogically derived, since – according to Roosevelt – that decision drew upon a historical parallel which has considerable resonance for those of the Muslim faith. 'This reminds me, as a good Moslem', the shah is reported to have said, 'Of Mohammed's Hegira in 622 A.D. by your calendar, year one by ours. He "fled" purely to dramatize his situation. I could do the same.'[77] According to Marvin Zonis, this account represents a misreading of Muslim history, since the Prophet's flight 'was not an act of "dramatization", but necessary to preserve his life'. Mohammed, like the shah, left because he was in grave danger.[78] The shah, moreover, may well have alluded to this analogy simply to rationalize an act which others might perceive as cowardly or self-serving, not least since the British were unaware of any contingency plans for the shah to flee the country.[79] All of this is difficult to establish after the passage of so much time, but what is clear is that in 1979 the shah, as in 1953, fled the country, thus evoking the critical historical image. If even the shah was deluded into thinking that Carter would order the CIA to intervene – or that America might act in some way short of this so as to magically re-establish his power base in Iran – it is little wonder that many ordinary Iranians made a similar error.

In fact, although the students could not have known this, the notion of a 1953-style coup was not entirely without its advocates within the Carter administration. National Security Adviser Zbigniew Brzezinski was the leading supporter of such a move, as he relates in detail in his memoirs.[80] Jimmy Carter, as one might expect, seems to have simply refused to consider this option. But it was not what was going on behind the scenes within the Carter administration that had such a

---

[75] Kenneth Love, 'Shah Flees Iran After Move to Dismiss Mossadegh Fails', *New York Times*, 17 August 1953.

[76] See Taheri, *The Unknown Life of the Shah*, pp. 140–2. See also Zonis, *Majestic Failure*, pp. 47, 52, 101–3.   [77] Roosevelt, *Countercoup*, p. 161.

[78] Zonis, *Majestic Failure*, p. 101.

[79] See Christopher Woodhouse, *Something Ventured* (London: Granada, 1982), p. 127.

[80] Brzezinski, *Power and Principle*, especially pp. 382–98.

negative effect upon Iranian perceptions, since this was obviously hidden from view at the time. Rather, it was its overt and visible actions in the public sphere which had this effect.

Human rights versus realism

Why did the student radicals ignore evidence – mostly rhetorical perhaps, but apparently sincere – that the Carter administration was different to most post-war American administrations? Clearly, it would be wrong to assert that the answer lies in ignorance. It would not be correct, for instance, to claim that none of the Iranian hostage takers had any familiarity with the workings of American politics. Some had reportedly studied in the United States,[81] and it is reasonable to assume that others were familiar with the ways in which Jimmy Carter's professed foreign policy principles differed from post-war American practice. The real reason seems to have much to do with the Carter administration's behaviour towards Iran from 1977 onwards. In his inauguration speech, Carter famously highlighted the pursuit of human rights as the central objective of his foreign policy, setting a marked contrast between his own presidency and those of Nixon and Ford. 'Our commitment to human rights must be absolute', he declared. 'Because we are free, we can never be indifferent to the fate of freedom everywhere. Our moral sense dictates a clear-cut preference for those societies which share with us an abiding respect for individual human rights.' At a stroke, Carter thus raised hopes in Iran, as elsewhere, that the containment of 'un-American' ideals would not now form the basis of the new president's policy towards them. And yet the radicals were to find good reasons in Carter's actual behaviour to discount his words.

In reality, the human rights policy was never applied to Iran. Perhaps under the influence of Zbigniew Brzezinski, Carter – much like his predecessors – came to appreciate the strategic importance of the oil-rich Middle East to the Cold War fight against communism, and hence considerations of *Realpolitik* crept in early and came to swamp other, more liberal idealist notions (such as the argument that the shah ought to hold free and fair elections). Although the Carter administration had warned the shah publicly that his human rights record must improve, in practice it continued to turn a blind eye to the repressive and often

---

[81] Massoumeh Ebtekar was one notable example. She had lived for some time in Philadelphia, and attended the University of Pennsylvania. At the time of writing, she is now a vice-president of Iran.

brutal tactics of SAVAK, the shah's secret police, and the administration was itself internally divided on the desirability of cracking down on internal dissent in Iran. Privately, Carter made it clear that he would like domestic reform in Iran but also that he would support whatever the shah chose to do, including the option of setting up an unelected military government in Iran.[82]

On 22 November 1977, not long after the shah had returned to Iran from a visit to the United States at which the White House accorded him a warm welcome, a peaceful meeting of those opposed to the shah's rule was ended with great violence by SAVAK forces. This certainly did not help Carter's effort to be 'seen differently' by modern Iranians, but there was worse to come. On his only visit to Iran during the final days of 1977, Carter had toasted the shah with champagne on live Iranian television and had famously described Iran as 'an island of stability . . . a great tribute to the respect, admiration and love of your people for you'.[83] These words were spoken, ironically, just as Iran was about to become anything but an island of stability, and they would of course return to haunt Carter in the years to come. But the principal effect of this simple action – obviously intended to shore up the shah's domestic political support – may actually have been to convince even Iranians familiar with the workings of American politics that Carter was really no different from the long line of US presidents who had preceded him. And as Ioannides notes, when one considers 1953 and all that had happened since 'it was not unreasonable for most Iranians . . . to see in the Shah's admission [to the United States] a mortal threat to revolution, and in the hostage taking the ultimate if even desperate defense to this threat'.[84]

The roots of the hostage crisis

Of the available explanations for the seizure of the embassy in 1979, only the analogical reasoning approach can convincingly account for the behaviour of the students once they had entered the embassy, their frantic search for spies, how the behaviour of the United States may have encouraged the misperceptions which led to the hostage taking and how the shah's departure fed conspiratorial images, based in part on historical fact, in the heads of ordinary Iranians. Of the four explanations noted earlier, this is also the only one which can account for why

[82] Carter, *Keeping Faith*, p. 447.   [83] Quoted in Moin, *Khomeini*, p. 186.
[84] Ioannides, *America's Iran*, p. 108.

the shah convinced himself that America would again rescue his throne. While the instrumental or domestic politics explanation is perfectly valid as an account of Khomeini's behaviour several days after the seizure, there is no evidence that he actively planned the event or encouraged the hostage takers originally. The statements of those who did plan the takeover, as well as those in Khomeini's immediate circle, are at one on this.

The finding that psychological forces exerted a key impact upon those who seized the embassy is potentially of broad interest because it suggests that cognitive models developed originally in the United States – drawn from experimental research in which American undergraduates were the subjects – do in fact have a wider applicability in terms of what one may observe through the use of qualitative case studies such as the one examined here. In particular, it reinforces the earlier 'pre-theory' generated by James Rosenau, which stresses the importance of individual psychological forces in Third World foreign policy decision-making.[85] It is also consistent with the approach adopted by analysts of Middle Eastern foreign policy like Adeed Dawisha:

> The phenomenon of the principal decision maker predominates in all Middle Eastern states except for Israel and Turkey . . . in the rest of the region, the institutionalised structure, particularly as it relates to the domain of foreign policy, tends to be dominated by a strong and central figure. It could thus be persuasively argued that a better understanding of Middle Eastern foreign policy making can be facilitated through analysing leaders' personalities, perceptions, values and needs than by examining organisational procedures of bureaucratic competition.[86]

This has certainly long been the case in Iran, Ayatollah Khomeini and the shah being but two of the most recent historical examples of dominant, charismatic and centralized leadership in the country.

By the same token, the factors underlying the hostage seizure – while obviously unique in some respects – cast some doubt upon the claim made by both Weinstein and Korany that psychological forces play a secondary role in underdeveloped states.[87] If anything, the role of

---

[85] James Rosenau, 'Pre-Theories and Theories of Foreign Policy', in Rosenau, *The Scientific Study of Foreign Policy* (New York: Nicols, 1980), pp. 115–69.
[86] Adeed Dawisha, 'The Middle East', in Christopher Clapham (ed.), *Foreign Policy Making in Developing States: A Comparative Approach* (Westmead: Saxon House, 1977), pp. 62–3.
[87] Weinstein, 'The Uses of Foreign Policy in Indonesia'; Korany, 'The Take-off of Third World Studies'.

individual psychological factors is probably greater in the Middle East than in the United States for the reason above given by Dawisha and others, and hence one can expect the beliefs and analogies used by these leaders to exert a particularly forceful impact. Just because a political system allows for more active leadership, of course, it does not logically follow that the actions of a leader in such a system have major consequences in political outcomes. In discussing the role of psychological forces in politics, Fred Greenstein makes a distinction between what he calls 'actor indispensability' and 'action indispensability' which is of critical relevance here.[88] In order to show that the individual cognitions of leaders matter, one has to show first of all that the cognitions or beliefs were different from those which might be expected of another actor who has, or might have, held the same institutional position ('actor indispensability'). Secondly, one must also demonstrate that the actions taken by the actor in question had some material impact on the outcome one is interested in, and that this outcome would not have occurred had the actor not pursued the action he or she did ('action dispensability').

Generally speaking, structural theory suggests that while Third World leaders may exert an indispensable effect upon their own policy processes, their actions are quite dispensable in the sense that their policies and decisions have little impact on outcomes in the international system. While in general this proposition is probably true, there are enough examples of Third World leaders exerting an indispensable impact upon outcomes *vis-à-vis* powerful adversaries to conclude that this is a gross oversimplification. Applied to the Iranian case examined here, we can see that the actions of Khomeini and the students differed from those advocated by Iranian moderates such as President Abolhassan Bani Sadr, who opposed the continuation of the hostage crisis.[89] Certainly, Iran's previous leader, the shah, would not have pursued the policy course Khomeini did on the hostages issue, had the incident occurred during his reign. Khomeini's actions were also clearly indispensable to the outcome – the humiliation and eventual electoral defeat of an American president – in that he clearly managed to impose his preferences over those of the United States.

If the students who seized the embassy in November 1979 are to be believed – and there are few good academic grounds to disbelieve

---

[88] Fred Greenstein, 'The Impact of Personality on Politics: An Attempt to Clear Away the Underbrush', *American Political Science Review*, 61: 629–41, September 1967.
[89] See Moin, *Khomeini*, pp. 227–8.

them, since their accounts are so consistent with one another – the whole train of events which led to American hostages spending 444 days in captivity was due in part to simple cognitive misperception. The students invaded the Tehran embassy essentially because they misinterpreted the signals they were receiving from Washington. Signs and messages designed to reassure the fragile new regime had precisely the opposite effect, and in large part because they evoked memories of events which most members of the Carter administration assumed had long since lost their relevance. As we shall see in the chapters which follow, the Iranians of the late 1970s were not the only hostages to history, for other (rather more recent) events helped shape the parameters of the policies which the Carter administration would use to try to get the hostages back.

4 The waiting game

When the embassy was overrun on 4 November, the first reaction among the American decision-makers in Washington DC was stunned surprise. Officials from both the embassy and the moderate Iranian government had warned the administration that admitting the shah might produce such a reaction – indeed, Carter himself had anticipated it, overriding his own reservations on humanitarian grounds – but such dire warnings had seemed misplaced after 22 October.[1] The reaction in Tehran had appeared muted on its face, since nothing of consequence happened for nearly two weeks. This, however, proved to be merely the calm before the storm.

Secretary of State Vance was roused from his bed at 3 o'clock that Sunday morning, and over the course of the next few hours a number of advisers and experts assembled at the State Department and the White House. Meetings within the US government began almost immediately, with the goal of defining the nature of the situation and developing a response to it. The SCC (or Special Coordinating Committee)[2] first met the day after the crisis began, on Monday 5 November. At this stage, very little was known about why the embassy had been overrun, or even about the identity of the captors. Nevertheless, it is now clear that few of the participants on the American side expected the whole affair to last very long. Indeed, Gary Sick believes that 'everybody felt that

---

[1] Carter, *Keeping Faith*, p. 463.
[2] The SCC was a foreign policy crisis management group used by Carter to handle problems which cut across the interests and concerns of the individual Departments. Its members included the secretary of state, the national security adviser, the secretary of defence, the vice president, the chairman of the Joint Chiefs and the CIA director, and other members were added as and when this was deemed necessary. Its meetings were chaired by Zbigniew Brzezinski.

way'.[3] As Warren Christopher later explained, in previous instances where embassies were occupied by hostile forces, the host governments had swiftly stepped in to restore order and return control to the United States. When Jimmy Carter first learned that the embassy had been overrun, 'I thought they might have abused or gone into the embassy or something but I never dreamed that the government would not eventually, maybe over a period of hours, come on in there.'[4] Similarly, 'nobody was aware of any example of a case where an embassy had in fact been run over, taken over by demonstrators or what have you, when it went on much more than a few days', according to Sick.[5]

Those inside Iran – including many of the hostages themselves – appear to have shared the expectation that it would all be resolved swiftly. US chargé d'affaires Bruce Laingen – trapped in the Iranian Foreign Ministry throughout the crisis – recalls that 'neither we nor probably any of our colleagues in the chancery thought then that the affair would be anything more than a symbolic occupation that would be terminated and somehow put right within a matter of hours'.[6] Consular officer Richard Queen says: 'I was sure that the Iranian government would come in and clean them out. It was just an interesting experience, something I could write friends and parents about. In a letter home I could say, "We were captured today . . .".'[7] Joe Hall, warrant officer inside the embassy, remembers that he 'pretty much figured someone would come over with a rescue force . . . and take care of the situation', and very similar recollections have been voiced by communications officer Bill Belk, economics officer Malcolm Kalp and chief political officer Victor Tomseth.[8]

Such unanimity of thought seems rather remarkable. Why did all these individuals – both in Washington and Tehran – simultaneously come to the conclusion that the whole episode might be over so quickly, and why in particular did the president and others expect it to end 'over a period of hours'? In part, this had to do with general historical precedent, to the fact just alluded to that most of the decision-makers could not think of an historical example where such a crisis had not been quickly resolved. But there was also another, much more specific, historical exemplar which contributed to the general sense that there

[3] Zbigniew Brzezinski, *Power and Principle*, p. 477; Gary Sick, interview with the author.
[4] Interview with Jimmy Carter, Miller Center Interviews, Carter Presidency Project, Jimmy Carter Library, 29 November 1982, p. 38.　　[5] Sick, interview with the author.
[6] Bruce Laingen, *Yellow Ribbon: The Secret Journal of Bruce Laingen* (Washington, DC: Brassey's, 1992), p. 13.　　[7] Quoted in Wells, *444 Days*, p. 85.
[8] See Wells, *444 Days*, p. 44 (Hall), p. 49 (Belk), p. 62 (Kalp) and p. 78 (Tomseth).

was little to be concerned about; 14 February of that year had seen a very similar incident, when another Iranian mob stormed the embassy and took control of the building for a short period in what became known as the 'Valentine's Day Open House'.[9]

At about 9.30 in the morning the embassy was attacked by armed Iranian militants firing on the building. This time the attackers came from the Fedayeen or Marxist faction within the revolutionary forces, rather than the Islamic Followers of the Line of the Iman who would be responsible for the November takeover. After large numbers of gunmen began clambering over the walls, the then US ambassador, William Sullivan, ordered the marines guarding the embassy to fire only in self-defence, and to use tear gas to hold the attackers at bay. As the situation got out of hand, Sullivan requested the assistance of the provisional government. As would happen in November, the embassy staff shut themselves inside the communications vault, and began destroying documents. When the Fedayeen militants threatened to kill those inside the vault and to set fire to the building, Sullivan ordered the embassy personnel to surrender. Within a couple of hours, however, the provisional government authorities – headed by Iranian Foreign Minister Yazdi – arrived on the scene. Yazdi successfully persuaded the Fedayeen to leave the embassy compound, and by 12 o'clock noon the provisional moderates had control of the building.

An American embassy guard named Sergeant Kenneth Kraus was kidnapped by the mob shortly after the initial assault on the embassy. Kraus was injured during the attack and taken to a local hospital. He was then thrown into jail, but released after intensive pressure from the US embassy staff. This incident aside, however, in February the Iranian government had quickly taken steps to remove the militants from the embassy building itself, which was swiftly restored to the jurisdiction of the United States.[10] As Yazdi recalls, 'I was able to control the situation. I thought that it was the obligation of the new government to protect the security of the foreign citizens, and therefore I went to solve the problem and to apologize for what had happened.'[11]

By analogy, when the embassy was again overrun on 4 November, almost everyone expected the Iranians to do the same this time. As Turner recalls, at the SCC meeting of 5 November: 'Everyone assumed the Iranians would come to their senses, as they had in February, and

---

[9] The phrase 'Valentine's Day Open House' comes from Daugherty, 'A First Tour Like No Other'. [10] Turner, *Terrorism and Democracy*, pp. 20–4.
[11] Interview with Ibrahim Yazdi, Iran Project, Antelope Productions.

step in to free the hostages. Most thought it would be a matter of hours or, at most, a few days.'[12] At a senior staff meeting that same morning, Hamilton Jordan told those assembled not to worry about the hostage situation. 'Don't forget', he noted, 'this same thing happened last February. We're talking to our diplomats at the embassy and Foreign Minister Ibrahim Yazdi and Prime Minister Mehdi Bazargan at the Foreign Ministry. As soon as the government gets its act together, they'll free our people.'[13]

Lloyd Cutler sums up the feeling the decision-makers shared at this early stage:

> In the beginning, of course, all our efforts were to . . . assist the Iranian government in recapturing the embassy. We first thought of it very much like the Columbian situation that came along later or other terrorist seizures of embassies as happened in the Sudan, where the local government deplores what happened just as much as you do and does everything it can to bring it to an end.[14]

Many of the hostages themselves were also clearly thinking of the February analogy in reaching the conclusion that the situation would be swiftly resolved. As Victor Tomseth recalls, for example, 'it was our great hope that he [Yazdi] would do what he had done in February: go to the compound, preferably with an armed force, and get the people to give it up to us'.[15] Others inside the embassy at the time, such as Warrant Officer Joe Hall and Economics Officer Malcolm Kalp, also mention the comparison.[16] Most, if not all, the Americans – including Carter, Cutler, Brzezinski, Jordan and Turner – used a very recent analogy in order to 'define the situation', and they concluded on this basis that the events occurring in Iran did not represent a crisis. 'We always thought it was going to last just a relatively short period of time',[17] Cutler recalls, and Vance notes that 'the general expectation throughout the day and even into the next was that the release would be obtained within a few hours once the Iranian authorities intervened'.[18]

With the benefit of hindsight, this unanimity of opinion now seems foolhardy and more than a little complacent to some. Among other things, however, the weight exerted by the February analogy on the

[12] Turner, *Terrorism and Democracy*, p. 29.
[13] Hamilton Jordan, *Crisis: The Last Year of the Carter Presidency* (New York: Berkley, 1983), p. 15. [14] Lloyd Cutler, Exit interview, 2 March 1981, Jimmy Carter Library, p. 16.
[15] Quoted in Wells, *444 Days*, p. 78.
[16] Both are quoted in ibid. For Hall, see p. 44 and for Kalp, p. 62.
[17] Cutler, Exit interview, p. 17. [18] Vance, *Hard Choices*, p. 375.

minds of the decision-makers demonstrates a long-established psychological tendency among decision-makers operating under conditions of high uncertainty and low levels of hard information: that is, how the recency of events enhances their cognitive availability, and makes it more likely that analogies will be drawn using these events. As noted in chapter 3, Kahneman and Tversky have identified the prevalence of an availability heuristic which tends to operate under conditions of high uncertainty, a tendency to draw disproportionately upon recollections that are most readily available when predicting the likely course of future events. Rather than something unusual or 'foolhardy', then, the decision-makers appear to have engaged in a practice common to most decision-makers placed in comparable situations. What the hostages and the American decision-makers overlooked in drawing upon the February analogy, however, was that the political situation on the ground had changed substantially in just nine months. The power of the secular nationalist forces within Iranian society – represented in the provisional government by Bazargan, Bani-Sadr and Yazdi – had been substantially weakened by the return of Khomeini and the growth of the clergy's power. Yazdi's efforts to release the hostages did not work this time, and probably could not work, because the political tide had turned against him. 'No one realized how completely responsive the mob was to religious extremists, or understood the fact that Bazargan's and Yazdi's political authority had been diminished', Vance notes.[19]

Having already received a body blow from Yazdi's inability or unwillingness to repeat his actions of February on 4 and 5 November, the decision-makers' original definition of what was occurring was shattered on 6 November, when Ayatollah Khomeini not only refused to help turn the embassy back, but actually endorsed its capture by the Iranian militants. In the eyes of the policy-makers, this turned what could have been a minor (if troublesome) incident into a full-scale policy crisis. The confrontation was not now a disagreement between the US government and a group of conspiracy-minded 1953 analogists, but one between the United States and the state of Iran.

Some immediately perceived general parallels between what was occurring and past American foreign policy episodes. Hamilton Jordan, for instance, recalls speculating about whether this would be 'Carter's

---

[19] Ibid. This was also, as noted earlier, a different revolutionary faction. This was significant, since the Fedayeen did not enjoy the same level of support in Iran as the followers of Khomeini did.

Vietnam or his *Mayaguez'* on 6 November.[20] But it was at this point that the president and the great majority of his advisers came to see the hostage crisis as an 'unprecedented' situation, in which history could presumably provide little guidance. Early on in the crisis on 28 November 1979, Jimmy Carter called the hostage seizure

> an unprecedented and unique occurrence. Down through history, we have had times when some of our people were captured by terrorists or who were abused, and there have obviously been instances of international kidnapping which occurred for the discomfiture of a people or a government. So far as I know, this is the first time that such an activity has been encouraged by and supported by the government itself, and I don't anticipate this kind of thing recurring.[21]

Subsequent accounts of the hostage crisis decision-making by the actual participants indicate that this viewpoint was not confined to the president. Then Deputy Secretary of State Warren Christopher similarly emphasized the profound 'uniqueness' of the whole event, and he echoes Carter's sentiment in his edited volume about the crisis:

> While hostage situations are not unprecedented in the diplomatic community, in other cases host governments quite promptly have recognized their obligations under international law to protect foreign embassies against hostile elements in their populations. Here, however, the host government condoned and then embraced what the terrorists had done, and thus made the crime their own – an almost unprecedented act and one of extraordinary repugnance.[22]

Similarly, for Stansfield Turner, 'the idea of capturing sovereign territory seemed to defy all the rules of diplomacy'.[23]

The critical SCC and National Security Council (NSC) meetings – which would set the agenda for much of the later discussion and debate – occurred on 6 November. The first full meeting of the NSC on the hostage issue took place that afternoon, and the battle lines began to be drawn in a crisis which would drag on not for hours but for 444 days. Secretary of State Vance made it clear from the outset that he favoured a negotiated settlement to resolve the crisis, while National Security Adviser Zbigniew Brzezinski argued for a more 'forceful' stance, initially favouring negotiation but wishing to back this up with tougher action if talks did not produce swift results. At this meeting and the

---

[20] Jordan, *Crisis*, p. 19.
[21] Jimmy Carter, 'The President's News Conference on November 28 1979', *Public Papers of the President*, 1979, p. 2167.
[22] Warren Christopher, 'Introduction', in Christopher and Kreisberg, *American Hostages in Iran*, p. 1.   [23] Stansfield Turner, interview with the author.

SCC meeting which preceded it, Vance suggested two options which might be used to pressurize the Iranians into releasing the hostages: (1) encouraging the shah to leave the United States, and (2) negotiating with the Ayatollah Khomeini.

Brzezinski focused instead on possible military options, suggesting a number of alternatives, which included launching an Entebbe style rescue mission.[24] Added to Vance's proposals, this in effect gave the decision-makers a list of seven options to consider:

(1)　Encourage the shah to leave United States.
(2)　Negotiate with Khomeini.
(3)　Institute a naval blockade of Iran.
(4)　Launch an air strike on the oil refinery at Abadan.
(5)　Mine the Iranian harbours.
(6)　Seize the oil depots on Kharg Island.
(7)　Launch a rescue mission.

Of these seven options, only options (2) and (7) had been tried successfully in the past as a means of resolving a hostage incident – at least to the knowledge of the decision-makers – and it is probably no coincidence that debate would quickly centre on these two alternatives. The decision-makers were especially interested from this early stage on in possible parallels with the Israeli raid on Entebbe. As Gary Sick has pointed out, 'it was quite an obvious thing . . . Entebbe was famous as an operation, it was sort of the model of all rescue missions, so obviously it definitely came to mind.'[25] On 27 June 1976 a group of pro-Palestinian terrorists hijacked an Air France jet bound for Paris via Athens. Included among the 160 passengers on board were 103 Israeli nationals. The plane was diverted to Entebbe, Uganda, where it landed, and the hostages were disembarked and held at gunpoint in the airport terminal. The Palestinian hostage takers then demanded the release of various terrorists being held in Israel and elsewhere in return for the lives of the hostages, threatening to blow up the plane and the hostages if their demands were not met.

Within the Israeli government, Prime Minister Yitzhak Rabin and Defence Minister Shimon Peres wrestled with the agonizing problem of how to get the hostages back. As in the Tehran case, the government initially attempted to negotiate with the hostage takers. These

[24] Turner, *Terrorism and Democracy*, p. 31.
[25] Gary Sick, interview with the author. For a theoretical analysis of the decision to mount the Israeli operation, see Maoz, 'The Decision to Raid Entebbe'.

negotiations were abandoned much more swiftly in this case, however. Three days into the hostage crisis the terrorists decided to release all the non-Israeli hostages, who had been separated from the others in a measure that reminded Rabin and his advisers of Nazi 'selektion'.[26] While pretending to continue the negotiations to release the hostages, on 3 July – less than a week after the plane had been hijacked – Israeli commandoes carried out a famously daring rescue mission to release the hostages in what is generally agreed to have been one of the most successful operations of its kind in recent memory.

A Boeing 707 claiming to be an Air France airliner was used as a decoy to distract the attention of the airport radio tower, while the Israeli rescue force – travelling in four Hercules C-130 transport planes – landed quietly at the end of the runway. In order to get close enough to the terminal to neutralize the hostage takers, the initial force travelled in a black Mercedes similar to that used by the Ugandan president, Idi Amin, with whose blessing the terrorists were operating. The rescuers swiftly took control of the terminal, and killed the hostage takers with relatively few casualties among the hostages. They returned safely to Israel, to huge national and international acclaim. The daring exploits of the rescuers soon inspired no less than three different Hollywood movies, which told the story in predictably dramatic fashion, and a number of hurriedly written books. Understandably, by the late 1970s most Americans were familiar with the episode because its details had been so widely disseminated in this way.

Confronting the equally vexing problem of getting the hostages out of Tehran three years later, Brzezinski came out strongly in favour of option (7) – the rescue operation – over and above the others. 'I don't remember whether I did specifically mention Entebbe', Brzezinski has said, 'but I do recall feeling that we ought to start looking at the option of a rescue mission early on . . . in all probability, I would have either thought of or referred to the Israeli rescue mission as a point of reference.'[27] Vance also recalls: 'I think Zbig felt quite strongly that one ought to think about the Entebbe thing, because he thought it was similar to the kind of situation that we were facing in Iran at that time.'[28]

---

[26] Unlike the African American and female hostages released early on in the Iran hostage crisis, the non-Israeli hostages were able to furnish the rescue planners with details about the location of the other hostages. The Tehran hostage takers, for whatever reason, decided to keep many of the hostages in separate rooms, which prevented them being of much help to the Carter administration's rescue planners.

[27] Zbigniew Brzezinski, interview with the author.

[28] Cyrus Vance, interview with the author, New York City, 14 February 1995.

In what sense did Brzezinski think that the two causes were comparable? Clearly, he realized that no two situations are ever identical, and that there were important differences between the two. 'No one thought it was Entebbe', he notes. 'The point of Entebbe is not that this is Entebbe: the circumstances are very different. The point of Entebbe, however, is that sometimes you take risky decision s and you execute them.' The Israeli raid, Brzezinski believed, 'was a demonstration that daring works, and that of course it's chancy, but son etimes the costs of not doing anything are even higher than a chancy undertaking'.[29] He would echo this same thinking in April 1980, shortly after the failure of the rescue operation, when he said – in apparent al lusion to Entebbe – 'everyone recognized that the operation was risky. We also know from history that there are moments in which a certai n amount of risk is necessary.'[30] This, then, was the key lesson to be drawn: even though there were very real differences between the two s ituations, these were at their root barriers which could be overcome. A well-planned operation along the general lines of the Entebbe operation would have a good chance of releasing the hostages and preserving (and perhaps even enhancing) the national honour and integrity of the United States.

Brzezinski was especially attracted by the analogy with the Entebbe raid in this sense. Like the other decision-makers, h e assumed initially that the embassy would soon be returned to US ju risdiction. He also drew on unspecified historical lessons in tempor arily ruling out a military response, arguing that 'experience indicated that kidnappers were most volatile and trigger-happy in the early stages of hostage-taking'.[31] Yet he also believed very strongly that America's national honour was at stake during the crisis, and that more aggressive measures ought to be tried if negotiating the release of the hostages involved a diminution of this. Brzezinski soon became the leading advocate of a rescue mission within the administration, and according to Destler, Gelb and Lake, he 'promoted and nurtured this venture'.[32]

Since Entebbe was of course an Israeli operation, no American official was involved – either directly or, so far as we know, indirectly – in its planning. And yet the national security a dviser did have a personal link of sorts to the raid. In July 1976, Gerald Ford was still president, and

[29] Brzezinski, interview with the author.
[30] Zbigniew Brzezinski, interviewed on ABC's ' Issues and Answers', 27 April 1980.
[31] Brzezinski, *Power and Principle*, p. 477.
[32] I. M. Destler, Leslie Gelb and Anthony Lak e, *Our Own Worst Enemy: The Unmaking of American Foreign Policy* (New York: Simon & Schuster, 1984), p. 224.

Brzezinski, not yet in government, was a political science professor at Columbia University and an adviser on foreign policy matters to then Democratic party presidential candidate Jimmy Carter. Nevertheless, by this time it was widely recognized that Brzezinski would be offered a major position in any future Carter administration, should the then Georgia governor win the presidential election due to be held in November. Brzezinski was already active in meeting foreign leaders and in making trips abroad, and by the purest coincidence happened to be not only in Israel during the Entebbe hostage crisis, but dining at the house of Shimon Peres, the Israeli defence minister, only the day before the Israelis decided to launch the mission.

Peres was intensely embroiled in discussions within the Israeli government on the hostage issue, and a dress rehearsal for a possible rescue operation was going on that night. Since the dinner appointment had been made some days or weeks in advance, it would obviously have aroused suspicion to have cancelled it, and so the event went ahead as planned. As Brzezinski relates, 'dinner was a private, hospitable affair at his house, despite the enormous tension that was in the air: as we dined the lives of some 100 Israeli hostages were being threatened by reckless kidnappers at an airport in distant Uganda. The terrorists were making demands on the Israeli government which it was apparently getting ready to accept.'

At one especially memorable point in the evening, Brzezinski pointedly suggested to his hosts that they mount a rescue mission rather than give in to the kidnappers' demands. 'Why don't you send some commandos down to Uganda and storm the damn airport terminal?,' he asked.[33] 'I don't remember exactly whether I embellished my observation with any fanciful stratagem or design as to how it ought to be executed . . . but I do remember the reaction of the Foreign Minister and of . . . I think the Chief of Staff was present then. They both froze.' Shimon Peres himself looked 'stunned and suspicious'.[34] 'Their reaction was such that the moment the dinner was over, when I went back I was going to call the ambassador and say "they're going to stage a rescue mission". And then I said to myself, "well, if they are, let them go ahead and do it, why fuck it up . . . so I didn't do it". And when I landed in Rome or some place, a few hours later, I learned the rescue mission had been initiated', Brzezinski remembers. Peres and the other

[33] Brzezinski, *Power and Principle*, p. 84.
[34] Ibid.; Brzezinski, interview with the author. William Stevenson also tells the story of Brzezinski's visit in *90 Minutes at Entebbe* (New York: Bantam, 1976), pp. 56–7.

Israeli officials, Brzezinski later discovered, had actually considered delaying his departure from Israel, because he had 'smoked out the fact that they were going to do it, and this might leak'.[35] In the event, however, the Israeli defence minister merely responded to Brzezinski's suggestion by listing the difficulties involved in mounting such an operation, attempting to leave no hint that the raid was imminent. This was a strategy Brzezinski himself was later to employ, and to urge on the president, before the Tehran mission.

Brzezinski freely admits that this episode probably did impact upon his thinking about the Iranian hostage crisis. When the Entebbe raid turned out to be a great success – both in a military and political sense – it naturally had a reinforcing effect upon his belief that such operations could work, given the right conditions and careful planning: 'because of that, in the back of my mind, there was that experience somewhere, driving me towards the idea that we ought to start looking at the rescue mission early on', Brzezinski reports.[36]

It was probably inevitable that in the early meetings on the crisis a discussion of parallels with the Israeli raid on Entebbe would take place. At the 6 November gatherings, the possibility of mounting this kind of mission was discussed, in Sick's words, 'in considerable detail'.[37] However, even though Entebbe became an immediate topic for discussion, 'what came to mind immediately after invoking the parallel was how different this really was'.[38] Especially important here were the contributions of Defence Secretary Harold Brown and chairman of the Joint Chiefs, David Jones. Brown had previously discussed the possibility of a rescue operation with then Israeli Defence Minister Ezer Weizman, and the latter had reportedly poured cold water on the notion that something similar could be tried in this instance. During the first days of the crisis, officials from the Carter administration, working through an intermediary, had reportedly asked Israeli intelligence to examine the feasibility of an Entebbe style raid, but Weizman reported that 'they could see no way to conduct a successful rescue mission'.[39]

[35] Brzezinski, interview with the author. Interestingly, Daniel Patrick Moynihan – then US ambassador to the United Nations – was also dining with one of the rescue mission's planners – Foreign Minister Yigal Allon – that night. Allon apparently did as good a job as Peres at keeping his American guest in the dark about the imminent operation. See Stevenson, *90 Minutes at Entebbe*, p. 57.   [36] Ibid.
[37] Gary Sick, 'Military Options and Constraints', in Christopher *et al.*, *American Hostages in Iran*, p. 145.   [38] Sick, interview with the author.
[39] Terence Smith, 'Putting the Hostages' Lives First ', *New York Times Magazine*, 17 May 1981, p. 78. Sick refers to a meeting between Brown and 'a high Israeli official intimately associated with the Entebbe rescue operation', in Christopher *et al.*, *American Hos-*

This clearly had an effect on America's defence secretary. At the NSC meeting of 6 November, Brown explicitly rejected the Entebbe analogy, arguing that a rescue mission would take considerable time to plan. Adequate intelligence would need to be gleaned before the administration could even consider mounting such an operation.[40] As Sick recalls, 'I remember vividly in one of the early meetings that this whole subject [of Entebbe] came up, and Brown said that he'd talked to the Israelis and they had said this is no Entebbe, this is a very different set of circumstances.'[41] Hamilton Jordan's recollection is very similar, as recorded in his diary: 'Brown cautioned [that] Tehran wasn't Entebbe, where the Israelis had been able to fly in and snatch up their citizens from the airfield where they were being held. Our hostages, he explained, were locked up in a compound in the middle of a city of more than four million people, with the nearest airport nine miles away.'[42] The secretary of defence was to express this view again just after the failure of the rescue mission, when he told reporters that 'Tehran is not Entebbe.'[43]

Similarly, when it came to David Jones's turn to speak, the chairman of the Joint Chiefs noted that the situation in Tehran was different from Entebbe in several very significant respects: the Tehran embassy where the hostages were being held was not an airport, it was situated inland, and it was located a long way from any US military base. Furthermore, Tehran was a major city, a densely populated urban centre, and previous rescue operations had almost all been conducted in sparsely populated rural areas. As Vance recalled a couple of years later, 'the Joint Chiefs reminded us that downtown Tehran was not the same thing as Entebbe Airport. There was no way to get a rescue team into the middle of the city, with thousands of demonstrators milling about, without getting the hostages killed in the process.'[44] Brzezinski notes that 'Vance and Christopher were noticeably cool to any serious consideration of military options',[45] and Vance in particular was quite resistant to the idea that the Entebbe and Tehran situations were in any real sense

tages in Iran, p. 145. Stansfield Turner has confirmed that there was definitely 'communication going on' between the Carter administration and the Israelis at the time, although he did not participate directly in this (Turner, interview with the author).

[40] Sick, 'Military Options and Constraints', p. 145; see also Carter, *Keeping Faith*, pp. 459–60 and Powell, *The Other Side of the Story*, pp. 225–6.
[41] Sick, interview with the author.   [42] Jordan, *Crisis*, p. 43.
[43] Harold Brown statement to reporters on 25 April 1980. See 'Secretary Brown's News Conference, April 25 1980', US Department of State Bulletin, 80 (June 1980), p. 41.
[44] Quoted in Smith,'Putting the Hostages' Lives First', p. 78.
[45] Brzezinski, *Power and Principle*, p. 482.

comparable: 'I thought clearly about Entebbe, and I felt it to be a very, very different situation. Very different. And therefore trying to strike some kind of parallel about Entebbe to me was irrational.'[46]

When the Israeli analogy was discussed during the very first days of the hostage crisis, David Jones was clearly considering the possibility of mounting 'another Entebbe'. As Sick reports, 'General Jones had had lunch with Israeli Chief of Staff General Raphael Eytan, who happened to be in Washington, and they had discussed the possibility of a rescue mission. General Eytan, after reviewing the location of the embassy in an urban environment far from an airport, had concluded that such a mission would be more difficult than the Entebbe raid.'[47] Moreover, as Paul Ryan put it, 'there was only a limited amount of useful information that could be drawn from the raids at Entebbe and Mogadishu,[48] as they were so unlike the Iranian rescue plan. These rescues were relatively simple; no helicopters were involved and the time in enemy territory was short. In the absence of any precedent, how was the decision reached to go ahead?'[49]

Jones's reluctance to move forward quickly probably related not simply to Eytan and Weizman's advice, however, but also to his own experience as acting chairman of the Joint Chiefs and chief planner for the *Mayaguez* rescue mission four years earlier. On 12 May 1975 a US merchant ship, the SS *Mayaguez*, had been seized by the Cambodians in international waters, some 60 miles off the Cambodian coast. Its crew of thirty-nine were taken hostage; taken off the ship, they were placed under guard on nearby Koh Tang Island. The crisis lasted only three days, for – mindful of the fact that the *Pueblo* crisis only seven years before had dragged on for almost a year – President Ford and his advisers quickly decided to launch a bold rescue attempt. Unfortunately, by the time the raid was launched the crew of the *Mayaguez* were already in the process of being released; eighteen US Marines died in the rescue mission and in a subsequent punitive strike launched against the Cambodian mainland, fifty more were wounded and twenty-three members of the Air Force died in a related crash.

Mayaguez is remembered in different ways, and different analysts have drawn different lessons from it. According to Seymour Hersh, the

---

[46] Vance, interview with the author.   [47] Gary Sick, *All Fall Down*, p. 425.
[48] The latter is a reference to the successful October 1977 rescue of the passengers of a Lufthansa airliner by a German anti-terrorist unit. The plane had been hijacked and flown to Mogadishu, Somalia.
[49] Ryan, *The Iranian Hostage Rescue Mission*, pp. 25–6.

operation was a 'slaughter' and a 'tragedy'. Ford himself, on the other hand, continues to this day to see it as a great success. '*Mayaguez* provided us with a shot in the arm as a nation when we really needed it . . . It convinced some of our adversaries we were not a paper tiger.'[50] Despite this disagreement, it is fair to say that Ford's and Kissinger's raid on the Cambodians had been a political success – Ford's popularity ratings went up in the aftermath of the operation – but a failure from a *military* standpoint. Moreover, it had been a failure on David Jones's watch. In dealing with Iran, Jones not unnaturally wished to avoid 'another *Mayaguez*' this time, and his stake in doing so was a good deal more personal than it was for Vance or Carter. Richard Neustadt and Ernest May note that Jones actually referred to *Mayaguez* repeatedly during the implementation stage of the Iran rescue mission: 'General Jones looked back on the *Mayaguez* as a model of how not to plan a rescue mission. When he next faced such a task, in 1980 . . . he would insist on controlling the timetable and on centralizing both planning and command in his own Joint Staff. In doing so, we are told, he would sometimes refer explicitly to the *Mayaguez* analogy.'[51]

Jones felt unduly rushed in the *Mayaguez* case, and his pessimism about the prospects for a successful mission at the outset seem to have reflected his determination not to be pushed into another hasty or ill-considered operation. On 14 May 1975, Jones attended the NSC meeting at which President Ford made the decision to push ahead with the rescue option, but his argument that the military needed more time to do the job to the best of its ability was overriden. As Lucien Vanden-broucke relates, 'explaining that US troops were poised to take the *Mayaguez* and Koh Tang, [Jones] observed that by waiting another twenty-four hours, US forces would be better prepared. Command and control would be more firmly in place, giving the mission a better chance of success.'[52] Although Jones was worried about inadequate intelligence on the whereabouts of the hostages and the nature of the resistance the enemy was able to put up, he 'never voiced forceful reservations'.[53] Pressured by Ford and Kissinger to launch the rescue mission on 14 May instead of the following day, Jones argued that it would be difficult, if not impossible. The various forces involved in a

[50] Seymour Hersh, *The Price of Power: Kissinger in the Nixon White House* (New York: Summit Books, 1983), p. 639. Ford is quoted in Walter Isaacson, *Kissinger: A Biography* (New York: Simon and Schuster, 1992), p. 651.
[51] Neustadt and May, *Thinking in Time*, p. 65.
[52] Lucien Vandenbroucke, *Perilous Options: Special Operations as an Instrument of US Foreign Policy* (Oxford: Oxford University Press, 1993), p. 82.   [53] Ibid., p. 163.

rescue bid would have to be coordinated properly, and many of the necessary forces had not yet even arrived in the area.[54] Nevertheless, Ford decided that the mission should be launched immediately.

At various points in the Iran hostage crisis – especially at the planning of the rescue mission stage – *Mayaguez* was alluded to as a reminder of the perils of mounting such operations. As Sick recalls, 'there were examples and references to the *Mayaguez*, of people saying we launched a rescue mission only to discover that we should just wait until they were in the process of being released, that you ought to be very sure that you know what you're doing', although, as he points out, the topic of the *Mayaguez* 'was not something people dwelt on'.[55] In his opposition to any repetition of the *Mayaguez* mission, Jones was most explicitly supported by the secretary of state and the president himself. Vance looked back on the *Mayaguez* affair as a fiasco, but drew a more basic lesson from it, seeing it as an example of what can happen when policy-makers attempt to use military force to extricate hostages: 'the last thing we need is another *Mayaguez*', he reportedly said of proposals to mount a military rescue mission.[56] And throughout the Iranian crisis, Jimmy Carter was to repeatedly attack Gerald Ford's actions in ordering the 1975 rescue mission. In an interview conducted in March 1980, he expressed this view clearly.

> I have a very real political awareness that at least on a transient basis the more drastic the action taken by the President, the more popular it is. When President Ford expended 40 American lives on the *Mayaguez* to save that many people who had already been released, it was looked upon as a heroic action, and his status as a bold and wise leader rose greatly. This is always a temptation.[57]

In subsequent interviews he has again criticized Ford for his military adventurism and for the loss of life which resulted from his decision to go ahead with the *Mayaguez* operation.[58]

Jones concluded that a rescue mission was 'nearly impossible' in Tehran at this time, and 'the whole concept of a quick rescue mission was basically ruled out'.[59] President Carter nevertheless ordered that

[54] Richard Head, Frisco Short and Robert McFarlane, *Crisis Resolution: Presidential Decision Making in the Mayaguez and Korean Confrontations* (Boulder, Colorado: Westview Press, 1978), p. 118.   [55] Sick, interview with the author.
[56] See *Newsweek*, 12 May 1980, p. 38.
[57] Quoted in *Washington Post*, 29 March 1980, p. A13.
[58] See Reginald Ross Smith, 'A Comparative Case Analysis of Presidential Decision-Making: The *Pueblo*, the *Mayaguez* and the Iranian Hostage Crisis', unpublished MA dissertation, Emory University, Atlanta, 1984.   [59] Sick, interview with the author.

contingency planning for a rescue operation proceed, since he recognized that this measure might become a practical necessity should the Iranians begin executing the hostages or putting them on trial.[60] On 6 November, therefore, Brzezinski 'telephoned Secretary of Defense Harold Brown and instructed him to have the Joint Chiefs of Staff develop a plan for a rescue mission'.[61]

According to CIA Director Stansfield Turner, there was 'almost no interest' expressed in the other military options that Brzezinski had proposed at the 6 November SCC and NSC meetings, something he attributes to the fact that 'no one expected the crisis to last long'. At the SCC meeting, Harold Brown outlined various measures that could be taken to try to compel the militants to release the hostages. Most of these options centred on cutting off Iran's supply of oil or its ability to sell it overseas. Kharg Island, the place from which most of Iran's oil was shipped, could be captured by American forces; the main Iranian oil refinery at Abadan could be bombed; the Iranian military's fighter aircraft could be destroyed from the air; or the ports at Abadan, Bushehr and Bandar Abbas could be mined.[62] Lastly, a naval blockade of these ports could be instituted.

The fact that none of these options held any real appeal for the decision-makers was probably not just due to the expectation that the crisis would not last, however. The decision-makers also felt that these options were less than satisfactory in two principal ways. First, it was hypothesized that none of these options would lead *directly* to the release of the hostages. Secondly, the hostage takers might conceivably retaliate by killing some of the hostages in retaliation for such punitive actions.[63] The seizure of Kharg Island was rejected because it might lead to significant casualties on both sides of the conflict, and might well bring the Soviet Union into the situation if the Iranians turned to them for help. The mining of Iranian harbours, it was reasoned, might lead to similar effects and would be considered an act of war, as might a simple naval blockade. Bombing the oil refineries, on the other hand, was seen as a purely 'punitive' action to be taken if all else failed.[64]

At least one analogy that we know of was used at this stage by the president himself. At the SCC meeting that morning, Stansfield Turner suggested placing the USS *Midway* off the Iranian coast, so that it would

[60] Jordan, *Crisis*, p. 242.
[61] Brzezinski, 'The Failed Mission: The Inside Account of the Attempt to Free the Hostages in Iran', *New York Times Magazine*, 18 April 1982, p. 28.
[62] Turner, *Terrorism and Democracy*, p. 32.
[63] Sick, 'Military Options and Constraints', p. 145.   [64] Ibid., pp. 145–6.

be ready were a military strike against Iran deemed necessary. This idea garnered little support, but the issue was raised again in the NSC meeting that afternoon. Carter dismissed Turner's idea, however, alluding to an episode which had occurred the previous year. As Turner recalls:

> the President reminded us of an incident in late 1978. When it had become clear that the Shah was in serious trouble, the President placed an aircraft carrier on alert to proceed into the Indian Ocean from the Pacific. The order immediately leaked, making it clear to the world we though the Shah was in so much trouble that the United States was bringing up force. That only exacerbated the Shah's problems. Now the President obviously did not want to risk a similar misfire.[65]

It is not entirely clear from Turner's account what lesson Carter had drawn from the 1978 incident, or what the latter expected to happen in this instance were the *Midway* to be placed off the coast of Iran. Who or what is the analogue to the shah in this comparison? Obviously, Carter would not have been worried about destabilizing Khomeini, so perhaps he was mapping the 'United States government' or 'the hostages' onto 'the shah' here. The most likely explanation is that Carter feared that the leaking of this second order would place the hostages' lives in jeopardy. The meaning of the analogy, however, is less significant for our purposes than the simple fact that it was used. And what *is* fairly clear is that that a rescue mission of such obvious difficulty lacked any recent analogical 'base'. With the Entebbe analogy thus weakened – at least for the time being – the way was left open for other analogies and policy preferences to take hold.

Cyrus Vance did not share the view, widespread within the administration, that the hostage crisis was an 'unprecedented' event. As he would state later, 'those kind of things have happened before . . . we have had other embassies that have been seized or hostages that have been seized in the past on this side of the [Atlantic] ocean, so it wasn't the first time'.[66] Two particular precedents sprang to Vance's mind at the very outset of the Iranian crisis: the *Pueblo* incident from 1968 and the Angus Ward affair of 1949. Vance recalled in his memoirs that he

> believed strongly that the hostages would be released safely once they had served their political purpose in Iran. I found support for this conclusion in what had happened in two similar cases where Americans were held hostage. These were the Angus Ward incident,

---

[65] Turner, *Terrorism and Democracy*, pp. 34–5.   [66] Vance, interview with the author.

involving the seizure of our consular staff in Mukden at the end of World War II, and the case of the USS *Pueblo*.[67]

In January 1968, during the presidency of Lyndon Johnson, the North Koreans seized an American spy ship called the USS *Pueblo*, and took its crew of eighty-three hostage. The hostages remained in captivity until December of that year, when they were released after extensive negotiations. In order to win the release of the crew, the United States negotiators working in Panmunjon agreed to sign a bizarre confession of wrongdoing, while simultaneously openly disclaiming its validity. The use of military force was not considered a viable option by the president or his secretary of defence, Clark Clifford, and was rejected at an early stage in the administration's deliberations. The North Koreans enjoyed substantial military capabilities, and had signed a defence treaty with the Soviet Union, meaning that a military strike by the Americans might well provoke Russian involvement and would probably at the very least be costly in terms of human life. The alternatives of mounting a naval blockade, mining Wonsan harbour, attacking the North Koreans directly, intimidating them with US fighter flights and replacing the *Pueblo* with another intelligence gathering ship were all rejected as too costly or unlikely to achieve the release of the ship's crew.[68]

The *Pueblo* incident differed from the Tehran crisis in that the former had not involved the seizure of a US embassy. An even more direct precedent, however, was to be found in the Angus Ward case, a hostage taking episode which occurred during the Truman years. Angus Ward – consul general at the US Consulate in Mukden, China – was held captive along with his wife and staff for almost exactly a year, from November 1948 to November 1949. The seizure of the hostages was apparently undertaken at the instigation of the Chinese government itself – or, at least, by factions within it – and as Russell Buhite notes, 'in making this move, Chinese Communist forces were challenging diplomatic practices that had evolved over several centuries'.[69] Initially, quiet moves were made to pressure the Chinese into respecting these traditional practices, but negotiations only resulted in American frustration. Like the Iran hostages three decades later, Ward was caught in the kind of complex and unstable political situation which tends to follow any major revolution, and found himself at the centre of a

[67] Vance, *Hard Choices*, pp. 408–9.
[68] Russell Buhite, *Lives At Risk: Hostages and Victims in American Foreign Policy* (Wilmington, Delaware: Scholarly Resources, 1995), p. 149.   [69] Ibid., p. 120.

factional tug-of-war within the Chinese government. By May of 1949 the local authorities had begun accusing Ward and his entourage of espionage activities, and they were subsequently imprisoned on trumped-up charges. Having received jail sentences initially, their sentences were commuted to deportation and the crisis was effectively over. Even though the use of military force to rescue the hostages was ultimately rejected, it was actively considered by an angry President Truman in the early stages of the crisis.[70] As public pressure to act mounted, Truman initially thought of mounting a military rescue mission and then suggested a naval blockade of China. However, all the military options were soon ruled out as impractical or likely to lead to a major escalation of hostilities.

Of the parallel with the *Pueblo* and Carter's knowledge of it, Vance says that 'I remember calling it to his attention quite early on',[71] in the Iranian hostage crisis, probably during the first few days. Moreover, Vance drew the analogy with Brzezinski, Brown, Jordan and the president present at the foreign policy breakfast of 9 November 1979. At that meeting, Vance placed the *Pueblo* strategy on the table as his proposed 'definition of the situation' and solution to the crisis. The secretary of state was first to speak, outlining the efforts which had been made thus far to effect the release of the hostages. Brzezinski followed, contending that the president's highest duty and responsibility was to 'the honor and dignity of our country and its foreign policy interests', rather than to protect the lives of the hostages. 'At some point that greater responsibility could become more important than the safety of our diplomats . . . if they're still in captivity at Thanksgiving, what will that say about your Presidency and America's image in the world?', Brzezinski asked.[72]

Vance clearly disagreed with the thrust of Brzezinski's argument and its implications, as Jordan reports: 'The hostages have been held only five days', he said. 'We're dealing with a volatile, chaotic situation in Iran, and negotiation is the only way to free them. The President and this nation will ultimately be judged by our restraint in the face of provocation, and on the safe return of our hostages', he argued. 'We have to keep looking for ways to reach Khomeini and peacefully resolve this. He harked back to the *Pueblo* incident, which had plagued the Johnson administration but which had finally been resolved honourably and without loss of life.'[73]

[70] Ibid., p. 131.   [71] Vance, interview with the author.   [72] Jordan, *Crisis*, p. 36.
[73] Ibid., pp. 36–7.

Vance's direct experience of the *Pueblo* hostage crisis helps explain why he repeatedly and consistently opposed any rescue mission, and why he remained so wedded to a diplomatic solution even when almost everyone else had thrown up their hands in exasperation. Vance was sent to South Korea as a special emissary of President Johnson during the *Pueblo* affair in 1968. Although not directly involved in the negotiations to free the hostages going on in Panmunjon at that time, Vance helped to calm the South Koreans. He successfully dissuaded President Park from attacking North Korea in retaliation for *Pueblo* and for a recent attack on Park's presidential palace – the Blue House – by the North. The United States had received information that Park was considering military reprisals against the North, but Vance successfully persuaded him not to involve himself in this situation or in the hostage negotiations, since Vance and Johnson 'felt that to bring the South Koreans into the discussion at this point might jeopardize the success of the discussions'.[74] Eleven years later, in dealing with the Iranian crisis, Vance looked back on *Pueblo* as a model of what can be achieved by dogged negotiation, since the American hostages were eventually re-turned without the use of military force. In essence, Vance saw the hostages as an indispensable political tool for the groups fighting it out for control of Iran after the fall of the shah, and reasoned that the Americans were probably reasonably safe for that reason. Once a 'winner' had emerged from this process and a political settlement put in place, the Iranians would have no further use for their captives and would therefore release them.

The impact of *Pueblo* on Vance's thinking about the Tehran crisis is quite clear in Vance's own mind, for when the latter crisis came along in late 1979, *Pueblo* 'made me think that this isn't a one time thing that hasn't happened before. This is similar to difficult situations, to say the least, that had happened on other occasions.' The chief lesson of the *Pueblo* incident, as he saw it, was

> try to proceed with care and caution in trying to achieve a solution which could be done without spilling bloodshed, and particularly the bloodshed of our hostages who were still being held. And I obviously thought about this from time to time as I watched what happened and I saw on television what was going on, and I read in the papers what was going on. As time went on, I was more and more convinced that

[74] See Cyrus Vance, second oral history interview, Lyndon Johnson Library, Austin, Texas, 29 December 1969, p. 15.

the right thing to do was to do what we were doing: namely, not to use force.[75]

Very early on in the Tehran crisis, Vance had also drawn Carter's attention to the similarities between the Angus Ward affair and the situation in Iran. As Vance later wrote:

> the Ward case had many similarities to the seizure in Iran, as is clear from the memorandum of the Joint Chiefs of Staff to President Truman recommending against the use of military force. I had sent a copy of this memorandum to the President shortly after the hostages were taken. I was convinced that as time passed the chances of physical harm to the hostages diminished.[76]

The memorandum to which Vance refers was initially sent by Truman's chairman of the Joint Chiefs, Omar Bradley, to the secretary of defence of that time. Close attention to this document – which was reprinted in Vance's memoirs[77] and reproduced below – reveals that the two situations do exhibit a number of rather striking similarities.

MEMORANDUM BY THE CHAIRMAN OF THE JOINT CHIEFS OF STAFF (BRADLEY) TO THE SECRETARY OF DEFENSE (JOHNSON)

Washington, 18 November 1949

The following are the views of the Joint Chiefs of Staff in response to your oral question as to what might be done by the Department of Defense to assist the Department of State to extricate Mr. Angus Ward from his predicament in Mukden:

(a) The Department of Defense can, at little risk and cost, assist the Department of State to extricate Mr. Angus Ward from Mukden by providing transportation by sea or air for a duly accredited Department of State representative to any point for which diplomatic clearance for the visit has being obtained;

(b) Other military alternatives involve either threats by the United States government, coupled with a present apparent intent to carry out the threatened action, or direct military action as may be necessary in the circumstance. In either of these two courses of action, there are military implications of such deep significance that they should be examined in detail;

(c) Mukden, the locale of Mr. Ward's confinement, is the seat of government for Manchuria, this government being subordinate to the

[75] Vance, interview with the author.   [76] Vance, *Hard Choices*, pp. 408–9.
[77] Ibid., pp. 498–500. See also *Foreign Relations*, 1949, vol. VIII, pp. 1007–19.

Chinese Communist Government at Peking. According to intelligence sources, Mukden is also the headquarters of a Chinese Communist army;

(d) In accordance with the rights granted under the Sino-Soviet Treaty of 1945, the USSR has established operating facilities for submarines and for surface vessels at Dairen and Port Arthur. Considerable quantities of Manchurian goods are exported from Diaren by sea; lesser quantities of goods are exported from Manchurian ports in the Gulf of Chihli and in Korea Bay. There is no overt United States trade with Manchuria;

(e) It is recognized that political considerations could affect the military considerations involved. Such political considerations would include the nature of the warning and the color of authority (United Nations or the duly recognized Chinese Nationalist Government) under which military action might be initiated. Regardless of the political considerations, however, there are, broadly speaking, only two possible courses of military action; namely:

(1) Forcible measures to remove Mr. Angus Ward from Mukden; and

(2) Military redress;

(f) The physical removal of Mr. Ward from Mukden would require the employment of military forces in sufficient strength to force a landing, either by sea or by air, to effect rescue, and to fight their way out of Manchuria or, alternatively, it would require covert operations for the removal of Mr. Ward from Manchuria, after forcibly extricating him from custody. The strength of the military forces required to force a landing and overtly to remove Mr. Ward from custody must be adequate, from the inception of the operation, to ensure its success under all contingencies, and such strength is probably greater than that presently available. The undertaking of such military action would involve a conflict with the civil forces in that area, and probably the military forces as well. Thus such action might well lead to open war with the Chinese Communist Government. Furthermore, failure of the USSR to become involved, particularly in view of Soviet strategic interests in Manchuria and the presence of USSR units in the Dairen–Port Arthur area, can be regarded only as a remote possibility. In view of the foregoing considerations, there is a likelihood that overt United States military action might lead to global war. It is understood that covert measures to remove Mr. Ward from Manchuria would probably require action beyond the capabilities of the covert strength available to the United States government. In the case of either overt or covert action for the removal of Mr. Ward, there would be grave doubts as to whether he would be allowed to survive. Moreover, covert action, even if successful, would not sustain the attitude of the United States with respect to the treatment of its consular representatives and other nationals, and might be construed as a tacit admission of Mr. Ward's guilt;

(g) The second course of action; namely, redress, would involve the application of retortion, reprisal, or some form of sanction such as embargo or blockade;

(h) Since there are no diplomatic representatives of the Chinese Communist Government in United States territory, simple retortion is not possible. Retortion, however, could be accomplished through the kidnapping by covert forces of one or more highly placed officials of the Manchurian government. Even if such an operation were within the capabilities of United States covert forces, this action would establish a highly undesirable precedent in United States international relations and, by the very nature of its covert form, would fail to provide a clear-cut basis for the extrication of Mr. Ward without at least tacit overt approval by the United States of an unfriendly act carried out by covert forces. Furthermore, retortion of this nature might not alter the decision of the Manchurian government to hold Mr. Ward rather than to negotiate an exchange. In addition, our covert action or our subsequent retortion might jeopardize the safety of other United States nationals in Communist China;

(i) Reprisal would call for seizure or destruction of Manchurian property or that of its citizens. Since there is no Manchurian property in the United States or its possessions, acts of reprisal would have to involve military operations directly against Manchuria and this again would probably lead to war;

(j) A United States embargo would be futile in the absence of Manchurian trade with this nation or with nations subject to our influence; and

(k) *Pacific blockade*. A pacific blockade is a blockade established by one or more states against the ports of another to enforce certain demands, without the intention of going to war. As a rule only vessels of states whose ports are blocked are seized. The United States has never been a party to a pacific blockade.

It is generally conceded –

(1) That a pacific blockade is a legitimate means of constraint short of war.

(2) Those parties to the blockade are bound by its consequences.

(3) As a matter of policy it might be advisable to resort to pacific blockade in order to avoid declaration of war.

(4) That states not party to a pacific blockade are in no way bound to observe it.

Currently British interests control the greater percentage of ships entering China ports. They would not be affected by a United States declaration of a pacific blockade.

(1) Blockade. A blockade is normally employed only in time of war and its institution is commonly considered a belligerent act. It affects

shipping regardless of nationality. Such blockade to be recognized would have to be effective. It would involve either coercion of or prior agreement with the British and might eventually necessitate the commitment of strength adequate to deal with the Soviet naval and air forces in the Far East.

In view of all the foregoing considerations, the Joint Chiefs of Staff are of the opinion that direct military action to assist the Department of State in extricating Mr. Angus Ward from his predicament might lead to war and would not of itself ensure his timely and safe extrication. They do, however, point out that the Department of Defense can assist by supplying appropriate transportation for the accredited representatives of the Government to negotiate for Mr. Ward's release. Consideration might also be given to designating a military officer, such as the Commander of the Seventh Task Fleet, to negotiate locally for the release of Mr. Ward.

For the Joint Chiefs of Staff:
OMAR N. BRADLEY

Several of the similarities between the two cases are worth bringing to the reader's attention. Ward was, like the hostages in Iran, embroiled in a post-revolutionary power struggle in which his own role had become that of a helpless pawn, and in common with the Tehran captives he had been accused of espionage activities. It is also one of the ironies of American diplomatic history that before arriving in his post at Mukden, Ward had been stationed in Tehran. But the most striking similarities relate to the military or strategic commonalities between the two cases. As in the Iranian case, President Truman had expressed interest in a possible rescue mission, but Omar Bradley concluded that: (1) a rescue operation would be extremely difficult given the location of the hostages; (2) 'the undertaking of such military action would involve a conflict with the civil forces in that area, and probably the military forces as well'; (3) 'failure of the USSR to become involved . . . can be regarded only as a remote possibility'; and (4) 'covert action, even if successful, would not sustain the attitude of the United States with respect to the treatment of its consular representatives and other nationals'. In other words, there was a good chance that the Chinese would react to a successful operation by seizing other US citizens.

Vance was to echo many of these exact same concerns both before and after the decision to go ahead with the rescue mission. Like Bradley, he was somewhat concerned that the Soviets might intervene should the US engage in military operations in such a politically sensitive region, and that a rescue operation (whether successful or unsuccessful) might push Iran into the hands of the Soviets; and he also feared that even a successful operation might backfire on the United States, in the sense that Iran might react by taking more US hostages as replacements. This seemed a very real possibility to Vance, since many representatives of the American media were encamped in Tehran at that time.

The number of hostages held in Mukden was a great deal smaller than the number in the Tehran case, but Vance felt that this difference actually enhanced the appropriateness of the analogy, for the need to proceed cautiously was even greater in Iran given that so many more lives were now at stake.

> We were also dealing not only with one person, as was the case in the Angus Ward case, but we were dealing with some fifty people at that period of time, and some sixty-odd people before we got the thirteen out.[78] So we were dealing with a lot of lives that might very well be lost. So it was even, in a way, a more difficult situation in which to think of using force.[79]

In a later interview, Gary Sick spontaneously recalled this analogy being used in the decision-makers' deliberations, although he doubted whether it had a formative impact upon anyone's thinking. According to Sick's recollection, 'we all learned of this [the Ward affair] well after the event. The morning that this happened, nobody was saying "aha! This is like such and such a case." It was only quite a long time later that anybody came up with that.'[80] Yet while this may well be true of the non-State Department staff – Sick was employed by the National Security Council at that time – Cyrus Vance was clearly thinking of the parallel from day one of the crisis. 'I had heard about it before', he recalls. While he does not now remember exactly when he first learned the details of the Angus Ward affair, he does recall that this was a case he had become familiar with at some point in his earlier life, and that this was not something which needed to be drawn to his attention by someone else after the Tehran crisis had started, or something which State Department officials scrambled around to look for after the event. 'I know it was one of the things that leapt to mind', he maintains. He believes that both the *Pueblo* and the Angus Ward incidents had a

---

[78] A reference to the thirteen original hostages who were released early on in the hostage crisis, all of whom were black or female.   [79] Vance, interview with the author.
[80] Sick, interview with the author.

genuinely formative impact upon the way he thought about the crisis in Tehran, and his impression was that 'it did have an effect' on Jimmy Carter, once the president had read the memorandum and seen the parallels for himself.[81] As Buhite notes, Bradley's study in 1949 'was the first systematic assessment ever made of the options available – or not available – in hostage crises. As such, it foreshadowed responses in future situations and pointed up the dilemma that the nation faced throughout the twentieth century.'[82]

The public record supports Vance's recollection of the point at which the Ward case grabbed the attention of those at the top of the decision-making process, showing that Jimmy Carter was aware of the Angus Ward precedent by at least the middle of December, for the president was to mention the case in public on 13 December 1979, only nine days after the crisis had begun. On that occasion, Carter stated: 'I've re-read the history on it and even the private memoranda that were exchanged within the White House.' He also noted that 'President Truman did ask the Joint Chiefs of Staff and others to analyze how he might, through physical action if necessary, cause the release of our Ambassador and his staff. It was not done, and eventually the Ambassador was re-leased.'[83]

It is unlikely, as Brzezinski has suggested, that Carter was aware of the Ward analogy before it was brought to his attention. Nevertheless, the secretary of state's active lobbying on behalf of the Ward precedent certainly made the president conscious of it, for Carter publicly alluded to the impact it had on his thinking on at least two recorded occasions. Apart from the president's 13 December parallel between the Iranian crisis and the Ward affair, at a press conference on 19 April 1980 Carter stated that he had examined three earlier crises – including the 1949 precedent – in order to draw lessons from them:

> *Interviewer*: Mr, President, turning for a minute to Iran, I just wondered, as you assess what to do in Iran, do you draw upon any kind of historical parallels between either the *Pueblo* incident or the *Mayaguez* . . .?
> *The President*: I have studied all the previous occurrences in my lifetime where American hostages have been taken – in Mongolia, when President Truman was in office, and the *Mayaguez* incident under President Ford, and the *Pueblo* incident under President Johnson – to learn how they reacted and what the degree of success

---

[81] Vance, interview with the author.   [82] Buhite, *Lives At Risk*, p. 132.
[83] See Jimmy Carter, Public Papers of the President, 1979, p. 2242.

was, and also the legalities involved in dealing with countries that either directly or indirectly participated in the holding of hostages.[84]

Jimmy Carter's belief that he could negotiate with Khomeini for the release of the hostages may also have been aided by other, less observable analogies or general schemata. For instance, since both were religious men, Carter may initially have reasoned that this apparent affinity gave him some insight into Khomeini's character and that he could 'work' with him on this basis. In the beginning, at least, it is not fanciful to believe that he may have transferred onto Khomeini the characteristics one would expect of a Southern Baptist clergyman. One wonders perhaps whether such an impression might have led him into a similar schematic error to that committed by Harry Truman in his initial dealings with Stalin. As Deborah Welch Larson notes, Truman initially misperceived Stalin because he saw him as similar to his old party boss, Tom Pendergast. She refers to the construction of 'personae', mental categories into which people place unfamiliar individuals in order to simplify their understanding and dealings with that individual.[85]

Regardless of the effect that such initial impressions may or may not have had, Carter does seem to have been impressed by the similarities between the Ward, *Pueblo* and Iran cases at the outset. This cannot be said of several of the other decision-makers, however, at least two of whom were clearly *not* convinced that the *Pueblo*–Ward strategy was something to be replicated this time. As his remarks at the 9 November breakfast reveal, Zbigniew Brzezinski looked upon *Pueblo* and Angus Ward as sacrifices of America's interests and national honour. When Vance suggested following the *Pueblo* precedent that morning, Brzezinski's reaction was to point out forcefully 'but that went on for a year!'.[86] The national security adviser saw the Johnson administration's response to the *Pueblo* affair as a failure, since it took so long to get the hostages back and the United States lost a good deal of national 'face' in the encounter. Brzezinski recalls: 'I did not think that [a repetition of the *Pueblo* strategy] was desirable. I did not think that we would be able to sustain that, even though I did not expect that the television, for example, every night would lead the news with the statement that this is the 142nd, 143rd, 144th day of the hostage crisis.'[87] The political cost,

---

[84] Jimmy Carter, Question and Answer session with reporters from Pennsylvania, 19 April 1980, Public Papers of the President, pp. 744–5.

[85] Larson, *Origins of Containment*, p. 178.   [86] Jordan, *Crisis*, pp. 36–7.

[87] Brzezinski, interview with the author.

in other words, would be too great to simply 'wait it out', as Vance was suggesting. As Reginald Ross Smith, who interviewed the former national security adviser in the early 1980s, notes:

> Brzezinski has remarked that the *Pueblo* and Iranian situations were very different because of the publicity which surrounded the Iranian hostage crisis and the resultant pressure on the Carter administration to act to free the hostages. He believes that the media did not display an equal interest in the *Pueblo*, primarily because the Tet offensive in Vietnam was receiving all of the media attention.[88]

Even more explicitly than Brzezinski, White House Chief of Staff Hamilton Jordan also pointed to the unfavourable political ramifications of following a *Pueblo*-based strategy. When Brzezinski objected to the wisdom of being guided by the *Pueblo* analogy, Jordan backed him up, adding that 'Johnson wasn't in the middle of a re-election campaign' during the *Pueblo* crisis.[89] Jordan's remark – which clearly implies that Lyndon Johnson could afford the political costs of negotiating for a more extended period of time – is a curious one, since Johnson was in fact embroiled in the campaign of 1968 at the time the *Pueblo* was seized in January of that year. Nevertheless, it does illustrate the character of his objections. According to Brzezinski, Jordan remarked at the foreign policy breakfast of 9 November that 'if it drags out that long, you can forget about a second term'.[90]

CIA Director Turner seems to have been somewhat set against following a *Pueblo*-style policy also. Turner avoided playing an 'advocacy' role during the crisis unless directly requested to do so by the president. As Frank Carlucci, Turner's deputy at the time, has pointed out, 'the rescue attempt . . . was not mine (or Stan's) to bless or oppose since in the Carter administration the CIA was quite properly confined to a non-policy role; and we were never asked whether we favored or opposed a particular policy decision'.[91] Initially, Turner was even kept out of the secret meetings at which the military options were being explored (although at his own insistence he was included afterwards, once he discovered the existence of these discussions).

However, Turner's account of the hostage crisis makes clear that he did have policy preferences of his own, and that he favoured military options over diplomatic ones. He viewed *Pueblo* as a bad precedent to

---

[88] Ross Smith, 'A Comparative Case Analysis of Presidential Decision-Making', p. 109.
[89] Jordan, *Crisis*, pp. 36–7.   [90] Brzezinski, interview with the author.
[91] Frank Carlucci, personal correspondence with the author, 11 March 1994.

follow in the Iranian crisis, albeit one that the administration would be forced to follow in the absence of other realistic options. When it became clear that Carter was going to try peaceful, negotiated means to get the hostages out, Turner privately believed that:

> We were back to Lyndon Johnson's futile efforts to use diplomacy for the release of the crew of the *Pueblo*. He had called on nations and organizations to intercede on our behalf . . . He had approached the South Koreans, hoping to arrange an exchange of *Pueblo*'s crew for North Korean military prisoners held in South Korea. He had sought adjudication by the International Court of Justice and mediation by several third parties. Nothing had worked.[92]

Turner does not seem to have expressed this opinion at the time, at least not in official forums. Given his absence of input into policy formulation during the early stages of the crisis, his view on this matter probably played little role in decision-making at this stage. What it illustrates, however, is how widespread resistance to the *Pueblo* analogy was from almost every quarter. Yet, in spite of such opposition, the president appears to have followed the *Pueblo* and Angus Ward precedents for some time, although he never seems to have been entirely convinced by their longer-term applicability, and his humanitarian concern for the hostages and their families made him disinclined to wait as long as Johnson had to get the hostages back. Obviously, Carter's own belief system predisposed him towards a peaceful resolution of the crisis, which in practice would mean negotiating with the Iranians in some manner. With the Entebbe analogy weakened – and with the other military options also ruled out by Carter as 'impractical or unlikely to succeed without considerable loss of life on both sides'[93] – *Pueblo* and Angus Ward won the analogical war virtually by default, since there appeared to be no practical policy alternative to the bargaining option. 'We were almost forced to consider Cy's strategy of less obtrusive diplomatic pressures combined with patient negotiations', as Stansfield Turner explained.[94] Similarly, as Vance himself has admitted, the receptivity of Carter to the *Pueblo* analogy 'was certainly reinforced by the fact that the Joint Chiefs came up with the decisions they came up with right at the outset'.[95] Equally, it was clear that those who

---

[92] Turner, *Terrorism and Democracy*, p. 37.
[93] Carter, *Keeping Faith*, p. 459. These options included a bombing of selected Iranian targets, a naval blockade and mining the Iranian harbours.
[94] Turner, *Terrorism and Democracy*, p. 60.   [95] Vance, interview with the author.

had not been intimately involved in the *Pueblo* crisis, and had no familiarity with the Angus Ward case, would not be as willing to adhere to the perceived lessons of these two episodes as the secretary of state was.

third parties, took the issue to the United Nations and sent aircraft carriers to the region.

Carter later acknowledged the *general* impact of *Pueblo* on his own strategy in an interview with Reginald Ross Smith in January 1984, when he compared the Iranian situation to the *Pueblo* and *Mayaguez* crises, and stated that he considered himself 'to have followed the Johnson example in being restrained and trying through peaceful means to gain the release of the Americans'.[5] In Vance's judgement, the effect of the *Pueblo* on the Tehran strategy was general in character as opposed to specific, however. Rather than providing a highly detailed blueprint as to how the decision-makers ought to conduct themselves, 'it was more of a general lesson, I think, that we'd learnt from that'.[6]

At the negotiation stage, Carter's approach took a number of different forms. Initially, the strategy was to send someone to talk directly to Khomeini and his entourage. This would obviously involve sending a presidential emissary loyal to the United States, but who would also appear sufficiently 'independent' to gain the trust of the other side. At a meeting of the SCC on 5 November and at the instigation of Vance, the decision-makers had agreed to send two emissaries to Iran – former Attorney General Ramsay Clark and Senate Intelligence Committee staff director William Miller – to negotiate the release of the hostages.[7] When the Iranian authorities refused to admit Clark and Miller, Carter took a series of steps designed to increase the diplomatic pressure on the hostage takers. On 12 November he ordered the suspension of all oil imports from Iran, and two days later instructed American officials to freeze all Iranian assets held in US banks. On 29 November, the United States asked the International Court of Justice to order the release of the hostages. Again, this measure – like Carter's later appeal to the UN Security Council to impose economic sanctions – was designed to increase the leverage on Iran and thereby reinforce the negotiations which were being undertaken by Vance and the State Department.

A substantial number of attempts were made to negotiate with the revolutionaries in Iran. Carter and Vance tried anything and everything they could think of within the negotiation track, consistent with what Carter in particular saw as the maintenance of America's national honour, to get the hostages back. As Gary Sick notes, the United States issued 'an onslaught of messages, pleas, statements, personal emissaries, condemnations, and resolutions of all kinds from governments

---

[5] See Ross Smith, 'A Comparative Case Analysis of Presidential Decision-Making', p. 144.
[6] Vance, interview with the author.   [7] Turner, *Terrorism and Democracy*, pp. 29–30.

and individuals around the world, descending in torrents on Iranian officials and representatives wherever they might be'.[8] A full account of these attempts has been provided by others, and lies beyond the scope of this book. However, several of the approaches stand out by virtue of their documentation in the literature on the hostage crisis.[9] Most notable among these are the Waldheim approach, the Cottam channel and the so-called 'French connection' associated with White House Chief of Staff Hamilton Jordan.

At an SCC meeting on 28 November, the decision-makers decided to increase the economic pressure on Iran, and Vance paid a visit to Europe in December designed to garner support for this. When little came of this venture, the United States asked United Nations Secretary General Kurt Waldheim to go to Tehran to negotiate the hostages' release, or at least to determine whether there was a chance that negotiations could be opened. In the event, Khomeini refused to grant Waldheim an audience, just as he had done with Clark and Miller. In Turner's words, 'not only had Khomeini shown his disdain for the United Nations by refusing to meet with him, but twice the Secretary General believed his life was threatened by angry mobs'.[10] Prior to Waldheim's arrival in the country in December 1979, pictures had been published in the Iranian press showing him in conversation with the shah. On his arrival he was forced to fight his way through numerous street demonstrations, and was denied the opportunity to speak with the hostages themselves. He returned to New York in a state of shock, stating on his arrival that he was 'glad to be back, especially alive'.[11]

After the failure of the Waldheim attempt, another approach came through the political scientist Richard Cottam, a University of Pittsburgh expert on Iran who had also worked for the CIA and had been stationed at the Tehran embassy in the 1950s. He had initially been considered as a possible emissary to Iran at the 5 November SCC meeting, but since only Turner supported his candidacy, he was passed over in favour of Clark and Miller. Cottam had interviewed the Ayatollah Khomeini while the latter was living in exile in Paris, and he was also a friend of Sadegh Ghotbzadeh, then Iran's foreign minister, as well as of Ibrahim Yazdi. In many ways, then, he was an obvious choice as someone who might be able to talk directly to the Iranians. In December 1979, Cottam travelled to Iran and engaged in direct talks

---

[8] Sick, *All Fall Down*, p. 255.
[9] For a more comprehensive account of these attempts, see Sick, *All Fall Down*.
[10] Turner, *Terrorism and Democracy*, p. 85.   [11] Ibid.; Sick, *All Fall Down*, pp. 291–2.

with Ghotbzadeh, relaying reports on the situation to the State Department by telephone. Then, when nothing came of this, Cottam continued to talk to Ghotbzadeh by phone from his office in Pittsburgh. The president's chief of staff met with Cottam at Pittsburgh airport in January 1980, but by this time it had become clear that Cottam's approach, like all the others, had failed to produce the hostages' release.[12] While the State Department continued to consult with him, he was no longer the main point of contact between the US government and the Iranians.[13]

By late January of 1980 the Carter administration was trying another channel. A seemingly very promising line of negotiation opened up between Hamilton Jordan and the Iranians, mediated by two lawyer businessmen with whom he had earlier become acquainted during talks on the future of the Panama canal. Christian Bourguet, a French lawyer, and Hector Villalon, an Argentine businessman, were authorized by Foreign Minister Bani-Sadr, and then by Sadegh Ghotbzadeh when the latter replaced Bani-Sadr in this position, to represent the Iranian government in the negotiations over the hostages' release. This approach became popularly known as the 'French connection', since both Bourguet and Villalon were based in Paris. They worked out with Jordan an apparently simple and straightforward plan by which the United States would agree to creation of a United Nations special commission that would examine various wrongdoings committed by the shah of Iran during the years of his rule. The idea was to provide a forum in which the current Iranian regime would present its grievances. After this had been set up, the commission members would then be allowed to visit with the hostages. Once the commission had issued its report, the hostages would be released. Although the UN commission was formed as agreed, it was never allowed to visit the hostages, and by early March the whole plan had collapsed.

The essential problem in both the Cottam and the Bourguet–Villalon cases was that the moderates in the provisional government did not have the power or authority to deliver on their part of the deal. Both Iranian President Abol Hassan Bani-Sadr and Ghotbzadeh appear to have believed, for various reasons, that it was not a good idea for Iran to hold onto the American hostages; nevertheless, neither man was able to prevail upon the revolutionary militants holding the hostages to

---

[12] The story of Jordan's visit to Cottam is told by Jordan in *Crisis*, pp. 114–16.
[13] Clarke Thomas, 'Pitt Professor Tells of Role in Hostage Talks', *Pittsburgh Post-Gazette*, 25 July 1984, p. 7.

transfer them to the control of the provisional government, which was a prerequisite for getting the hostages back.

Jimmy Carter's frustration with the collapse of this channel in particular was immense. As Sick relates, over a hundred hours of meetings had been conducted between Jordan, working in collaboration with the State Department's Harold Saunders, and the two lawyers, but it had all come to naught.[14] The problem was not just that repeated efforts to get the hostages back via negotiation had yielded no concrete results. It was also that on several occasions it had seemed that the hostages were close to release, but then Carter's hopes had been *dashed*. In Carter's own disappointment-laden words, 'it was obvious to me that the Revolutionary Council would never act and that, in spite of all our work and the efforts of the elected leaders of Iran, the hostages were not going to be released'.[15] Vance, on the other hand, does not appear to have been anywhere near as frustrated by these events as Carter was. This was due in large part to the fact that he viewed the central lesson of the *Pueblo* and Ward as being the necessity of waiting. Since the hostages had a profound domestic political value to Khomeini, it stood to reason that negotiation efforts on the part of the United States might well be rebuffed; indeed, this was probably to be expected. Thus Vance's strategy did not depend simply on establishing a negotiation channel to the radicals in Iran. It rested, above all, on a willingness to wait until the hostages no longer performed this useful domestic role.

As Stansfield Turner has put it, 'Cy's approach required considerable patience.' It soon became clear that the other decision-makers had accepted the negotiation track with great reluctance, however, and that they were not prepared to wait it out in the manner which the *Pueblo* analogy suggested they ought to: 'We did not want to wait for them to come to their senses', Turner notes. 'We wanted to act.'[16] As early as 1 December, the patience of some members of the policy-making group was already wearing thin. Harold Brown sent a memorandum to the president that day outlining his view that military action of some sort could not be avoided for very much longer. Brzezinski was also pressurizing the president to take tougher action, and more generally 'put the pressure on' for faster action.[17]

Events beyond the president's control were also pushing Carter slowly but surely towards doing something of a stronger nature about

---

[14] Sick, *All Fall Down*, p. 297.   [15] Carter, *Keeping Faith*, p. 515.   [16] Ibid., pp. 59–60.
[17] Turner, interview with the author.

the hostages. The onset of the presidential campaign led members of Carter's White House staff in particular to express mounting concern about the president's re-election prospects and 'rising public pressure for more direct action against Iran'.[18] Moreover, the invasion of Afghanistan by the Soviet Union in December 1979 probably altered the strategic environment within which the advisers were working. Certainly, this event did not change Carter's basic view of the world, and Turner, for one, 'noticed no particular shift in his attitude towards the hostage issue' after this.[19] This event may nevertheless have been crucially important in tipping the balance in favour of Brzezinski's view of the world while correspondingly discrediting that of Vance, and no doubt this indirectly altered the reception of the analogies being proposed by each.[20] The *Pueblo* analogy implies a softly softly approach to international relations of the sort which seemed increasingly naive as the second Cold War began, while Brzezinski's aggressive advocacy of daring feats now seemed to fit the times, and his warnings about Soviet expansionism appeared deeply prophetic.

Planning the rescue mission

On 6 November, the president instructed Brzezinski to start preparing a rescue plan, recognizing that such a rescue might become a practical necessity if the hostage takers started killing their captives. The contingency planning for the rescue mission was quickly taken out of the NSC and SCC process and entrusted to a very small, *ad hoc* group. This group was usually composed of Zbigniew Brzezinski, David Jones, Harold Brown and Stansfield Turner, although Vice President Mondale also attended where possible. However, from the very first day the planners ran into an immediate problem: there were no standard operating procedures upon which the Joint Chiefs could rely in planning the mission. As Richard Gabriel notes, 'the seizure of the hostages came as such a surprise that no military contingency plan existed to deal with the situation'.[21] Rescue operations were not something the US military was used to planning for – in recent years, the only major rescue missions had been Son Tay in 1970 and *Mayaguez* in 1975 – and so the Joint Chiefs had never developed an office that would handle events

---

[18] Brzezinski, 'The Failed Mission', p. 30.   [19] Turner, interview with the author.
[20] Destler, Gelb and Lake, *Our Own Worst Enemy*, p. 223 and Sick, *All Fall Down*, pp. 341–3.
[21] Richard Gabriel, *Military Incompetence: Why the American Military Doesn't Win* (New York: Hill and Wang, 1985), p. 86.

such as hostage crises. This meant, as Gabriel notes, that 'once the decision was made to develop a military option, an entire staff structure had to be created from scratch'.[22]

Although there was no established JCS procedure for mounting rescue missions, there was already a rescue team in place: Delta Force. Delta Force was created in 1977 as an immediate response to the Mogadishu rescue operation, and was modelled on Germany's GSG-9 and on the British Special Air Services (SAS). Delta's leader, the unconventional Colonel Charles Beckwith, had spent a year on secondment with the SAS in 1962, and had long advocated the creation of a similar unit within the US armed forces. However, it was not until the successful Israeli and German raids of the mid-1970s that political pressures compelled the creation of Delta Force. On 13 October 1977, a Lufthansa airliner bound for Frankfurt was hijacked by Palestinian terrorists. The terrorists demanded the release of various Palestinian prisoners and ordered the pilot to fly the plane, with its mainly West German hostages aboard, to Rome. After various stops at airports around the globe, the plane landed at Mogadishu in Somalia. The German government then obtained the permission of the Somali government to put a rescue mission into effect, and on 17 October Germany's counterterrorist unit, GSG-9, stormed the aircraft. The raid was outstandingly successful: the terrorists were killed, and not a single hostage was lost (although a number were injured).

The success of the operation garnered international acclaim. On 18 October, President Jimmy Carter – obviously greatly impressed by the events at Mogadishu only the previous day and by those at Entebbe when he was a candidate for the presidency – told Brzezinski and Brown in a memorandum to 'find out how West Germany and Israel developed such effective counterterrorist measures'. He suggested that they ask then German Chancellor Helmut Schmidt and Israeli Prime Minister Menachem Begin how it was done, and requested that they develop 'similar US capabilities'.[23] A month later Delta Force was born.

By November 1979, Delta Force had been in training for almost two years. There was, however, a major problem with this training as preparation for the kind of circumstances they would face in Tehran: they had relied too heavily on the Mogadishu analogy. As Martin and Walcott relate, by November 1979

---

[22] Ibid.　　[23] Quoted in Martin and Walcott, *Best Laid Plans*, p. 39.

Delta had prepared for several different hostage scenarios . . . but they all had one thing in common. They occurred in foreign countries where the host government had invited Delta to end the standoff. The model for this so-called 'permissive environment' was GSG 9's Mogadishu operation. Delta never trained for the 'nonpermissive environment' the Israelis had encountered at Entebbe, where the host government was in league with the terrorists. Events would expose this predilection for the Mogadishu model to be a fundamental error.[24]

Presumably it was the recency of Mogadishu – and its status as a precipitating event in the birth of Delta Force – that inclined Beckwith towards this model, but it proved to be a problem when the rescuers were asked to confront a quite different scenario in Tehran, where the host government appeared to be as much a part of the problem as the hostage takers themselves. There was certainly no question of Delta Force being 'invited in' by the authorities in Tehran.

Given the absence of any habitual ways of doing things, it is not unnatural that from the earliest days of the military planning the group scrambled around for a plan on which to base the operation, for some historical comparison that would guide their actions. We still do not know all of the considerations which governed the actions of the planners, but at least some of the reasoning upon which they relied has entered the public domain in the years since the rescue mission was attempted. One useful source, for instance, is the report of Special Operations Review Group, set up in May after the failure of the mission and chaired by Admiral James Holloway. The group had a very limited purview – certainly it lacked the depth and breadth of the CIA report which examined the failure of the Bay of Pigs operation – but its port-mortem of the failed mission does contain some useful details.[25] In the years since 1980 various interviews have also been granted to researchers by members of the planning group, many of which help us piece together what occurred.[26]

In planning the mission, the decision-makers faced at least four major

---

[24] Ibid., pp. 40–1.
[25] The Special Operations Review Group's other members were Lieutenant Generals Samuel Wilson and Leroy Manor, and Major Generals James Smith, John Piotrowski and Alfred Gray. A declassified version of the report they produced was made public in August 1980. However, its terms of reference were sharply circumscribed in the sense that Holloway and his associates were not permitted to examine the reasoning and procedures adopted by the political decision-makers, such as Brzezinski, Brown or Carter himself. As Turner put it, this was 'like asking a doctor for a thorough diagnosis of a patient's health, but prohibiting mention of any one of several diseases that might be causing the patient's illness'. See Turner, *Terrorism and Democracy*, p. 134.
[26] Brzezinski and Turner have been particularly active in this regard.

problems, according to Stansfield Turner: 'firstly, how do we get the rescue force there; two, how to get them out; three . . . we needed to know their whereabouts, where they were in the embassy; and fourthly, how do we keep it secret'.[27] Added to these four problems was the difficulty involved in assaulting the embassy itself. We shall address each problem in turn.

(1) Getting the rescue force in and out

In the secret meetings at which the military options were discussed and a rescue plan formulated, the four-man group was inevitably compelled to concentrate on overcoming the central difference between Tehran and Entebbe: the 'airport problem', or the fact there was nowhere for a rescue team to land. Clearly, this hurdle would have to be cleared in a convincing fashion before a rescue operation could proceed. As Brzezinski put it, 'our target was far from the United States, remote from any American-controlled facilities, and helicopters were not usually used for long-distance assault missions'. Nevertheless, 'the military went to work overcoming these difficulties'.[28]

As the rescue planning proceeded, it became clear that long-range helicopters seemed to be the only way of getting the rescue force in and out of Iran undetected, but the distances involved would make the journey impossible without some means of refuelling them. At first the planners considered smuggling a military rescue team into Iran by increments, an idea modelled on a successful Tehran rescue operation previously ordered by the Texan billionaire and later US presidential candidate, H. Ross Perot. In February 1979, shortly after the Iranian revolution began, Perot – then head of the EDS corporation – had ordered the rescue of two of his employees being held in an Iranian prison. The rescue team, which reportedly included former CIA members, entered Tehran airport one by one using fake passports. Shortly before the two employees were spirited away, a revolutionary mob stormed the prison. According to one account, Perot paid local Iranians to 'foment' the uprising as a diversionary tactic, thus enabling the hostages to escape. They then sneaked out of Iran by bribing guards at the border.

While not everyone accepts this account of what occurred, Stansfield Turner argues that it is accurate, and maintains that it did initially affect

<hr>

[27] Turner, interview with the author.   [28] Brzezinski, 'The Failed Mission', p. 28.

the planning for the administration's mission.[29] The problem was somewhat analogous to the embassy situation in the sense that the captives were being held inside a compound under Iranian guard. Just as Perot's rescue force had entered the country through Tehran airport in piecemeal and clandestine fashion, for some days the planners seriously considered putting the rescue force in by similar means. On 11 November – a week after the hostages were seized – Perot was called in by the administration for secret talks with military officials about a possible mission. The famous businessman, together with a group of his employees who had been involved in the rescue, met with Turner and Jones to discuss how the Carter administration might repeat their successful strategy.[30] According to Turner, 'Ross and his people thought that if we infiltrated a military team into Tehran, it could canvass the territory, purchase its weapons, and then wait for the right moment to storm the embassy and release the hostages.'[31] However, it soon became clear that any attempt to rescue the embassy hostages would be of such a greater scale and magnitude that emulating the Perot strategy would surely end in disaster. In particular, it was thought highly probable that the rescuers would be identified as such by passport authorities in Tehran, who would certainly be on the look out for American citizens of suspicious appearance. An even more substantial problem, however, was getting the hostages and their rescuers out of Tehran once they had been released. Perot had smuggled his people out in trucks, but getting the much larger group that an embassy assault would involve out of the country was another matter entirely. According to Turner, however, 'we took some lessons from what Perot had done'. Even though the Perot model was rejected, 'Perot's idea of a clandestine approach had an influence', Turner maintains, as opposed to the more direct military approach eventually taken.[32]

On 12 November the planning group actively considered putting Delta Force into Iran the way Perot had suggested. Inevitably, however,

[29] Turner, interview with author. The favourable account of Perot's role can be found in Ken Follet's semi-fictional work, *On Wings of Eagles*. However, John Stempel – who worked in the US Embassy in Tehran between 1978 and 1979 – has argued that Perot's role in the release of the employees was minimal and coincidental. See 'Ross Who?', 'This Week', ITV, broadcast in Britain on 9 July 1992.

[30] There was no shortage of ideas – many of them amusingly far-fetched and sometimes bizarre – coming from members of the general public as to how the hostages might be released. A selection of letters to the administration in this vein is gathered among Lloyd Cutler's papers in the Jimmy Carter Library in Atlanta.

[31] Turner, *Terrorism and Democracy*, p. 41.   [32] Turner, interview with the author.

the rescue planning would be shaped on the whole by other forces and other lessons. One source of such lessons seems to have been the Entebbe experience, which had been conducted by overt military (rather than covert and clandestine) means. For instance, one aspect of Entebbe upon which the Iran planners appear to have drawn – a seemingly small yet nevertheless significant detail – relates to the effort to disguise the Americans' exit from Iran. Recall that in order to disguise their arrival at the Entebbe airport terminal in Uganda in 1976, the initial rescue force which was to storm the airport travelled in a black Mercedes designed to look like that used by Ugandan President Idi Amin, who was collaborating with the hostage takers. Approaching the airport terminal, the rescuers killed the guards outside with pistols fitted with silencers. The faces of the rescue force were also blackened, they were dressed as Ugandan guards and they carried pistols and AK-47 rifles similar to those used by the Ugandan military.[33] In similar vein, it is understood that – had the mission ever reached the later stages – the helicopters the rescue team would have used to escape were disguised to look as if they belonged to the Iranian military. As Martin and Walcott note, while stationed on the *Nimitz* seven of the eight helicopters were painted brown 'with Iranian markings'.[34] Moreover, according to a report based on interviews with Carter's military advisers conducted by *Washington Post* staff in 1982, 'Iranian agents accompanying the Delta team would be dressed in Iranian uniforms as well. This was expected to generate mass confusion near the embassy and create the impression that the military raiders were an Iranian military outfit responding to a rescue or coup attempt.'[35] As related by Charles Beckwith, the approach to the embassy was also strikingly reminiscent of the Entebbe raid. 'Between 11:00 P.M. and midnight', Beckwith states, 'a select group of operators would drive up to the embassy in the Datsun pickup and with .22-caliber suppressed (with silencers) handguns take down the two guardposts and the walking guards along Roosevelt Avenue.'[36]

For all the differences between the two cases, these were aspects of

---

[33] Stevenson, *90 Minutes At Entebbe*, p. 109.
[34] Martin and Walcott, *Best Laid Plans*, p. 13.
[35] Scott Armstrong, George Wilson and Bob Woodward, 'Debate Rekindles On Failed Iran Raid', *Washington Post*, 25 April 1982, p. A14. This would also undoubtedly have confused the hostages themselves, but this must have been deemed a risk worth taking.
[36] Charlie Beckwith and Donald Knox, *Delta Force* (London: Harcourt Brace Jovanovich, 1983), p. 254.

Entebbe that could readily be 'transplanted' to the Tehran case. Of course, it may have been no more than common sense to disguise the American helicopters as Iranian and to approach the embassy by car with silenced guns blazing, but given the effect of Entebbe on Brzezinski, it is plausible that he would utilize what lessons could be transferred from the original situation. Moreover, these similarities give some credence to the claim of Rehovam Zeevi – a former adviser to both Yitzhak Rabin and Menachem Begin – who has argued that the real reason the Tehran mission failed was that 'it was not imaginative enough and was modelled too closely on the rescue of Israeli hostages at Entebbe, Uganda'.[37]

Another major problem the planning group confronted was finding somewhere for the rescue team to land within Iran. The helicopters to be used in the raid would also need somewhere to refuel, since they could not cover the huge distances involved without some means of doing so. At first, the planners identified a military airfield outside the Iranian town of Nain as the best place to do this. However, this airfield was still in use and would therefore have to be seized by US forces prior to the arrival of the rescue team. It was soon realized that operational security might be severely jeopardized by problems encountered at this stage, and that the element of surprise vital to the success of the operation might be lost thereby. Eventually, therefore, the planners settled on another site, this time in Iran's Dasht-E-Kavir desert. One stretch of this desert – which according to one account was built by the CIA during the days of the shah[38] – was flat and firm enough to land aircraft on. It had the advantage of not needing to be seized by force. 'Desert One', as it would become known, was by no means a perfect choice, since the stretch of sand the planners identified was bisected by a main road regularly used by Iranian vehicles. However, it seemed to the group members that this option involved relatively *less* risk of jeopardizing mission security. It was selected as the initial landing site for the rescue force, and as the place where the helicopters would refuel prior to proceeding with the main part of the mission.

(2) Locating the hostages

Initially, plans for a rescue mission foundered on a lack of reliable intelligence as to where in the embassy the hostages were located. A

[37] Quoted in 'Israel Blames Poor Planning for Iran Raid Failure', *Los Angeles Times*, 27 April 1980, p. 20.   [38] Gabriel, *Military Incompetence*, p. 88.

major problem was that the CIA's top agents in Iran were themselves hostages, and so new contacts had to be built up almost from scratch. Understandably this took time, and therefore so, too, did the gathering of precise intelligence on the hostages' location. As Stansfield Turner relates, one significant problem which arose 'was knowing whether the hostages were still in the embassy compound and, if so, where. We remembered that a well-executed US raid on a prison camp at Son Tay in North Vietnam in 1970 had failed because the prisoners were not there.'[39]

The Son Tay raid had been ordered by President Nixon in November 1970 during the Vietnam War. For six months military planners had been working on a plan that would rescue American POWs being held behind enemy lines at the Son Tay camp in North Vietnam, and Nixon gave the go ahead for the plan on 18 November. The camp was deep inside enemy territory, little over 20 miles from Hanoi, and according to military intelligence approximately seventy US pilots were being held there. The intelligence for the operation came mainly from the Defence Intelligence Agency (DIA) – an arm of the Pentagon – since the military planners in Richard Gabriel's words 'felt much more comfortable using their own intelligence agency rather than relying on either the NSA or the CIA'.[40] On 20 November the rescue team, travelling in military helicopters from a base in Thailand, took off for Son Tay. The implementation of the plan was reportedly outstanding – as Lucien Vandenbroucke puts it, the raid itself was 'a masterful accomplishment' – and military resistance from North Vietnamese forces around the camp itself was successfully neutralized.[41] It must have been a great disappointment, to say the very least, when the rescuers discovered that the camp compound was entirely empty, and that the hostages had been moved elsewhere.

As Turner puts it, 'Son Tay came in here' as an analogy for the Iran rescue planners as they discussed the importance of reliable intelligence on the hostages' whereabouts, though he adds that 'I can't say that we discussed Son Tay very much.'[42] Since Son Tay had represented a notable case of the CIA being cut 'out of the loop' – something Brzezinski had already tried to do in the Iran case by also relying on the Defence Intelligence Agency – organizational memory may well have been at work here. There would no doubt have been voices within the CIA who remembered the events of 1970, and someone may

---

[39] Turner, *Terrorism and Democracy*, p. 71. [40] Gabriel, *Military Incompetence*, p. 39.
[41] Vandenbroucke, *Perilous Options*, p. 69. [42] Turner, interview with author.

conceivably have drawn the parallel to Turner's attention. Gary Sick, although not directly involved in the rescue mission planning himself, also recalls the Son Tay analogy being drawn. 'Another one of the parallels that was very much in people's minds was the very successful rescue mission in Vietnam . . . where they arrived with total surprise, only to find that there was nobody there.'[43]

In fact, one of the Delta Force team who would make up the rescue group – a former CIA agent called Major Richard Meadows, brought out of retirement for the occasion – had been intimately involved in the planning and execution of the Son Tay raid. His role in the Iranian rescue mission was somewhat exaggerated in the press, for as Turner has pointed out, Meadows went into Tehran only a few days before the mission was actually launched, and in his words 'took weeks to develop' and 'almost screwed up the whole operation'.[44] Nevertheless, the agent took considerable pains to gather information on the whereabouts of the hostages, not unnaturally wishing to avoid a repetition of his earlier experience.[45]

There was no shortage of hi-tech, satellite generated photographs of the embassy building viewed from overhead. However, all this told the planners was that the building was still standing. One participant noted that 'we had a zillion shots of the roof of the embassy . . . anything you wanted to know about the external aspects of that embassy we could tell you in infinite detail. We couldn't tell you shit about what was going on inside that building.'[46] There was, hence, a need for the kind of intelligence that only human beings can gather on the ground, but by January 1980 the CIA was at last, in Turner's words, 'reasonably sure that all the hostages were in the embassy compound'.[47] In the end, some vital intelligence came from what can only be described as remarkable luck. Shortly before the raid was launched, a CIA operative travelling on an international flight quite by chance encountered a Pakistani cook who until that day had worked at the US embassy and had even prepared the hostages' meals that morning. This individual knew the whereabouts of the hostages within the compound, and furnished information which would have been used by the rescue force had the operation ever reached that stage. 'Some people thought we had

---

[43] Sick, interview with author.   [44] Turner, interview with the author.
[45] See Philip Keisling, 'The Wrong Man and the Wrong Plan', *The Washington Monthly*, December 1983, pp. 51–8.
[46] Quoted in Steven Emerson, *Secret Warriors: Inside the Covert Military Operations of the Reagan Era* (New York: Putnam, 1988), p. 20; also in Vandenbroucke, *Perilous Options*, p. 127.   [47] Turner, *Terrorism and Democracy*, p. 87.

cooked up the story', Turner jokes, 'but it is true.'[48] The decision to proceed with the raid had by this time already long been made, but the information at least gave the rescue force confidence that their own mission would not be another Son Tay.

(3) Keeping the mission secret

The planners were also greatly concerned about operational security or OPSEC, as Holloway refers to it. They frequently worried about the possibility that the plans they were hatching would leak. In fact, to state that the group was 'concerned' about this aspect is something of an understatement, since the post-mortem studies conducted after the failure of the rescue mission indicated that the desire to maintain secrecy frequently bordered on obsession. The Holloway group found, for instance, that:

> Critical concern for OPSEC at all levels tended to dominate every aspect of mission planning, training and execution. From the outset, task force members were imbued with the absolute need for total secrecy. Planning was strictly compartmentalized; plans review was performed largely by those involved in the planning process; individuals were generally restricted to that information they actually required to play their particular roles.[49]

In Turner's words, the planning group had been 'excessively secretive' throughout its deliberations, and became 'almost paranoid' in the run-up to the mission itself.[50] One result of this was that, as the Holloway report puts it, 'there were pressures clearly felt by all involved to keep the force small in order to decrease the risk of detection'.[51] The obsession with secrecy also led to an unwillingness to subject the plan which the group had fashioned to the scrutiny of outside experts. The rescue force also never engaged in a full-scale dress rehearsal of the operation, again on the grounds that to do so would have risked detection before the raid was even launched.

It was the overriding emphasis on secrecy which led to a desire on Brzezinski's part to plan the mission in a small four-man group. In fact, the original group was even smaller than this, since Brzezinski had initially attempted to leave out Stansfield Turner and to by-pass CIA

---

[48] Ibid., p. 118; Turner, interview with the author.
[49] Special Operations Review Group, 'Rescue Mission Report', p. 13.
[50] Turner, *Terrorism and Democracy*, p. 115.
[51] Special Operations Review Group, 'Rescue Mission Report', p. 13.

involvement by relying on the DIA. When Turner found out about this he was, in his own words, 'livid'. He told Brzezinski that he was 'making it impossible for me to fulfil my responsibilities', and he insisted on being included in the planning group's deliberations. Brzezinski agreed to this, and the group was thus slightly enlarged.[52] Throughout the planning process, however, serious discussion of military options was avoided in the full SCC and NSC meetings, and the progress of this discussion was a closely guarded secret known only to a handful of people inside the administration. While this measure was effective in maintaining operational security, its major drawback consisted in the fact that those pursuing the negotiation option – most notably, Secretary Vance – were largely excluded from its deliberations until the rescue mission plan had already been formulated.

These shortcomings have often been alluded to in the write-ups on the failed mission, but it has rarely been explained *why* the concern with OPSEC was so overriding in this case. It is clear that all rescue mission planners have to be concerned with secrecy, but Holloway and his colleagues found that concern to be especially overplayed in this case. In previous rescue missions – again, Son Tay is a good example – the rescue team had been allowed to train as a single unit and in a single location, for instance, and discussion of military options had not been so jealously guarded or centralized in the White House. Why, then, was this particular group of planners led to claim that security considerations precluded such procedures?

The answer to this question is undoubtedly complex, but at least part of the priority given to this problem is probably attributable to Brzezinski's use of the Entebbe comparison. The need for both secrecy and surprise was one of the major lessons that the national security adviser had drawn from the 1976 episode. This became clear after the failure of the Tehran mission, when Brzezinski defended the small number of helicopters used in the Tehran raid by reference to the Entebbe analogy, suggesting that aspects of that precedent informed the planning of the Iranian rescue mission. 'Some have argued subsequently that the mission should have been composed of, say, twice as many helicopters', Brzezinski points out. 'But if the Iranians had discovered the mission as a result of the size of the air armada penetrating their airspace, we all would doubtless have been charged with typically excessive American redundancy, with unwillingness to go in hard and

---

[52] Turner, *Terrorism and Democracy*, pp. 38–9.

lean – the way, for example, the Israelis did at Entebbe.'[53]

The reason one ought to go in with a minimum of equipment, Brzezinski explains, is that 'otherwise you won't be able to keep it secret. One of the key elements in the success of the [Entebbe] mission was surprise and secrecy. If we were going to send an armada of helicopters in there . . . we could jeopardize the secrecy.' He points out that while he was 'not prepared to argue for a particular number of helicopters', his concern to keep the general figure on the low side was a lesson he had drawn from the success of the Entebbe raid.

Similarly, Pentagon officials argued at the time that the greater the number of helicopters in the air, the greater the likelihood that the rescue force would be detected before it reached its intended destination. Interestingly, after the failure of the Tehran rescue mission Shimon Peres was among those who most strongly defended the American decision to employ only eight helicopters. As he told a reporter from *Time* magazine, 'on an operation like this, one must be satisfied with the minimum of equipment. If you have too much, you blow the whole thing.'[54] In making this defence, Peres was clearly drawing upon his own experience of the Entebbe mission, which was of course a good deal more intimate than that of Brzezinski. At the same time, however, not all of those who had been involved with the Entebbe raid were quite so supportive. Yitzhak Rabin, for instance, suggested that the Tehran mission had failed due to inadequate planning, and Rehovam Zeevi has suggested that it was not imaginative enough in the sense that it borrowed too heavily from the Entebbe raid.[55] In short, the perceived lessons of Entebbe seem to have influenced the view Holloway found to be widespread among the planners, that 'complete security was essential to attain surprise'.[56]

(4) Storming the embassy

Relatively little attention, so far as we can ascertain, appears to have been paid by the planning group to the question of the assault on the embassy itself, which seems to have been left largely in the hands of the Joint Chiefs and Delta Force. According to Turner's account, the major problems to overcome related to how the rescuers would get in and out of the country. Secretary of Defence Harold Brown made clear after the

---

[53] Brzezinski, *Power and Principle*, p. 495.   [54] *Time*, 5 May 1980, p. 20.
[55] *Los Angeles Times*, 'Israel Blames Poor Planning for Iran Raid Failure'.
[56] Special Operations Review Group, 'Rescue Mission Report', p. 13.

failure of the Iran raid that the planners regarded the actual raid on the embassy, however, as the *easiest* stage of the mission, as the following extract from a press conference held on 25 April 1980 makes clear:

> *Interviewer*: How could you have secured the release of the hostages without massive bloodshed, given the fact that there is an estimated 150 armed Iranian militants guarding the embassy?
>
> *Secretary Brown*: I am not going to go into the details of any parts of the mission, beyond the parts that were actually carried out. I will say that the Joint Chiefs of Staff thoroughly reviewed this; I reviewed it, and the team itself was convinced that that was the part of the mission of which they were most confident.

Most people, like the questioner, imagine that the raid itself would have been the most difficult stage, and the process of getting the rescue force in the easiest, at least in relative terms. Brown and the other members of the planning group, however, contended that the opposite was true. Brzezinski and Jones, for instance, both expressed the view at a critical NSC meeting held on 22 March that 'the extraction of the hostages was probably the easiest part of the operation'.[57] Why were the planners so confident about the later stages?

Relatively little is known about this, so our answer must be in part speculative. Part of the explanation might relate to preparations which the CIA may have made for the rescue force. They may, for instance, have obtained the agreement of moderates to 'look the other way' while the raid was launched. It has long been known that an Iranian team had been recruited by the CIA to assist the military operation in Tehran. We know also that Richard Meadows had been sent in to supervise the Iranian agents, and to obtain a hideout and the trucks which would transport the rescuers into the city. According to Amir Taheri, this team of locals 'consisted of four air officers who had trained in San Antonio, Texas, and twenty-five cashiered members of the Imperial Guard who believed they were recruited for an anti-Khomeini operation which was to serve as a prelude to a *coup d'état'*. The four officers, Taheri says, would have been airlifted out of Iran with the embassy hostages.[58] Assuming that this information is accurate – it remains as yet unverified by other scholars of the hostage crisis rescue mission – it is not clear what role, if any, these officers would have played in the embassy assault itself. Charles Beckwith recalls that by March 1980 Delta Force

---

[57] Sick, *All Fall Down*, p. 337.
[58] See Amir Taheri, *Nest of Spies: America's Journey to Disaster in Iran* (London: Hutchison, 1988), p. 133.

had practised the assault stage on a mock-up of the embassy so often that it became 'drudgery'.[59] Some intelligence suggested that the students had become 'sloppy' and less vigilant in their guarding of the hostages over the last few months, and that their numbers had dwindled greatly from about 150 in November to around 25 by the time of the rescue mission. Yet none of these factors alone seems to justify the remarkable and widespread confidence the planners exhibited in the ability of Delta Force to raid the embassy.

One suggestive answer as to why this might have been the case is again provided by the analogical reasoning approach. The United States had in fact launched assaults on its Tehran embassy before, in mock attacks designed to test the compound's security. As Richard Gabriel notes, 'the Iranian embassy had been tested by an Army Special Forces team in 1974. Four attempts were made at that time to breach the security of the embassy compound, and in each case the assault force succeeded.' The rescue planners not unnaturally sought the help of this earlier team in planning the 1980 operation, and according to Gabriel this was why the planners 'regarded the actual assault on the embassy as probably the easiest part of the operation'.[60] The embassy's security had been augmented as a result of the first attempt to seize the building in February of 1979. Nevertheless, having raided the embassy compound in 1974 with relative ease, the planners appear to have reasoned that they could do so with similar ease in 1980.

The rescue option resurfaces

By the early part of 1980, the planning team was beginning to make progress in formulating what appeared to be a workable rescue plan. Moreover, just as the rescuers were making progress with the supply of a rescue option, so the *demand* for such an operation was increasing. The sense of exasperation with the faltering negotiations alluded to earlier led to three crucial meetings of March and April 1980 at which Jimmy Carter moved towards, and eventually gave his final approval for, the hostage rescue mission. While Carter himself says little about the decision-making process which led to the choice of the rescue option – he devotes barely five pages to this in his memoirs[61] – others have been rather more forthcoming over the past twenty years, allowing us to piece together the reasoning adopted by the key decision-makers.

[59] Beckwith and Knox, *Delta Force*, p. 241.   [60] Gabriel, *Military Incompetence*, p. 91.
[61] Carter, *Keeping Faith*, pp. 516–21.

The rescue planning had thus far been confined to the small planning group, though Vance and Christopher appear to have had some idea that it was progressing. By late March 1980 the rescue option resurfaced in broader discussion groups as a viable option. By this time it seemed to many of those around the president that negotiations could not, and would not, succeed in obtaining the release of the hostages. Accordingly, at an NSC meeting held on Saturday 22 March, the rescue option began to be discussed with real seriousness. What had seemed an impossibility to Brown and Jones back in November had now come to seem a real and viable possibility. Cyrus Vance, Zbigniew Brzezinski, Walter Mondale, David Jones, Harold Brown, Stansfield Turner, David Aaron and Jody Powell all gathered at Camp David that weekend for several hours. The meeting began with a review of the diplomatic efforts with which most of the decision-makers had now become weary and frustrated. General Jones then gave the NSC something which most of its members had never heard before: a summary of the rescue plan which the planning group had now produced.

The plan was highly complex and relied heavily on the use of helicopters, together with a fair measure of luck. It was planned to last two days in all. The first phase was designed to get the rescue team into Iran and to refuel the helicopters which would need to travel enormous distances during the mission. Eight RH-53 helicopters, Jones explained, would fly from the US carrier *Nimitz* to the remote site in the Iranian desert which had been designated 'Desert One', entering Iran under cover of darkness. Simultaneously, eight Hercules C-130 transport planes carrying the rescue force would take off from Masirah Island in Oman, and would rendezvous with the helicopters at Desert One. There, two things would happen: the C-130s would be used to refuel the RH-53s, and the rescue team would transfer to the newly refuelled helicopters.

The second phase, Jones believed, would be somewhat easier to undertake, though not without risk. The rescue team would be flown from Desert One to a hideout in the desert, codenamed 'Desert Two', where they would remain until nightfall. While the helicopters were hidden in the desert, the rescue team would be transported to the embassy by truck under cover of darkness, and would then raid the embassy. As the embassy raid was in progress, the helicopters would land at the nearby Amjadieh football stadium, and would take the hostages and the rescue force to an abandoned airfield once the raid had been successfully completed. From there they would be spirited out of Iran by plane, and would be provided with substantial aircover from US fighters. The essentials of the plan are depicted in the figure below (p. 126).

Cyrus Vance listened carefully to Jones's summary that day, but remained unconvinced that it could succeed. As he had done throughout the crisis, he again argued against the use of military force, drawing once more on the *Pueblo* and Angus Ward analogies as evidence that patience and resilience would pay off eventually.[62] The president's patience, however, was clearly almost exhausted. As Brzezinski recalls, 'the President asked [Vance] with some impatience whether that meant he was willing to sit and wait until the end of the year, while the hostages continued to be imprisoned'.[63] Clearly, Vance *was* prepared to wait. Jimmy Carter, however, was not, and at the same meeting the president finally gave his permission to launch a secret exploratory flight into Iran, in order to pave the way for a rescue operation (a measure which both Brzezinski and Turner had advocated for some months).

The decision-makers were now moving swiftly towards approving the plan, although at this point no final decision appears to have been reached. The second and probably most critical meeting occurred on Friday 11 April. The relative brevity of this meeting – it lasted less than two hours – indicates the extent to which it had been almost foreordained by the 22 March discussion, but this was the meeting at which Carter and the NSC finally made the formal decision to launch the rescue mission. In Carter's words, 'we could no longer afford to depend on diplomacy. I decided to act.'[64] Present at the meeting were Mondale, Brown, Brzezinski, Christopher, Turner, Jones, Jordan and Powell. Absent from this list, unusually, was Secretary Vance, who was away taking a short weekend vacation in Florida and was replaced on this occasion by his deputy, Warren Christopher. Carter began the meeting with the following words, according to Jordan:

> Gentlemen, I want you to know that I am seriously considering an attempt to rescue the hostages. As you know, the first week the hostages were seized, I ordered the Joint Chiefs to develop a rescue plan that could be used in dire circumstances. A team of expert paramilitary people now report that they have confidence in their ability to rescue our people. Before I make up my mind, I want to know your reactions.[65]

---

[62] Vance, *Hard Choices*, p. 408. [63] Brzezinski, *Power and Principle*, p. 487.
[64] Carter, *Keeping Faith*, p. 516. [65] Jordan, *Crisis*, p. 233.

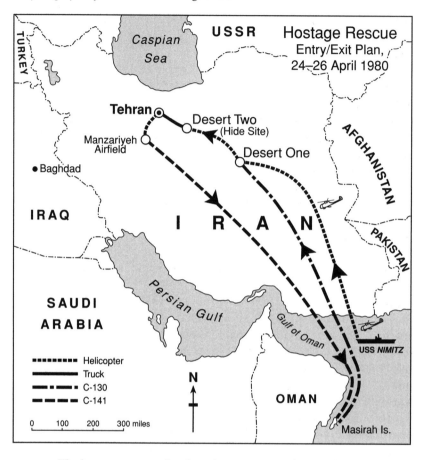

The hostage rescue plan: how it was supposed to work
Source: John Valliere, 'Disaster at Desert One: Catalyst for Change',
Parameters, Autumn 1992, p. 71.

Jordan got the very strong impression that Carter had already made up his mind in favour of the mission. Christopher was first to respond, and began by outlining various peaceful measures which he felt could still be used to free the hostages. The United States could try again to reach the Iranians through the United Nations, Iranian ships and aircraft could be blacklisted and the administration could lobby for the creation of an international telecommunications embargo on Iran. The deputy secretary of state was reportedly uncertain whether or not his boss had undergone a change of heart on the rescue mission, and did not push these alternative courses of action particularly hard. However, all of the other key decision-makers – notably Brzezinski, Brown, Turner and Jordan – spoke in favour of the mission, with Harold Brown in particular dismissing Christopher's proposals as 'not impressive'.[66] Walter Mondale also argued that the rescue mission represented the best of the options remaining, and Brzezinski was especially forceful in his recommendation that the raid go ahead. Thus, President Carter and his advisers reached the decision, in the absence of the secretary of state, that the military rescue mission would finally go ahead.[67] In Carter's words, 'it was time for us to bring the hostages home; their safety and our national honor were at stake'.[68] Brzezinski reports in his memoirs that at 12.48 the president announced 'we ought to go ahead without delay'.[69]

When Vance returned from his holiday on Monday morning, he was naturally angry that a foreign policy decision of such crucial import – and, moreover, a decision which went against everything he had been arguing for – had been reached in his absence. The secretary of state talked that morning with Carter, and expressed his deep reservations about the rescue mission. The negotiations, he said, needed to be given more time, and he insisted that the hostages would be released as soon as they were no longer politically useful to Khomeini and the other internal factions within Iran.[70] Speaking personally for the first time about the arguments he put to Carter during this meeting, Vance has recently recalled his feelings at that point.

> I said to him, I feel very strongly about this because I'm deeply concerned that taking any action by force as far as this is concerned may very well jeopardize the lives of a lot of our people. I don't think that it's foregone that if we don't act, that it's going to take forever in order to get them out, because I think the time is going to come, that they are going to be let out. There were indications already that that may well happen, and that's the way it did happen.[71]

The president remained unmoved by Vance's objections, but gave him an opportunity to express them at a third critical NSC meeting held the following day, on Tuesday 15 April, lasting just over 2 hours. At this meeting, Vance repeated the arguments in favour of continued negotiations he had used throughout the crisis. As Carter relates, 'his primary

---

[66] Brzezinski, *Power and Principle*, pp. 492–3.
[67] Vance, *Hard Choices*, p. 409. See also Brzezinski, *Power and Principle*, pp. 492–3; Turner, *Terrorism and Democracy*, p. 107.   [68] Carter, *Keeping Faith*, p. 517.
[69] Brzezinski, *Power and Principle*, p. 493.   [70] Vance, *Hard Choices*, p. 409.
[71] Vance, interview with the author.

argument was that we should be patient and not do anything which might endanger their safety'.[72] Again, Vance's misgivings seem to have related in general to the lessons he drew from the *Pueblo* and Angus Ward crises, but his specific argument against the rescue mission drew on even more personal events from his own policy-making past. As Lloyd Cutler has pointed out, Vance was opposed to the rescue mission 'on its merits, both because of the contingencies of success and the difficulties of accomplishing it and also the consequences even if you were successful',[73] and he explicitly drew upon his experience of analogous operations in Vietnam in order to assess the likelihood that the mission would work.

This recollection, of course, led him to highly pessimistic assessments in that regard. Reportedly, he believed that

> the mission was too difficult to pull off. Vance's years at the Pentagon had led him to believe that operations that look simple on paper are often far more complicated on the ground . . . Vance contended that the burden of proof was on the military to show that force was likely to be more successful than protracted negotiations, which had won freedom for the captured crew of the *Pueblo* in 1968.[74]

As Vance related to Jordan that day:

> generals will rarely tell you they can't do something. This is a damn complex operation, and I haven't forgotten the old saying from my Pentagon days that in the military anything that can go wrong will go wrong. I'm just opposed to the idea of a military operation as long as there is any chance of negotiating the release.[75]

Vance recalls that he did remark on this in the White House Situation Room that day. 'I had seen all kinds of things messed up', he remembers. 'I had seen real mess-ups, by people going in and trying to do things that hadn't really been thought through clearly enough . . . I've seen too many people screw up on things, because they're carried away by the situation of the moment and how it affects them.'[76] The recollection of Vietnam was naturally uppermost in Vance's mind here. Brzezinski, of course, viewed the lessons of Vietnam rather differently from the secretary of state: 'Cy is the ultimate example of a good man who has been traumatized by his Vietnam experience', he reportedly

---

[72] Carter, *Keeping Faith*, p. 517. The 15 April meeting is disposed of with particular brevity in Carter's book. He devotes only two sentences to it.
[73] Lloyd Cutler exit interview, Jimmy Carter Library, p. 19.
[74] See *Newsweek*, 12 May 1980, p. 36.   [75] Jordan, *Crisis*, p. 246.
[76] Vance, interview with the author.

said of the secretary's grim assessment of the prospects of success.[77] Many of those who had served under Johnson during the Vietnam years not unnaturally exhibited a strong desire to avoid 'another Vietnam'. As Brzezinski has pointed out, Vance

> obviously was affected by it, so were quite a few people in the State Department. . . . I was affected by it too, but perhaps in a different way, in the sense that one of the lessons I drew from it was that – if you're going to use force – use it consistently in relationship to objectives that are attainable, but use it also very assertively. So different people drew different lessons, but I'd argue that the dominant attitude was one of skepticism and reservation about the use of force.[78]

This latter lesson, of course, was the one drawn by Vance and many of his colleagues at the State Department.[79]

Vance voiced a large number of strongly felt concerns at the 15 April meeting. First, 'I was very worried about the helicopters', he remembers. 'It was entirely possible that we weren't going to be able to get in there without losing some helicopters, and what then?' Secondly, 'I was also very concerned that if we did get in, that we would have to bomb, and if we bombed, then the consequences of that in terms of the response that would take place', Vance says. Thirdly, he worried that 'we would have to do this without notifying our allies – particularly the British – about this, and I knew that this would have a very negative effect'. Fourthly, 'I was also worried about what the effects might be in so far as what the Russians would do in response to this'; and lastly, 'the climate which we were involved in at that particular period of time, the whole situation in that part of the Middle East, was extremely fragile, and that we might indeed cause a real breakout of major warfare. That worried me a lot.' For Vance, these five concerns added up to an inescapable conclusion: 'when you look at all of these things, you couldn't help but come to the conclusion that this is something that cannot and should not be done, because it's against the national interest. That was my view, and I said what my strong views were.'[80]

Vance failed to win over the other members of the group at the 15 April meeting, and after much soul searching he offered his resignation as secretary of state six days later. Carter accepted this, although Vance's departure was not announced until after the failure of the

---

[77] Ibid.   [78] Brzezinski, interview with the author.
[79] On this point, see also Michael Ledeen and William Lewis, *Debacle: The American Failure in Iran* (New York: Alfred Knopf, 1981), p. 66, and Brian Klunk, *Consensus and the American Mission* (Lanham, Massachusetts: University Press of America, 1986), p. 122.
[80] Vance, interview with the author.

rescue mission. Shortly after this decision, the rescue operation finally went ahead on 24 April 1980. In the last days before the mission was mounted, however, another analogy was to gain special importance for Jimmy Carter. Apart from his desire to avoid Ford's perceived errors, when he finally gave the go-ahead for the rescue mission the president saw a potential parallel between the Tehran raid and the Bay of Pigs fiasco under John Kennedy. Carter decided that, while he would retain overall control of the mission, he would not 'meddle' in its operational details while it was actually in progress, as Kennedy had. Instead, he would merely monitor the situation as an observer, by means of telephone reports relayed via General Jones and Harold Brown. At a final briefing on the rescue mission on 16 April, the president told his military officials: 'I know you'll be busy. Your mission comes first. If you have time to tell us what's happening, that would be nice. But don't feel you have to give us play by play status reports. I will not second guess or interfere.' Carter himself later noted in his memoirs that he 'made it clear that there would be no interference from the White House while the mission was under way'.[81] Given Carter's well-known predilection for micro-management – as well as his own past military experience in the navy – this unwillingness to get involved in the details seems rather out of character, but it was almost certainly an attempt to apply the lessons of the Bay of Pigs as Carter perceived them.

The Bay of Pigs episode is undoubtedly one of the best-known US foreign policy fiascos of all time. Indeed, in the opinion of Irving Janis it 'ranks among the worst fiascos ever perpetrated by a responsible government'.[82] While that may be something of an overstatement, it was certainly a disaster by any standards. On 16 April 1961 a group of Cuban exiles, trained and organized mainly by the CIA, attempted to invade the island of Cuba. John Kennedy's two major objectives in giving his approval for the plan – hatched originally during the Eisenhower administration – had been to topple the regime of Fidel Castro, while simultaneously leaving no hint that the hand of the United States was on the whole plan. Neither objective was achieved in practice, and in attempting to attain the latter goal the president intervened in the operational and military details of the plan. For what were largely diplomatic and political reasons, Kennedy decided to cancel the air

---

[81] Quoted in Schemmer, 'Presidential Courage – and the April 1980 Iranian Rescue Mission', p. 61; Carter, *Keeping Faith*, p. 517; Beckwith and Knox, *Delta Force*, p. 258.
[82] Irving Janis, *Groupthink: Psychological Studies of Policy Decisions and Fiascos* (London: Houghton Mifflin, 1982), p. 14.

strikes which the CIA told him were essential to provide air cover for the invading forces. He reportedly did not consult the military in reaching this decision, and the fact that he did not do so is often cited as a major reason for the failure of the landing at the Bay of Pigs.

The details of the Bay of Pigs episode had by the late 1970s been examined and re-examined in exhaustive detail, so this was a case with which Zbigniew Brzezinski – as a trained scholar of international affairs – was quite familiar. Brzezinski notes in his memoirs that President Carter

> emphasized particularly that he would not interfere with operational decisions, that he would give the military maximum leeway for doing what was necessary within the framework of the approved plans. He and I had earlier discussed John Kennedy's interference with military planning for the Bay of Pigs operation, and Carter was clearly determined to make certain that his personal concerns did not interfere with the mission's chances of success.[83]

As Brzezinski has recently explained, the point of the Bay of Pigs parallel

> was that if you're going to do it, and once you have made the political decision to do it, let the operational control be in the hands of the military . . . the execution of it was 100% in the hands of the military . . . so the Bay of Pigs analogy applied in the sense that Carter never interfered with the scale of the effort, nor shut off anything, nor ordered anything, beyond the plan.

The Bay of Pigs, on the other hand, 'involved Kennedy at the last minute altering the plan, reducing the direct American role, calling off the air cover, and things of that sort . . . and what I didn't want to happen in the middle of this operation was fiddling around with the plan'.[84]

Disaster in the desert

The events which occurred in the desert of Iran on 24 April 1980 have been endlessly analysed and dissected in the years since. At 6 o'clock in the morning Iranian time, the C-130s carrying the rescue team took off from Masirah Island in Oman, and at 7 o'clock the eight helicopters

---

[83] Brzezinski, *Power and Principle*, p. 495.
[84] Brzezinski, interview with the author. For a discussion of whether the failed mission represented a 'repetition' of the Bay of Pigs affair, see Maxwell D. Taylor, 'Analogies (II): Was Desert One Another Bay of Pigs?', *Washington Post*, 12 May 1980.

took off from the USS *Nimitz*, headed for the rendezvous point at Desert One. Various disasters ensued; some were major irritants, while others proved catastrophic. The main calamities are summarized below:

(1) The C-130s were supposed to enter Iran under cover of darkness. Due to a miscalculation of the flight time, the planes actually entered Iranian airspace while it was still daylight.

(2) At around 9 a.m., one of the helicopters had to be abandoned in the Iranian desert after a warning light flashed in the cockpit (although it was later found that it was still safe to fly a RH-53 helicopter with the indicator light flashing).

(3) At around 10 a.m. the helicopters entered a dust storm that meteorological reports had failed to predict. They consequently reached Desert One only with immense difficulty. Moreover, one helicopter pilot encountered such terrible conditions that he almost crashed, and consequently decided to return to the *Nimitz*. This left only six helicopters, all of which arrived at Desert One at least an hour late.

(4) The C-130s reached Desert One at around 10 p.m. Since the landing site was near a main road, however, they were forced to shoot out the tires of an Iranian bus which passed alongside the rescue team, and then take its passengers hostage; two trucks came along the road a short time later, one of which escaped.

(5) Once at Desert One, the C-130s and RH-53s created a dust storm of their own – together with an almost deafening amount of noise – a scenario which had not been envisioned because (for reasons of OPSEC) the rescue force had never trained together as a single unit.

(6) On arriving at Desert One, it was discovered that one of the remaining six helicopters was malfunctioning. The minimum number deemed necessary to take the hostages and the rescue force out of Iran had earlier been deemed by the planning group to be six. As military commander, Charles Beckwith was then compelled to cancel the mission.

(7) As the rescue team prepared to begin the long flight back to base, one of the RH-53 helicopters collided with one of the C-130s. The explosion lit up the sky. Eight members of the rescue force were killed in the resulting fire.

It is conceivable that Carter could have overriden the judgement of

Beckwith and ordered his commander to proceed with the mission, but he chose not to do so. Again, the reason seems to relate to the Bay of Pigs analogy. Following the conversations he had earlier conducted with Brzezinski, this precedent weighed so heavily on the president's mind during the Iranian mission that his first response after its failure was to ask what Kennedy did next, and to instruct Jody Powell to bring a copy of the post-Bay of Pigs speech; as *Time* magazine noted, 'at 2 a.m. on Friday, Carter asked his staff to find a copy of John F. Kennedy's remarks following the abortive Bay of Pigs invasion. Indeed, the phrases he used in his broadcast five hours later were highly reminiscent of Kennedy's remarks after the earlier failure.'[85]

Interestingly, as Jimmy Carter himself reports, on 24 April 1980 – the day the Tehran raid was launched – Shimon Peres was actually in the White House having what Carter describes as a 'private session', which is also referred to as one of several 'routine duties'.[86] Brzezinski does not allude to the irony of this meeting in his memoirs, for if nothing else this was indeed – as Brzezinski himself has recently remarked – 'an amazing coincidence'.[87] For one thing, it was and still is highly unusual for a US president to meet with an Israeli opposition leader, which was the position Peres then held. What is clear, however, is that Brzezinski saw the potential to repeat the political and policy success of Entebbe in the Iranian hostage case, and that the optimism derived from this image – which by April 1980 was shared by the vast majority of Carter's advisers – proved unfounded.

The failure of the operation has been traced to various factors, but the most frequently cited cause has been its sheer complexity, the 'too many moving parts' problem. The planners had attempted to overcome the various problems they encountered at the outset of the crisis by means of a complex and carefully crafted plan. The central problems they faced – the absence of an airport or landing place near the embassy, the absence of a convenient refuelling point, the distances involved and the problem of getting the rescue force into Tehran undetected and then out again – had been overcome on paper, but only at the cost of generating an operation which depended on every single stage going exactly as intended. In the event, very few did.

In the days and years afterward, many would express surprise at the form the rescue operation took. According to Philip Keisling, for instance:

[85] See *Time*, 5 May 1980, p. 19; Jordan, *Crisis*, p. 256.   [86] Carter, *Keeping Faith*, p. 514.
[87] Brzezinski, interview with the author.

its failure had almost been assured by the military's process of planning the raid, analyzing it for defects, and choosing the man to lead it. The military systematically ignored or downplayed intelligence that suggested the difficulty – if not the impossibility – of the task. The plan for the raid . . . violated a fundamental tenet of military strategy, which holds that the possibility of failure increases exponentially with a plan's complexity and size.[88]

In similar vein, Colin Powell – during the hostage crisis a military assistant at the Pentagon but not privy to the planning itself – has said that he was 'surprised at the way this operation had been conceived and conducted'. Powell notes that 'helicopters are notoriously temperamental. For a mission this demanding of men and machines, far more than eight helos should have been launched to make sure that six would still be airworthy to carry out the demanding second leg of the mission.' He identifies other shortcomings as well. 'Desert One also erred in counting on a "pickup" team drawn from all four services and brought together just for this mission in which men from one service flew helicopters of another. Weaknesses in the chain of command, communications, weather forecasting, and security further contributed to the failure.'[89]

Others have agreed with Powell's point about using a mixture of rescuers from different armed services. Edward Luttwak, for instance, notes that personnel from all four services were involved, and suggests that this was primarily due to each service wanting its slice of the action: 'not one of the services (except the Coast Guard) could be deprived of its share; the Army, Air Force, Navy, and Marine Corps were all present in the rescue force'. If the mission had been planned and executed by a single service, Luttwak implies, it would have stood a greater chance of success. British, French and Israeli experts, he notes, 'had learned long ago to avoid any mixture of men'.[90] Privately, the Israelis expressed astonishment at the manner in which the plan had been drawn up and implemented. Their officials had considerable

---

[88] Keisling, 'Desert One: The Wrong Man and the Wrong Plan', p. 52. Ironically, less than two weeks after the failure of the American rescue mission the British SAS successfully raided the Iranian embassy at Prince's Gate in London, which had also been seized by terrorists, and rescued a number of hostages. Although the operational circumstances were rather different, one wonders whether this event – had it occurred before the US attempt and not after – would have been used in some way as a historical analogy within the Carter administration. See 'A Rescue That Worked', *The Economist*, 19 May 1980.
[89] Colin Powell with Joseph Persico, *My American Journey* (New York: Random House, 1995), p. 249.   [90] Luttwak, *The Pentagon and the Art of War*, p. 44.

experience with the planning of these kinds of operations. The much celebrated Entebbe raid of 1976 had been conceived and executed over a few days, so the fact that the American team had had nearly half a year provoked particular surprise and incredulity. As one Israeli commentator connected with the Entebbe raid reportedly said, 'Six months. Can you imagine what you could do in six months? In that time you could find a house a mile from the embassy, bring in the compressors piece by piece, and tunnel your way into the compound.'[91]

Some attribute the failure of the operation to a misguided faith in the power of technology to overcome fundamental human frailties. Daniel Greenberg, for instance, opined not long after the failure of the raid that 'the risks and consequences of something going wrong get much bigger when desperate politicians turn hopefully to "technological fixes" for difficult political problems'. In the United States, he argued, there is a particular cultural belief in these kind of solutions, a popular notion that 'clever and vigorous application of far-out techniques and equipment can bring a desired solution out of an otherwise intractable problem'.[92]

What no one disputes either then or now is that the decision to mount the operation, at least in the form in which it was launched, was ultimately a grave mistake. Nevertheless, at least some of the subsequent critiques no doubt reflect the phenomenon of what psychologists term 'hindsight bias'. As Susan Fiske and Shelley Taylor note, 'work by Fischoff and others . . . indicates that it is very difficult to ignore knowledge of an actual outcome and to generate unbiased inferences about what could or should have happened'. People's tendency to be 'wise after the event' sometimes even extends to a habit of misremembering their own predictions to fit in with what actually occurred.[93]

We should probably avoid this same phenomenon when judging the worth of the analogies utilized by various Carter administration officials. Whatever historical analogy (if any) now seems relevant to the reader, we can see with the benefit of hindsight that the Joint Chiefs had been correct all along in seeing the airport and base factor as a significant barrier to any rescue operation. We can see that they ought to have viewed this as an insurmountable one in this instance, because it was

---

[91] Quoted in Dial Torgerson, 'US Blundered in Iran Mission, Israeli Military Experts Claim', *Los Angeles Times*, 2 May 1980, p. 6.

[92] Daniel Greenberg, 'Mission Improbable', *Washington Post*, 29 April 1980.

[93] Susan Fiske and Shelley Taylor, *Social Cognition* (Reading, Massachusetts: Addison-Wellesly, 1984), p. 376.

the attempt to overcome that barrier with eight helicopters and the refuelling base at Desert One which destroyed the mission. One can also see with the benefit of hindsight that Cyrus Vance was eventually proved 'correct' in using the *Pueblo* analogy, in the sense that, as he had expected, the hostages were indeed released once they had served their political purpose, which, as noted earlier, seems to have been to neutralize other internal factions within Iran. Hindsight, however, is something decision-makers obviously do not possess as they go about making their decisions in the present. They must operate in the dark, drawing upon their own judgements of probability, which in this instance as in others often meant using analogies.

Back to the drawing board

The Carter administration was now left with neither an overall policy on Iran nor a meaningful strategy for getting the hostages out. As Stansfield Turner puts it, 'having resorted to a rescue mission largely because we had run out of alternatives, we now had to study those alternatives all over again. Were any options we had discarded viable now? Were there any new ones?'[94] Predictably, the decision-makers' options continued to centre upon the two channels or tracks which had been identified all along as the realistic options: a revival of the negotiations, and plans for a second rescue mission. In the aftermath of the failed raid, Brzezinski and the others continued to believe that the April 1980 rescue operation had been both justifiable and worth a try. Interviewed on ABC's now defunct television programme *Issues and Answers* on 27 April, Brzezinski stated: 'Everyone recognized that the operation was risky. We also know from history that there are moments in which a certain amount of risk is necessary.' Although he did not mention Entebbe specifically, it was clearly at the back of his mind.

Almost as soon as the first rescue attempt had failed, planning for a second operation began. As before, the prime mover behind this option was Brzezinski. Such an operation would obviously be much more difficult to pull off than under previous conditions, for, as expected, the militants had reacted to the news of the failed mission by dispersing the hostages to other locations (they were now being held in sixteen different Iranian cities, according to some reports).[95] It would therefore be logically impossible to launch the same kind of operation. But as

[94] Turner, *Terrorism and Democracy*, p. 146.   [95] Ibid.

Brzezinski states, the second mission – which was never actually implemented – was modelled even more closely on the Entebbe raid:

> The second mission had some analogies with Entebbe while it was being planned, because the second plan involved going into the airport at Tehran, taking the airport, landing an armoured mobile force, driving into the city, shooting up anything in the way, bombing anything that starts interfering, storming the embassy, taking out anybody who's alive after that process and then going back and taking off.[96]

The first operation also provided a glaringly obvious analogy from which the planners could work. Stung by the criticism that the first mission had failed because not enough military firepower had been applied, Carter told the planners that they would have everything they needed to put a second operation into effect.[97] The second raid, according to Brzezinski, should be 'less complex and less dependent on high technology than the previous operation',[98] two criticisms which had immediately been levelled at the April raid by the press.

The second mission was codenamed 'Honey Badger', and was, as Martin and Walcott note, 'more an invasion than a rescue mission'.[99] Two batallions of Rangers would be sent into Tehran to capture the main airfield in Tehran. This time – to get around the unreliability of helicopters flying long distances – the helicopters would be brought in aboard C-141 transport aircraft. Recalling the Perot tactic, some of the rescuers this time would enter Tehran piecemeal via commercial flights using fake passports, while others would arrive across land by truck. While the rescue forces launched several separate rescues throughout Iran, the helicopters would arrive at these locations and spirit both rescuers and hostages out of Iran.

Despite Brzezinski's injunction to make it so, the new plan could hardly be described as less complex than the original. In all, it reportedly would have involved around 2,000 men.[100] This was probably dictated by the objective demands of the situation, since the task itself was now even less straightforward than before. Opposition to a second raid within the administration was widespread, moreover. Brzezinski had suggested that the CIA pour personnel into Iran in order to gather the extensive intelligence about the new whereabouts of the hostages that such a raid would require. However, as Turner admits, 'the CIA

---

[96] Brzezinski, interview with the author.
[97] Martin and Walcott, *Best Laid Plans*, p. 29.   [98] Sick, *All Fall Down*, p. 357.
[99] Martin and Walcott, *Best Laid Plans*, p. 29.   [100] Ibid., p. 30.

professionals saw the task as almost impossible and were not trying as hard as they could'.[101] And even within Brzezinski's own staff, the prevailing view seems to have been that such a raid would be virtually impossible. Gary Sick, in particular, expressed this opinion in a memorandum he sent to his boss at the time. As Sick relates, on the Sunday after the failure of the first rescue mission Brzezinski called the Middle Eastern specialist into his office. Reporting that he 'had obtained the president's permission to begin immediate planning for a second rescue mission', Brzezinski argued that 'we must go back in' and both asked Sick and William Odom, Brzezinki's military assistant, to come up with ideas for a second rescue.[102]

Sick, however, was quite sceptical that such a mission could succeed, noting the lack of reliable intelligence on the hostages' location and the conflicting reports the administration was receiving in this regard. He argued also that the hostage takers would now be expecting a second operation, would almost certainly have taken heightened precautions to guard against such a mission succeeding, and that the Middle Eastern governments which had assisted the Americans to undertake the first operation would probably be much less willing to repeat the same favour now. Egypt and Oman, for instance, had cooperated with the first operation, but had been stung by criticism from other Arab states as a result. 'For these reasons I regarded the prospects of a second rescue attempt as extremely dim', Sick argued. 'The nature of the situation had changed dramatically because of the failure of the raid, and there seemed to be no reasonable chance of conducting another rescue attempt for quite a long time.'[103] Brzezinski seems to have been quite dissatisfied with this response, and subsequently cut Sick out of the planning for a second mission.

The problem of the inherent unreliability and temperament of helicopters, of course, also remained. Any second attempt, it seemed, would similarly have to rely upon long-range helicopters to get the hostages out, and a landing site would have to be found for the rescue aircraft, preferably as near to the location of the hostages as possible. These were both barriers, we may recall, to the implementation of an Entebbe-style rescue. At least some of the planners, however, appear to have entertained the possibility that both of these problems could be overcome this time through a rather bizarre plan known as 'Credible Sport'. The idea behind this plan was to modify a Lockheed C-130

---

[101] Turner, *Terrorism and Democracy*, p. 146.
[102] Sick, *All Fall Down*, p. 357.   [103] Ibid., p. 360.

Hercules aircraft in a way that would enable it to take off and land like a helicopter! According to recently published films and documents, the modified plane was equipped with rocket thrusters which would lift it off the ground and also enable it to land in tight corners, in places where ordinary C-130 aircraft obviously could not. Perhaps unsurprisingly, the idea never came to fruition – an early prototype crashed on the runway – and Credible Sport was still under development in January 1981 when the hostages were finally released.[104] It is not known who the prime movers behind this idea were, but it is inconceivable that President Carter was not at least generally aware of it.

The plans for this second mission were never implemented, since it was generally conceded, as Carter puts it, that 'even with maximum intelligence effort, there was no way to tell exactly where all of them were' inside Iran.[105] As before, the lessons of Son Tay were uppermost in Turner's mind, and he realized that it would now be even more difficult to keep track of who had been moved where.[106] At the end of April 1980, the SCC again examined the non-rescue military options, but they were once again rejected as unlikely to produce results. These measures were judged correspondingly likely to result in the deaths of the hostages. In practice, then, it was the revival of the negotiation track which the decision-makers would return to, and which would eventually bear fruit.

After Vance's resignation as secretary of state, Senator Edmund Muskie of Maine was selected to succeed him. One of the great ironies of the debate within the Carter administration on the hostages, however, is that the decision-makers were essentially forced to return to Vance's policy of waiting it out after April 1980. Vance's policy continued without Vance, and as Turner puts it, 'waiting patiently probably would have done as much for the hostages as anything else, and it is the course we eventually followed'.[107] The administration was left, in Sick's words, 'waiting for the Ayatollah'.[108] According to Turner, however this was never spelled out in explicit terms, 'because none of us would admit that the United States could be stymied by a theocracy run by a group of extremist clerics. And we certainly did not want to acknowledge our impotence before the American public.'[109] It was

---

[104] See 'The Impossible Mission of Credible Sport', *Jane's Defence Weekly*, 5 March 1997. The existence of the plan was also broadcast by CNN after this article was published.
[105] Carter, *Keeping Faith*, p. 533.   [106] Turner, *Terrorism and Democracy*, p. 147.
[107] Ibid., p. 154.   [108] Sick, *All Fall Down*, p. 360.
[109] Turner, *Terrorism and Democracy*, p. 148.

ironic, too, that the issue would fall back in the lap of the State Department during the last eight months of the crisis, from whence it had been prized during the early part of 1980.

Secretary Muskie essentially left the negotiation and day-to-day handling of the hostage issue in the hands of Warren Christopher, who – though evidently disappointed not to have been promoted to the top job – continued to serve as deputy secretary of state. As Sick notes, the summer months of 1980 were quiet and uneventful, punctuated only by the death of the shah in Egypt on 27 July. As those who had argued that the shah was never the real issue predicted, his death seemed to provoke little reaction in Iran, and the event failed to kickstart negotiations. On 9 September, however, the Iranians – much to the administration's surprise – suddenly indicated their intention to resolve the hostage issue. They also indicated a softening of the terms of release, including Iran's willingness to drop its insistence on an American apology for the shah's wrongdoings or an international investigation into America's post-war role in Iranian politics, both of which had earlier proved stumbling blocks to an agreement.

Since Carter and his advisers had been so often disappointed before, they were initially slow to believe that the approach was genuine. No doubt the decision-makers recalled the failed French connection talks in March, when negotiations seemed to have come so far only to fail at the final hurdle. What was significant about this new channel, however, was that it apparently offered a direct link to Khomeini; the offer to negotiate had come from Sadegh Tabatabai, a relative of Khomeini whom the latter had authorized to negotiate on his behalf. Here, at last, was the opening the Americans had been looking for since November 1979. While previous channels had been to moderates like Bani-Sadr and Ghotbzadeh who lacked Khomeini's ear, Tabatabai possessed this access. This was confirmed on 12 September when the Ayatollah made a speech which mirrored the terms his relative had laid out in private.

Christopher was sent to Bonn, Germany to negotiate directly with Tabatabai, and the two met in secret – together with Hans-Dietrich Genscher, the German foreign minister – on 16 and 18 September. A 'core group' was also formed at this time under Christopher's direction that would eventually see the crisis through to its resolution. This was to be the beginning of the end, rather than the end itself, however. On 22 September Iran was invaded by Iraq. This appears to have had two major effects: first of all, it probably slowed down the pace of the negotiations in the short term, since the Iranians were momentarily distracted by an issue which held much greater urgency for them. In the longer term, however, it undoubtedly added impetus to Khomeini's desire to release the American hostages, since Iran needed the economic sanctions which had been placed upon it lifted in order to prosecute its new war. The pace of negotiations was still slow, since some in the Majlis (the Iranian parliament) seemed determined to stand in the way of a resolution of the issue before the November US presidential election. After these negotiations again foundered, the Algerians stepped in as mediators. While Carter's political advisers had ardently hoped that the hostages would be returned before the election, this was not to be.

Why did the Iranians finally decide to release the hostages? While this too remains clouded in mystery, it is too simplistic to trace this change of heart simply to the onset of the Iran–Iraq war, for Tabatabai's approach came a couple of weeks prior to the invasion. Probably as important, if not more so, was the declining political utility of the American hostages to Khomeini in the internal game of one-upmanship he was playing with other factions within Iran. Aside from the fact that Khomeini needed the sanctions lifted to arm Iran against Saddam Hussein's Iraq, a new Iranian government was by this time in place. On 28 May 1980 the new Majlis opened, in which the pro-Khomeini forces were very much in the ascendant *vis-à-vis* the moderates. By early September the creation of a pro-Khomeini government was imminent, and on 10 September – the day after Tabatabai's initiative through the West Germans – the Majlis gave their formal imprimatur to the new Cabinet under the leadership of Prime Minister Mohammad-Ali Rajai.

Morning in America

If the basic conditions for a release of the hostages had already been met two months before the presidential election of 1980, why was this action delayed until the following January? In the years since the release of the hostages, a more sinister interpretation of the last days of the negotiations has repeatedly emerged. Most notably, Gary Sick has alleged in his book *October Surprise* that representatives of Ronald Reagan's staff reached a deal with the Iranian radicals to delay the release of the hostages until after the 1980 election.[110] According to Sick, Reagan's

---

[110] Sick, *October Surprise*.

then campaign manager William Casey – a man who would later be revealed as one of the major figures in the Iran–Contra scandal – approached two Iranian brothers, Cyrus and Jamshid Hashemi, who arranged for him to meet with representatives of the Ayatollah Khomeini. Unbeknown to the Carter administration, Casey then met secretly in Madrid with these representatives in July and August 1980, and again in Paris during October. The deal, Sick says, 'was for Iran to hand the hostages to the Republicans (rather than Jimmy Carter) in return for some arms immediately (via Israel) plus the promise of future arms and political benefits once the Reagan administration came to office'.[111]

A full assessment of this theory lies beyond the scope of the present study. The political storm which accompanied the publication of *October Surprise* provoked a somewhat half-hearted congressional investigation which failed to reach definitive conclusions. Nevertheless, that the Reagan administration would have *sought* to delay the release of the hostages until after the November election seems quite plausible in the light of later events. What seems clear, as Stansfield Turner has noted, is that some sort of approach to allies of Khomeini by the Reagan campaign was made.[112] It is also far from implausible that a figure such as Casey would have been the instigator of, or conduit for, such an effort. This part of Sick's argument is also lent plausibility by the extent of the meticulous empirical research he undertook in support of the book. Whether the attempt to influence the timing of the hostage release actually succeeded, however, has been a matter of great dispute. A central problem for the theory involves the difficulty in determining what if anything – if one concedes that such an approach was made – the precise effect of this move was. This again evokes Fred Greenstein's question of 'action dispensability', referred to in chapter 3. One may prove that a given actor performed a certain action, but it is possible that the action in question did not materially affect the outcome in question. In this instance, it is quite conceivable that the Majlis under Khomeini's influence delayed the hostages' release for reasons other than an approach by Reagan officials, or that this motivation was a secondary one.

What is known with absolute certainty is that the negotiations which finally freed the hostages were fraught with obstacles until the very end. A deal was finally struck only two days before the inauguration of

---

[111] Ibid., p. 11.   [112] Turner, interview with the author.

Ronald Reagan, on terms which were remarkably favourable to the American side. The hostages themselves were released only hours after Carter officially left office, the timing being arranged in such a way that the release did not take place until word arrived that Reagan had been sworn in. Nevertheless, one cannot treat this deliberate 'coincidence' as evidence for the *October Surprise* theory. Sick, of course, realizes this and reports that this was something upon which William Casey had insisted.

There are, however, other plausible interpretations. The choice of timing has usually been interpreted simply as Khomeini's final slap in the face for a beleaguered president as he returned to his home state of Georgia, and this may have been the real motivation. And yet there was probably more to it than this, and a fuller explanation again relates to the events of 1953. According to Ibrahim Yazdi, Khomeini knew perfectly well that releasing the hostages before November 1980 would in all likelihood cause Carter to win the election and Reagan to lose. Conversely, he knew also that by holding on to the hostages, Reagan would probably win. There was a sense, therefore, in which he held – or believed that he held – the result of the American election in his hands. According to Yazdi, by holding on to the hostages until Reagan became president, Khomeini was symbolically and somewhat theatrically trying to show that Iran could determine political outcomes in the United States, just as the latter had done in the former in 1953.[113] He was exacting a kind of revenge. If this was the intended message, however, it has been largely lost upon most observers, who have simply imagined some sort of personal animosity between Carter and Khomeini.

Word of the hostages' release came as Carter flew back to Plains, Georgia. Arriving in his childhood home, an almost tearful Jimmy Carter – his voice breaking with emotion – announced:

> Just a few moments ago on Air Force One, before we landed at Warner Robins, I received word officially for the first time that the aircraft carrying the fifty-two American hostages has cleared Iranian airspace. Every one of the fifty-two hostages is alive, well and free.[114]

At last, at long last, the national trauma of the Iranian hostage crisis was over.

---

[113] Interview with Ibrahim Yazdi, Iran Project, Antelope Productions.
[114] Quoted in Jordan, *Crisis*, p. 384.

6   Hostages to history

The American and Iranian decision-makers, as we have seen, over-whelmingly drew upon the experiences and analogies known to them personally, reflecting the greater cognitive availability of these events. The Entebbe analogy – a then very recent political and policy success – played an enhanced (if only partially visible) role in the policy dis-cussions of the Carter administration, and probably influenced Carter's eventual decision to mount a rescue operation, while other analogies exerted an impact at various stages of the crisis. Jimmy Carter and those surrounding him clearly considered various analogous situations and searched through them for cause and effect patterns. The president and his advisers seem to have made an early effort – albeit perhaps an informal one – to gather together potential precedents, and to search these for usable lessons which could then be applied to the current case. According to Brzezinski's recollection, 'at some point early on, we simply collected previous cases in order to see what happened and how they were handled, so either my staff or I gave it to him . . . I doubt whether he would have known of all these cases himself.'[1] As Carter himself put it at a press conference on 21 April 1980, 'I have studied all the previous occurences in my lifetime where American hostages have been taken . . . to learn how they reacted and what the degree of success was.' In other words, he had analysed a number of cases and tried to disentangle the causes of success and failure, engaging in what sup-porters of attribution theory call 'intuitive science'. On the Iranian side, moreover, ghostly images of 1953 haunted the streets of revolutionary Iran, providing the major motivation behind the attempt to prevent a CIA coup the radical students believed was surely imminent.

[1] Zbigniew Brzezinski, interview with the author.

144

Even the American rescue team were made keenly aware of the historical analogies swirling around them. Perhaps rather surprisingly, the members of Delta Force were trained in the historical precedents deemed relevant to the Tehran operation by an academic working for the CIA. As this individual recalls, the analogies he discussed with the rescue force included Entebbe and Mogadishu. There is a sense in which the academic was 'putting analogies into the system', although he did not of course play any role in instructing the top decision-makers regarding the question of which analogies might be regarded as potentially useful or relevant.[2]

Viewed from the American perspective, the Iran hostage crisis also offers us some interesting insights into the question of what decision-makers do when confronted with a discrete foreign policy situation of high uncertainty, but are not simultaneously drawn (at least by widely accepted reputation) to the historical mode of analysis. The novelty of the situation meant that the only available analogous cases differed from Iran in important (and arguably, structural) respects. Furthermore, the lessons of many of these previous instances were interpreted in diverse ways by the decision-making group, so that different policy-makers offered competing accounts of what they meant (especially differing beliefs regarding the question of whether the responses to these crises had been successes or failures). On both sides of the conflict the memories drawn upon as analogies were also sometimes unreliable or misinformed. The shah of Iran did not go to the United States when he fled the country the first time in 1953, for instance, just as Lyndon Johnson was in fact still embroiled in a presidential campaign during the *Pueblo* crisis in 1968. But it was the perceptions that mattered, not some 'objective' reality.

Intuition or common sense suggests the existence of two classic 'archetypes' – the historical thinker and the ahistorical thinker – the first of whom uses analogies, the second of whom presumably does not. The cognitive psychological perspective, on the other hand, proposes that *all* individuals are in a sense 'historical'. While decision-makers come to policy-making with past experiences and knowledge, the character and extent of which will vary within a range, all have some experiences and knowledge. All, in other words, possess the prerequisites of the basic human ability to analogize. It is difficult to imagine a president more ahistorical by reputation than Carter, or a group of people considered

---

[2] Anonymous source, conversation with the author, 6 June 1996.

more inexperienced than the Georgians with whom he surrounded himself. The administration certainly did contain a particularly high number of officials who either had no past experience of federal government or who thought in non-historical ways, or both. Yet it also contained enough veterans of the Kennedy and Johnson administrations to tap personal and institutional memories which seemed to have some bearing upon the case at hand. What this suggests is that no group of decision-makers is so ahistorical or blind to the perceived lessons of the past that it will fail to make use of analogies – whether appropriate or inappropriate – when it faces the kind of conditions encountered in the Iranian case. While there will always be those who will never be disposed towards the practice of analogizing, there are probably enough in any administration who *are* so disposed to reduce the overall impact of style. Moreover, if the Carter officials employed analogies in this instance, then we may reasonably assume that an administration more cognizant of the lessons of history would have thought of and been influenced by as many analogies, if not more.

The fact that historical analogizing was so extensive during the hostage crisis, then, suggests not that style is unimportant *per se*, but that almost any administration contains individuals with the requisite past experiences to use analogies. Those who had any first-hand experience or detailed knowledge of a previous hostage crisis – notably Cyrus Vance, Zbigniew Brzezinski and David Jones – invariably used this experience in the form of analogies. Those who had no direct experience of previous episodes, on the other hand, generally displayed a much lesser propensity to analogize. Stansfield Turner, for instance, recalls: 'I don't remember thinking of the problem in those terms. I wasn't involved in the *Pueblo* affair or the *Mayaguez* incident.'[3] The influence of style, then, seems to be on some of the decision group's parts but not on its whole.

If the Iran case suggests that we may effectively rule out individual style as an inhibition (or inducement) towards the use of analogical reasoning, it also propels us towards a conclusion regarding the availability of precedents or 'supply' of analogies. Our finding that analogies were so widespread in this case study even under such relatively unprecedented circumstances suggests rather strongly that analogizing is a demand- rather than supply-driven process. Although not as unprecedented as the Cuban missile crisis – there had been many hostage

---

[3] Stansfield Turner, interview with the author.

taking episodes before, but very few involving American embassies or the geographical and strategic position of Tehran – the hostage affair was quite novel in the sense that a host government had never (to the knowledge of almost everyone except Vance) condoned or endorsed the seizure of an American embassy overseas. It seems, however, that even under conditions such as these human beings in effect have no option but to search for the closest analogical 'match'. The Carter decision-makers exhibited the inherently human habit of attending to the past as a means of understanding and dealing with present dilemmas, even though the past seemed at best only a partial guide to the present.

Moreover, a pattern of analogical debate emerges in the Iran case similar to that observed by Yuen Foong Khong in the Vietnam case. Khong argues that in the latter instance

> someone would propose an analogy to Vietnam. Its validity would almost always be questioned. A critic would have little difficulty pointing out differences between the analogy and Vietnam . . . Interestingly, such criticisms and enumerations of differences seldom registered: the proposer of the analogy would either dismiss the differences or pay lip service to them and continue to believe that his analogy was valid.[4]

Although we lack the kind of documentary record available to Khong in his case study, the same sort of pattern is clearly evident in this example. Once the February analogy was rendered inapplicable by the ayatollah's endorsement of the embassy takeover, the decision-makers began by discussing the possible relevance of the Entebbe experience. The Entebbe analogy was invoked – probably by Brzezinski – but Jones and Brown then proceeded to outline the differences between Entebbe and Tehran. Vance countered with his own analogies – Angus Ward and *Pueblo* – but Brzezinski and Jordan both pointed to differences here as well. We do not yet know how actively each analogizer sought to rebut the arguments of their critics in policy discussions, but it does seem clear that those decision-makers who analogized continued to cling to their analogies in the face of counter-arguments.

It might be supposed that when a policy-maker is forced to confront a highly novel and non-routine problem, he or she is compelled to resort to creative or entirely hypothetical forms of reasoning. Unable to anchor the problem in some existing knowledge structure, it becomes impossible to 'look backwards' through history since nothing generates

---

[4] Khong, *Analogies at War*, pp. 219–20.

a usable match. It is precisely under these kind of conditions, however, that the demand for cognitive short cuts is greatest. Confronted with this kind of cognitive problem, the Carter decision-makers seem to have utilized partial analogies, drawing upon different analogies at different stages of the policy-making processes and piecing these together in the manner of a jigsaw puzzle.

Cognitively speaking, the key decision-makers appear to have responded to the novelty of the situation they faced by doing two principal things: each first of all – either consciously or unconsciously – sought to identify one or more analogical bases from which to operate; and secondly, each sought by various means to make the current situation or target match the base more closely, attempting to increase the cognitive 'fit' between the two. Logically, since one's perception of the past is relatively fixed, there are only two ways of doing this: one can make the base seem more like the target, by simply rationalizing away the dissimilarities between the latter and the former. Or, alternatively, one can seek to influence the target situation itself in ways which make it structurally more similar to the base instance.

The novelty of the situation first of all required the policy-makers who used analogies to screen out or downplay the differences between the target and the base. The use of the *Pueblo* analogy by Vance, for example, downplayed a number of differences between the two cases. First of all, in contrast to the North Korean situation, there was for a long time no established political authority in Iran with which to negotiate, no power which could 'deliver' on a deal to return the hostages; moreover, since the hostages by Vance's own estimation had become a political pawn in Khomeini's domestic struggle for power – and none of the major players in this struggle could afford to appear 'pro-American' – it seemed unlikely that anyone would engage in negotiations until this struggle had been resolved. In the *Pueblo* case, on the other hand, the negotiators could talk directly to a stable, established government.

The use of *Pueblo* as an analogical base also overlooked the fact that the crew of the *Pueblo* had been tortured during their captivity in 1968. As Russell Buhite notes, 'the North Koreans treated them most severely. The *Pueblo*'s officers and crew were held in primitive, drafty, louse-infested cells: they were periodically beaten almost to death (kidney chops with flying feet and blows to the head and shoulders with rifle butts were the most common tactics).' Their diet was also exceptionally poor, and injured Americans among the hostages were even initially denied medical attention.[5] The use of the *Pueblo* analogy also failed to take account of the different *political* environments in which Johnson and Carter were operating. In dealing with the *Pueblo* crisis, Lyndon Johnson could afford to negotiate for an extended period of time; like 1980, 1968 was a presidential election year. However, in 1968 public and mass media attention was distracted (to say the least) by the war in Vietnam. For this reason, the *Pueblo* hostage crisis never became a central, priority issue in the minds of most Americans, and never captured the public's attention, in the way that the Iran hostage crisis would. Few 'yellow ribbons' were tied around trees on the *Pueblo* hostages' behalf. One can argue, therefore, that simply waiting until the hostage takers had no further political use for the hostages was a *politically* viable strategy in 1968, while it probably was not in 1980. This was one reason why both Jordan and Brzezinski considered this strategy 'unsustainable'.

A final difference relates to the manner in which the *Pueblo* crisis was resolved. In order to obtain the release of the hostages in the *Pueblo* case, the United States agreed to sign a confession of wrongdoing. The signatory – the US negotiator General Gilbert Woodward – issued a written repudiation of the North Korean document just before he signed it. Nevertheless, in the eyes of many critics the US government had sacrificed America's national honour in resolving the crisis this way. Interestingly, when the captain of the *Pueblo* and former hostage Lloyd Bucher was asked what Carter should do in the Iran case in 1980, he argued emphatically that it was 'wrong for the United States to get us out of Korea that way. And it would be wrong for the United States to get the hostages out of Iran that way, too. It would be perceived (like the *Pueblo* incident) by the rest of the world and by history as weakness, and betrayal of principle.'[6] More importantly for our purposes, however, is the fact that repeating this strategy was simply unacceptable to Brzezinski, and – most importantly – it was unacceptable to Jimmy Carter. Similarly, the use of Entebbe as an analogical base first of all obscured the fact that the Tehran embassy was just that – an embassy – while most successful rescue operations had been conducted at airports. Secondly, Tehran was situated in a densely populated urban centre many miles from a US military base. As Turner notes, Entebbe

---

[5] Russell Buhite, *Lives At Risk*, p. 143.
[6] Quoted in 'Bucher Compares *Pueblo*, Iran Plights', *Los Angeles Times*, 8 May 1980, Part II, p. 4.

also did not involve the use of helicopters, which were of course an integral part of the Iran mission.[7]

In short, both Vance and Brzezinski were forced to employ historical analogies which one can recognize with the benefit of hindsight to have been only partially applicable to the case. However, viewed from a cognitive viewpoint, such screening operations are probably honest attempts to exclude what appears unimportant to an analogy, in the sense that the policy-maker distinguishes between those dissimilarities which are deemed to be merely contextual ('superficial'), and those which are more fundamental (or 'structural') in character. For Brzezinski, the differences between Entebbe and Tehran were ultimately surmountable, and he viewed the basic 'lesson' he derived from the former – namely, that risky moves are sometimes necessary in major crises – as entirely relevant here. Similarly, Vance believed that as long as the hostages were not being mistreated in the *Iran* case, and as long as Carter was prepared to put human life before national face and prestige, the basic lesson he drew from *Pueblo* – that patience and doggedness is the best way to resolve hostage crises – obtained here.

Secondly, some of the decision-makers did seek to influence the target situation in ways intended to increase its similarity to the base. The eventual 'victory' of Brzezinski's Entebbe analogy suggests that even when no direct match exists between a current situation and a previous one, policy-makers may try to manoeuvre and adapt the current situation until it can be made to fit the previous one more closely. In other words, a poor fit between the past situation and the case in hand does not automatically lead to the analogy being dropped, because the situation in hand can be manipulated until its structural features more closely resemble the past situation, thereby rendering the analogy 'operative'.

When policy-makers perform these kind of mental operations, they are probably endeavouring to preserve the perceived causal relationship which existed in the base, so that this relationship will be judged likely to hold in the target situation also. For example, for Brzezinski it was vitally important to identify those characteristics of the Entebbe raid which made it such an outstanding success, and then to transfer these to the target situation in Tehran. The rescue planners' central task was to find some means to overcome the differences between Entebbe and Tehran, since only by doing this could the success of Entebbe

---

[7] Turner, interview with the author.

potentially be repeated in Iran. If key causes of the successful policy outcome are present in the base but missing from the target, this decreases the likelihood that the same outcome will be reproduced again. Analogical debate hence frequently centres upon disputes about which elements are structural and which superficial. What, in other words, is fundamental to a particular outcome, and what mere background detail?

The choice of analogy: availability and representativeness

Even more striking is the relevance of the availability and representativeness heuristics discussed in chapter 2 to the use of analogies in the Carter administration (we have already discussed the evidence on the Iranian side in chapter 3, so will here confine ourselves to the American side). Three points seem most germane in this regard. First of all, out of the seven options generated by the decision-makers – get the shah to leave, negotiate, mount a naval blockade, launch an airstrike on the Abadan oil refinery, mine Iranian harbours, seize Iranian oil depots and launch a rescue mission – the available evidence is unambiguous on the point that, while all were discussed to some degree, only *two* were given serious consideration: negotiation and the rescue option. What is striking about this is that these were the only two options which had *analogical* precedents of any kind as methods of resolving hostage disputes. It is not beyond human imagination, for instance, that a naval blockade of Iran, by sending a message of American resolve to use greater military force if necessary, might have hastened the release of the hostages, and Carter might most obviously have recalled that this option was used by Kennedy to compel the removal of Soviet missiles from Cuba. But a hostage crisis had never, to the best knowledge of the participants themselves, been resolved successfully in such a manner; they had only been resolved either by dogged negotiation (*Pueblo*, Angus Ward) or military rescue missions (*Mayaguez*, Entebbe, Mogadishu), so that the historical analogies available for these options lent them some degree of plausibility and predictability. The other options were harder to imagine as solutions to the problem, and so lacked this plausibility. Put differently, the non-analogical options would be shots in the dark, in the sense that following them would greatly increase the uncertainty of the situation rather than diminish it.

Human decision-makers, it seems, not unnaturally prefer to pursue a strategy which has met with success in the past over one which has never been tried in such circumstances.

Secondly, the February analogy initially seems to have had a striking effect on practically all the decision-makers. None of the major players (with the possible exception of Vance) expected the embassy takeover to last very long. To an outside observer, the relative lack of concern expressed initially by the Carter decision-makers looks with hindsight very much like complacency. Why were the decision-makers so taken in by the February analogy? Why did some other historical comparison not spring to mind, perhaps offering a rival prediction to that offered by the February comparison? One likely explanation relates to the use of the availability and representativeness heuristics. Of the available analogies, February 1979 was obviously the most recent and therefore the most immediately recallable from memory. There was also arguably a strong 'fit' between the February incident and the November one: they involved the same embassy, the same city, and (at least at the outset) appeared to involve the same kind of revolutionary group, and so the representativeness heuristic may well have played a role here as well. Assuming that it did, it is easy to understand why the image of February 1979 exercised such a pull on the minds of intelligent men if one realizes that both heuristics may well have been at work in this instance.

The third piece of evidence which lends strong credence and support to the theoretical claims and empirical work of Kahneman and Tversky is the fact that the Tehran rescue mission was conducted in a political climate that was highly conducive to the launch of such operations. Again, the recency of Entebbe – the successful Israeli raid had occurred less than three years before the Tehran mission was launched – may have enhanced its attractiveness as a cognitive reference point. The Tehran raid occurred in the aftermath of two highly successful missions at Entebbe and Mogadishu, and the climate in both political and military circles was more favourable to such missions than it would otherwise have been. The problem with this, however, is that these two operations are unrepresentative of the wider population of cases. The painful fact is that military rescue operations have a high statistical probability of failure. Abraham Ribicoff has noted that 'the Israeli raid of the Entebbe airport is the rare exception in being highly successful in terms of rescuing all the hostages with a minimum of casualties to friendly personnel'.[8] As Alexander Scott said in similar vein, 'to put the Tehran raid in perspective, an average of at least three out of four commando, British intelligence and OSS operations in the European theater in World War II were "failures" by any standard, and a good third might politely be described as disasters'.[9]

The fact that the Tehran operation went ahead despite the high mathematical odds against it provides support for Kahneman and Tversky's contention that probability is rarely calculated on a statistical basis. Recall Gary Sick's observation, quoted in chapter 4, that the parallel with Entebbe was 'quite an obvious thing' and 'famous as an operation . . . so obviously it definitely came to mind'.[10] In contrast, rescue operations like the 1970 Son Tay raid in North Vietnam – though more typical and statistically representative of rescue missions in their results – were less well known and written about, and so it is quite conceivable that they would also be less cognitively available as reference points. As Scott notes, 'for every Entebbe, rescue of Mussolini or attack on Eben Emael, there are two or three failures like Dieppe'.[11] But like car crashes or terrorist attacks, it is the successes that get most attention.

Surprisingly, there is not much evidence at the time of writing that the famous German Mogadishu rescue of 1977 was ever explicitly mentioned as an analogy by the rescue planners.[12] Nevertheless, there is compelling evidence that Jimmy Carter was very much aware of that operation, that other members of the SCC knew about it, and that it had an effect upon Carter in particular. As Turner notes, the day after the successful Mogadishu raid, Carter – clearly impressed by the German action – sent Harold Brown a memorandum in which he asked 'Do we have the same capability as the Germans?' As noted in chapter 5, Mogadishu acted as a major impetus to Delta Force's development, so much so that it even appears to have shaped the hostage scenarios for which the rescuers trained.[13]

Just as the heuristics approach can account for why Entebbe may have been more attractive, it can also explain why analogies such as

---

[8] Abraham Ribicoff, 'Lessons and Conclusions', in Christopher (ed.), *American Hostages in Iran*, p. 386.
[9] Alexander Scott, 'The Lessons of the Iranian Raid for American Military Policy', *Armed Forces Journal International*, June 1980, p. 26.   [10] Sick, interview with the author.
[11] Scott, 'The Lessons of the Iranian Raid', p. 73.
[12] In interviews with the author, Vance, Brzezinski, Turner and Sick all failed to mention the Mogadishu raid.   [13] Turner, *Terrorism and Democracy*, p. 47.

Pueblo and Ward were comparatively *unattractive* to most of the deci-sion-makers. One reason why *Pueblo* was never fully accepted by Jor-dan and others, we have suggested, may well have been its domestic political implications. But there is also a *cognitive* explanation for this. Contrast the significant cognitive availability of the Entebbe and Mogadishu rescues with that of the *Pueblo* and Angus Ward incidents. As previously noted, the *Pueblo* crisis was not given much attention by the mass media in the United States in 1968, due to the fact that Vietnam essentially 'crowded it out'. It is therefore plausible that its structural attributes and details would be less available to the Carter decision-makers than, say, Entebbe, which was widely trumpeted in the United States and celebrated as a heroic success. Vance was of course directly involved in some aspects of the *Pueblo* crisis, but of the remaining decision-makers in the top echelons of the Carter administration, only Christopher and Brown had been in government during 1968. Most of the other decision-makers, then, would only have known about that hostage incident what they read in the newspapers. For instance, al-though Hamilton Jordan knew of the *Pueblo* crisis – he recalled that it had lasted about a year – he did not know much about the circumstan-ces surrounding it. Most notably, he claimed that Lyndon Johnson was not involved in a re-election campaign at the time of the *Pueblo* crisis, whereas in fact he was.[14] If Entebbe was 'an obvious thing', one could say that *Pueblo* and Angus Ward were, by contrast, 'non-obvious things'. Both hostage incidents were also not very recent, so it is not surprising for this reason also that they were less available in the memories of most of the decision-makers. Brzezinski said of the Angus Ward analogy that he doubted whether Carter would have been aware of it before it was brought to his attention.[15] We know that he was most certainly aware of both Entebbe and Mogadishu, however.

What the approach can and cannot explain

To summarize our findings thus far, we have suggested that analogical reasoning first of all informed the choice of both the negotiation and rescue options, and that analogical thinking affected some of the par-ticulars as well, notably the manner in which Delta Force trained prior to November 1979 (the Mogadishu analogy), the methods by which the rescuers would get in and out of Iran (Entebbe and Perot), the confi-

---

[14] Jordan, *Crisis*, p. 37.   [15] Brzezinski, interview with the author.

dence the planners had in the embassy assault (1974), the concern about having reliable intelligence concerning the hostages' whereabouts (Son Tay), the overwhelming priority given to secrecy and surprise and the 'lean' nature of the force used (Entebbe), and finally the choice of President Carter not to interfere in the decision of his military commanders to abort the mission (the Bay of Pigs).

What can the analogical reasoning explanation *not* account for, however? It is fair to say that the detailed particulars of the negotiation strategies employed are not explained or predicted by the *Pueblo* and Ward analogies. While these analogies seem to have conditioned Vance and Carter's decisions to negotiate, they do not appear to have influenced the precise form which the negotiations took (although they do appear to have influenced some details, such as how long Vance was prepared to be patient with the Iranians before concluding that other options had to be tried). In short, the administration did everything in its power to reach Khomeini and to open up a direct negotiation channel to him, rather than being constrained by the details of one analogy or another.

It would be surprising indeed if analogical theories were able to explain all aspects of the Iran decision-making, since individuals use several different forms of reasoning in complex decision-making situations. On occasion, the Carter people seem to have reasoned more or less hypothetically, without making reference to any obvious historical precedent or parallel. On 6 November 1979 the SCC and NSC met to discuss a range of options, but they ruled out a number of military options as being unlikely to lead to the hostages' release, likely to result in the deaths of some of the hostages, likely to bring the Soviet Union into the conflict, or all three. However, on what basis were such predictions made? How was the degree of likelihood assessed? The decision-makers seem to have reasoned in an entirely hypothetical manner in doing so, since as far as we can tell no one used a historical analogy in reaching these conclusions.

There is another trend which seems to emerge in the Iran case study: the incidence of analogizing seems to decrease as time passes. While a flood of analogies – the February incident, Entebbe, *Pueblo*, the Perot operation and so on – appear at the early meetings, after the failure of the rescue mission there is not much evidence that those responsible for reviving the negotiation channel drew on any historical analogy in deciding how to proceed (although memories of the failed 'French connection' may well have made the decisions-makers sceptical when the Tabatabai channel originally opened a link to Khomeini). This may be a simple artefact of the way in which information and data have been gathered in this study. For understandable reasons, the period up to and including the rescue mission has proved an attractive topic for researchers, while the period from April 1980 to January 1981 has not, and hence we know far more about the first period than we do about the second. Nevertheless, the finding that analogical reasoning tends to predominate in the critical early stages of a decision-making episode is supported by evidence drawn from other cases. Ernest May and Philip Zelikow find that, of the variety of historical analogies used by the ExComm during the missile crisis, most were used at the early stages. Analogies to Munich, Pearl Harbor, Suez–Hungary and World War I are heard early on in the missile crisis, but the frequency of these comparisons appears to tail off as time passes.[16] This trend may occur because levels of information are especially low during the early stages of a crisis or other stressful decision-making episode, placing a special premium on cognitive shorts-cuts like analogies. Conceivably, though, as decision-makers obtain 'harder' or more reliable information on the case in hand, the cognitive demand for such short-cuts may decrease. We still do not know enough about this to be able to say with any certainty whether this pattern actually exists, but the findings observed in the Iran and Cuba cases are at the very least suggestive.

Thus far, we have assumed that historical analogies are cognitive devices for making sense of the world around us, and that the Carter decision-makers in this sense 'meant' the historical comparisons they used and genuinely thought them helpful in dealing with the situation they faced. However, the thoughtful reader will have noticed that this central assumption is potentially flawed and perhaps altogether incorrect. In particular, there is at least a reasonable possibility – based perhaps on common sense expectation – that historical analogies are generally used merely as *ex-post justifications* for policies which have been arrived at by some other means of reasoning. Yuen Foong Khong in his book *Analogies at War* convincingly argued that the analogies used by Lyndon Johnson and his advisers were genuinely employed as *ex-ante*, rather than *ex-post*, devices. However, there is arguably no *a priori* reason to assume that this finding also applies here, so we shall address this issue in the following section. In confronting this question it will occasionally be helpful to illustrate the arguments made by

---

[16] Ernest May and Philip Zelikow (eds.), *The Kennedy Tapes: Inside the White House During the Cuban Missile Crisis* (London: The Belknap Press, 1997), pp. 699–700.

comparing the Iran decision-making with other cases, such as the missile crisis. Since we now know so much about that case, it provides an especially reliable point of comparison.

Mere *ex-post* justifications?

Sceptics often contend that historical analogies are solely persuasive devices, designed to win others over in a 'Machiavellian' fashion, as opposed to tools for understanding new events and situations. In the Iranian case, for instance, there is a possibility that each decision-maker arrived at his definition of the situation and preferred policy response *prior* to having thought of any analogy at all, and merely used history in order to bolster his policy preference after the fact and to sell his position to the other policy-makers. Cyrus Vance, for instance, might have decided that negotiation should be the strategy adopted for gaining the release of the hostages on some other, non-analogical grounds – for instance, he might have reasoned that this would best serve the Department of State's interests within the administration – and might then have looked around for analogies that would support this position. In a recent research note, Taylor and Rourke contend that the January 1991 congressional debate over whether to authorize the use of force in the Persian Gulf War shows that 'analogies legitimize, not drive, the policy choices of members of Congress . . . analogies are used by members of Congress as *post-hoc* justifications for policy choices and do not help determine them'.[17] They suggest, moreover, that this is probably the role analogies normally play.

Briefly stated, Taylor and Rourke find that there is a much stronger relationship between ideology and the choice of the Munich/Vietnam analogy among members of Congress than there is between age or experience and the choice of analogy. In order to operationalize the difficult concept of 'experience', however, they are compelled to utilize a rather rigid conceptualization of what that concept means to FPDM scholars. Their analysis assumes, for instance, that those who were politically formed during the Vietnam War, or who fought in it, ought to use the Vietnam analogy, while those who were politically formed during or after World War II ought to use that analogy. This ignores or downplays the fact that many individuals may subsequently have been exposed to crucial influences other than this initial one. More problem-

---

[17] Andrew Taylor and John Rourke, 'Historical Analogies in the Congressional Foreign Policy Process', *Journal of Politics*, 57: 460–8, 1995, p. 466.

atically, it also ignores the fact that – as scholars like Robert Jervis have long argued – different members of the same generation often take markedly different lessons from the same event, so that one should not *expect* two different individuals who happen to be of the same age to agree on key political questions.[18] The fact that ideology is strongly related to choice of analogy also comes as no surprise to scholars of political cognition, because many psychologists argue that analogizing plays a key role in the formation of beliefs. As discussed in chapter 2, schemas – including those containing judgements about political information and causation – are probably formed from having gone through the same kind of problem on several occasions, which then leads to the construction of generalized beliefs about the world. In Vance's case, for instance, Vietnam had a critical influence on the development of a system of beliefs which emphasized the need for conciliation and diplomatic compromise as a means of resolving disputes.[19]

Taylor and Rourke's note is a thoughtful and praiseworthy effort to grapple with a difficult area, but in the end what they have uncovered is the perhaps unsurprising finding that people who agree with one another in terms of their beliefs are a lot more likely to use the same analogy than are people born in the same year. What this demonstrates, perhaps, is that this is an area where only in-depth use of the interpretive case-study method and cumulative case study comparisons can yield meaningful results. Taylor and Rourke also take care to note that their findings do not necessarily apply to members of the US *executive* branch. It is perhaps more plausible that members of Congress would use analogies in an *ex-post* way because of the temptation to 'grandstand', and to take symbolic positions on issues that constituents care about.

The *ex-post* interpretation has an immediate intuitive appeal, however, not least because scepticism about government and its officials is currently at an all-time high in the United States and Europe. Moreover, if proven correct, this view would undermine a central assumption upon which we have proceeded in this study. The perspective we have adopted here allows that analogies are used for persuasive purposes or as bureaucratic weapons, but assumes that the analogizer has first of all used the same analogy as a cognitive device to make sense of the situation, or to propose some policy response to it, or both. This perspective can conveniently be termed the *ex-ante* view, while we shall

---

[18] On this point, see Khong, *Analogies at War*, p. 33.
[19] This of course raises the question of why study analogies at all, if generalized beliefs determine behaviour. This question will be addressed in chapter 7.

label the sceptics approach the *ex-post* view.[20] Simply put, the *ex-ante* view implies that analogies are *both* sources of understanding *and* persuasive devices designed to win over one's colleagues, and does not preclude the possibility that analogies are used for the purpose of persuasion. The *ex-post* view, on the other hand, contends that this is *all* that they are used for.

Which viewpoint is the correct one? A little preliminary thought reveals that – as with most interesting questions in politics – the debate is not ultimately resolvable by reference to any hard empirical criteria and that it resists rigorous or direct testing. Nevertheless, we can test it indirectly by developing criteria which can be used to judge the *likelihood* of whether analogies are generally employed as *ex-ante* sources of understanding and persuasion, or solely as *ex-post* justifications. By thinking out the implications of each of these rival explanations, one can arrive at hypotheses about the conditions under which one or the other interpretation is most likely to paint an accurate picture of reality.

Three criteria seem particularly useful in this regard. First of all, if analogies are solely justifications designed to win one's colleagues over to a pre-selected strategy, there is no reason why the analogies used by the decision-maker should be drawn from his or her *personal* experience. We expect the *ex-post* justifier to draw on the most persuasive analogy, from the widest pool of experience, and there is no reason why that pool should be limited to analogies which derive from the individual's personal background. On the other hand, if analogies are cognitive mechanisms for dealing with structural uncertainty – for making the unfamiliar familiar, in other words – we expect decision-makers to draw upon what is *most* familiar in doing this; and what is most familiar, of course, is personal experience, the events which have formed one's own political beliefs and makeup. If the policy-maker does limit himself or herself in this way, the likelihood that the analogy is genuinely believed in is correspondingly increased.

Examining the hostage crisis case study again, we can readily observe that the analogies used by the decision-makers do persistently relate to their own personal experiences; Brzezinski's use of the Entebbe analogy was related to his meeting with Shimon Peres and the Israelis just before the Entebbe raid, Vance's use of the Vietnam and *Pueblo* analogies to his intimate involvement in those two seminal episodes in America's political history, and Jones's use of the *Mayaguez* analogy to

[20] These terms are borrowed from the discipline of economics, where they are used to describe different conceptualizations of public and private expenditure and savings.

his role in the planning of that mission under Ford. It is probably difficult to argue that these decision-makers did not genuinely believe in such personal analogies. Vietnam had a particularly shattering effect upon Cyrus Vance, who has stated that he still finds it both difficult and painful to discuss the war in interviews.[21]

The same observation can equally be made in other cases drawn from American foreign policy. The Cuban missile crisis provides us with a prominent example which may conveniently be used as a basis for comparison. The evidence is overwhelming that the Pearl Harbor analogy was used repeatedly by Robert Kennedy during the deliberations in the ExComm over whether to launch a 'surgical' airstrike during the October 1962 crisis, and the World War I analogy was also used repeatedly by the president.[22] What significance ought we to attribute to this, though? Had RFK decided that he did not wish the United States to mount an air strike against Cuba before even thinking of the analogy and before suggesting it to his brother and his colleagues? Perhaps the attorney general had determined that he was opposed on ideological grounds to taking the missiles out this way, and then searched around for some alternative argument that would convince the hawks not to go along with the air strike option. Obviously, this would achieve his desired goal if successful, but would also avoid simultaneously alienating hard-liners with 'doveish' talk. Or perhaps he had decided against the air strike *solely* on the grounds that it might not work and that it risked escalation of the conflict. He may then, in similar fashion, have grabbed a justification from the history books which he thought would convert those who had more faith in the ability of the military to accomplish what it promised. In both of these instances, talk of Pearl Harbor would constitute an *ex-post* justification, designed to persuade the other ExComm members after the fact, rather than an *ex-ante* source of understanding and categorization.

While it is admittedly difficult to ascertain with any absolute degree of certainty more than three decades on, the available evidence suggests that RFK did genuinely believe in the analogy he employed in this instance, for the comparison drew on a personal experience of a formative kind. Pearl Harbor did constitute an event of considerable importance in Robert Kennedy's early life. As Arthur Schlesinger notes, the young Kennedy wrote regularly to his parents while at school, and did so on this subject:

[21] Cyrus Vance, interview with the author.
[22] See Richard Neustadt and Ernest May, *Thinking In Time*, pp. 1–16.

Pearl Harbor found Robert Kennedy, just turned sixteen, in his third year at Portsmouth Priory. The school, only a few miles from the naval base at Newport, responded quickly to the tremors of war The headmaster decreed a blackout. 'We all had to go sit in the basement for 20 minutes.' When the aircraft carrier *Ranger* steamed into Narragansett Bay, the boys watched planes practicing dive-bombing in the hazy distance.[23]

Much as many middle-aged Americans nowadays can remember being placed under emergency conditions at school during the Cuban missile crisis, RFK could clearly recall the same thing happening in relation to Pearl Harbor during his own youth. We therefore have every reason to believe that the cognitive availability of this vivid event – and not simply the desire to find a persuasive argument for the blockade – was what caused Kennedy to think of the parallel. The *ex-post* view also runs into theoretical difficulties in disputing the causal impact of analogies in this case, for where did RFK's preference for the blockade as opposed to the air strike come from, if not from the Pearl Harbor analogy? This perspective leaves a hole in the argument while proposing nothing in its place. Perhaps RFK had been a 'dove' from the start and simply did not want an air strike for that reason. Yet this argument too runs into difficulties on closer examination. He had begun the missile crisis by seriously contemplating the relevance of other historical parallels such as 'sinking the Maine', behaving very much like a hawk at the outset. And finally, none of the other decision-makers seriously doubted that Kennedy 'meant' the Pearl Harbor analogy; there were those who thought it greatly misplaced and even silly, of course, but no one doubted the attorney general's sincerity.

Another analogy which reportedly influenced the thinking of the Kennedys during the missile crisis was the World War I analogy, used in private by John Kennedy in discussions with the inner circle of his advisers. If this was an *ex-post* justification, who was the analogy intended to persuade? JFK was the president, after all. He could just as well have proceeded in the same fashion and given other, less specific reasons for not launching an air strike. The evidence shows that he confined talk of this analogy to a very small circle of confidants, to whom he seems to have expressed how he really felt about the missile situation.

In one sense, of course, in taking an analogy from Barbara Tuchman's

---

[23] Arthur Schlesinger, *Robert Kennedy and His Times* (Boston, Massachusetts: Houghton Mifflin, 1978), p. 40.

work the president appears to have done just what the *ex-post* justification school claims policy-makers do: he seems to have been grabbing an
argument from a history book. And yet, as in his brother's case, the
analogy JFK used seems strongly related to his earlier personal experiences. Ted Sorensen notes that:

> A favorite Kennedy word from my earliest association with him was
> 'miscalculation'. Long before he had read Barbara Tuchman's *The
> Guns of August* – which he recommended to his staff – he had as a
> student at Harvard taken a course on the origins of World War I. It
> made him realize, he said, 'how quickly countries which were com-
> paratively uninvolved were taken, in the space of a few days, into
> war'. After the missile crisis, Kennedy would refer to a 1914 conversa-
> tion between two German leaders about how WWI began, in which
> one said 'how did it all happen?' and the other replied 'ah, if only we
> knew'. JFK did not want a similar, even more devastating scenario to
> occur this time, after which one American might ask another 'how did
> it all happen'.[24]

Even more tellingly, the president did not actually attempt to persuade others of the utility of this analogy. He did not mention it in any
of the ExComm meetings, so far as we are aware. How, then, could it
constitute an *ex-post* justification? If he did not genuinely believe in the
analogy, why was it used at all?

Aside from the correlation between personal experience and the
choice of analogy, a second consideration which seems useful in thinking about the *ex-ante* versus *ex-post* question relates to the persuasive
power of analogies. It is reasonable to suppose that if analogies are used
solely in the *ex-post* fashion, we would not expect policy-makers to
employ analogies which are *obviously* non-persuasive in character,
given the intended audience towards which they are directed. Given
the substantial range of historical events and experiences upon which
policy-makers of all ideological persuasions can draw, if the *ex-post*
interpretation is accurate then one would expect decision-makers to
select analogies which fit the predispositions they know a given audience is likely to favour. For instance, if one is speaking to a room full of
'presidential supporters' – advisers around the president whose primary interest lies in looking after his interests and (in a first term) in
securing his re-election – one ought not to advocate an analogy which

---

[24] Taken from Theodore Sorensen, *Kennedy* (New York: Harper and Row, 1965), p. 513.
The same story was recounted by Robert Kennedy is one of his oral history interviews
for the John F. Kennedy Library. See Edwin O. Guthman and Jeffrey Shulman (eds.),
Robert Kennedy: In His Own Words (New York: Bantam Books, 1988), p. 168.

implies a solution associated with political pain. It makes sense to find another analogy somewhere in the history books which implies the same policy options, but rather less risk to the president's political prospects. Conversely, if one doggedly persists in arguing an analogy which is hard to sell, this is probably a good indication that one does genuinely believe in the analogy and is honestly using it in order to make an unfamiliar situation intelligible.

Looking again at the hostage crisis decision-making, the advocates of the analogies did persist in using analogies which proved unpopular, even in forums in which they knew full well that their chosen analogy and its supposed lessons would prove unconvincing to the audience towards which it was directed. Most notably, Cyrus Vance used the *Pueblo* analogy in the effort to persuade his colleagues to use negotiation, even when it became abundantly clear that a *Pueblo*-style policy conflicted with the bureaucratic interests and ideological world-views of those he was trying to win over to his cause. If analogies are just tools of persuasion, why did Vance select an instrument which was obviously not going to serve this function in an effective way?

Vance was probably unable to sell the *Pueblo* analogy to Carter and Georgian presidential supporters like Powell and Jordan for more than a few months because the *Pueblo* analogy implies that even though negotiation can produce the release of US hostages if combined with patience and dogged determination, such a policy success is likely to be obtained only at the cost of political and electoral failure. For Vance, this was an acceptable price to pay, since he did not intend to serve as secretary of state for a second term and apparently valued principle over all else. It was not an acceptable cost for the president, however, who in late 1979 was about to enter an election year, or for the other Georgians whose primary responsibility lay in ensuring that Jimmy Carter was elected to a second term. Given their different hierarchies of values, a conflict between Vance and the presidential supporters was probably inevitable. On the other hand, Brzezinski was offering the promise of political *and* policy success, with his conviction that an Entebbe-type scenario was now a distinct possibility, after so much planning designed to overcome the critical differences between Entebbe and Tehran.

Returning again to the missile crisis example, Robert Kennedy repeated the Pearl Harbor analogy again and again in both the ExComm meetings and in private consultations with the president, and he defended the parallel in the debate over its applicability with foreign policy heavyweight and former Secretary of State Dean Acheson. Why – if his aim was solely to win over his fellow policy-makers, rather than to make them see the merits of a comparison he thought genuinely useful in making sense of a complex situation – did he persist in using the analogy even after it became abundantly clear to everyone concerned that several ExComm members thought the parallel nonsensical? Why not search around for some other comparison which might be more persuasive?

Thirdly, if historical analogies are used solely in an *ex-post* fashion, then there is no logical reason why the structural features of an analogy should affect subsequent policy behaviour. In other words, if analogies are simply persuasive devices, then once the policy has been accepted in principle there is no logical reason why its subsequent details – how it is implemented and so on – should be affected by the analogy. The comparison will not necessarily be dropped altogether, but an analogy which is not honestly believed in should not impact upon the detailed features of the policy as it emerges. If, on the other hand, the analogy *is* an inspirational source of understanding and guidance, we should expect the policy-makers to use the analogy in designing the details of the policy, not just in arguing for its overall desirability.

The extent to which the analogies influenced the particular details of the strategies employed is rather more difficult to assess with precision, but the two main analogies employed in the Iran case – *Pueblo* and Entebbe – do appear to have impacted upon at least *some* of the subsequent details of Carter's policy as it was worked out. In its early stages, the State Department's response to the Iranian crisis was at the very least consistent with that of the Johnson administration during the *Pueblo* affair, in the sense that – at the prompting of his secretary of state – Carter employed a strategy of graduated response similar to that used in 1968, and used similar measures designed to reinforce and strengthen America's negotiating hand. *Pueblo* seems to have influenced the character of the Iran policy in that specific way, but also more generally in suggesting that patient and dogged negotiation would bring success in the end, and without loss of life. It also suggested that it might be many months (or even a year) before the hostages were released from captivity, suggesting a time limit beyond which more stringent action would have to be considered.

Similarly, Entebbe appears to have influenced the rescue mission in a number of ways. In general, it suggested that a daring and well-planned mission can bring both political and policy success. More specifically, however, it seems to have influenced decisively consider-ations having to do with OPSEC, which in turn led to a whole range of results, such as the crucial consideration of keeping the rescue force light, and perhaps may even have influenced the deceptive manner in which members of the administration conducted themselves in the run-up to the rescue mission. For instance, the kind of diversionary tactics which Shimon Peres employed during Brzezinski's visit to his house – and which fooled the Polish American so successfully – were later used by Brzezinski, Powell and Carter in their dealings with the American press prior to the rescue mission, and one may speculate as to whether this behaviour drew in part on the perceived lessons of Entebbe.

Obviously, the more conditions which are met in favour of a given interpretation, the greater the likelihood that this interpretation is the correct one (and conversely, that the other interpretation is incorrect). The evidence gleaned from the Iran case study arguably favours the *ex-ante* interpretation for the reasons given above, but there is an even more fundamental reason for adhering to that perspective. Our analysis has proceeded from the assumption that analogies tend to be used only in *certain* cases and under certain circumstances. This in and of itself lends credence to the *ex-ante* view, for since analogies are potentially useful as argumentative devices in virtually all policy contexts, we ought to see them being *used* in all policy contexts if supporters of the *ex-post* approach are correct. And yet there are many examples of policy-making situations in which people employ more general beliefs or standard operating procedures instead of historical analogies to define a situation and generate responses to it. The *ex-post* view has difficulty explaining why analogies were not considered useful in these cases, while the cognitive perspective can trace this to the differing contextual conditions under which a given set of decision-makers are working. Again, while we cannot directly prove that the analogies used in the Iran case were genuinely being used to make sense of reality, the balance of the evidence arguably does favour the argument that they were.

7 Some alternative explanations: non-analogical accounts of the Iran decision-making

Having addressed the question of how historical analogies are used by decision-makers, we now need to direct our attention to other, more concrete kinds of criticism which might be raised against the argument presented in the previous few chapters. One obvious potential problem with the analysis presented in chapters 3–5 is that we may have misrepresented events in the case study analysed here, and in so doing may have missed key variables accounting for the decisions taken. Other explanations are certainly possible as accounts of the decisions arrived at. Indeed, the hostage crisis has already been examined from a wide variety of theoretical angles in the existing literature, the vast majority of which offer 'non-analogical' accounts of the hostage crisis decision-making. Although much of this more narrowly seeks to explain the decision to mount the rescue mission, it seems sensible now to compare the ability of these explanations to account for as many aspects of the Iran decision-making as the account we have offered here. Doing so, we shall argue, helps to place the analogical argument in relation to other explanations which have been offered in the literature, and suggests that the former is not necessarily at all incompatible with some of the latter. Not all of the theoretical accounts examined here, we shall argue, should properly be considered *rival* explanations *per se*. The meaning of this statement should become clear as we move through the various theoretical accounts, and we shall return to the point having done so.

Clearly, any analyst attributing a central role to the individual level of analysis in the study of international relations runs the risk that factors lying at other, 'higher' levels of analysis can explain the decisions he or she is trying to account for in a satisfactory way, so that knowing the details of the reasoning processes employed by each decision-maker in a given case – while these may seem interesting in and of themselves –

actually contributes little of *theoretical* importance to our account of why a decision was made. Equally, there may be other individual level forces that we have overlooked in the preceding analysis, which may similarly account for more of the variance than the variable selected. In time honoured fashion, we shall proceed down the ladder of analysis, beginning with structural explanations and concluding with the individual level.

External factors and the international system

The first and most immediate possibility that would occur to a conventional theorist of international relations is that structural, systemic or external pressures might have forced President Jimmy Carter to act as he did, or might at least have formed the critical ingredient of the decision-making process. One can argue that *any* administration would have acted as the Carter administration did when placed in this particular 'objective' situation. Such counterfactuals are difficult to disprove. What makes this particular counterfactual doubtful as an explanation for the hostage crisis decision-making, however, is the simple fact that different American presidents through history actually *have* reacted in different ways when confronted with hostage problems broadly similar to the one under discussion. Different occupants of the White House have viewed such situations differently and have been motivated by noticeably different policy considerations in dealing with them. To take one particularly striking example, President Gerald Ford reacted in a manner radically different to Carter when faced with the seizure of American hostages during the 1975 *Mayaguez* episode. While one president viewed the situation primarily as a threat to US credibility and 'face' in the world, the other saw it primarily as a threat to human life; while one resorted almost immediately to the use of military force, the other tried negotiation for several months before selecting a military option that was probably the least forcible of the available alternatives. Ford's actions and reasoning were also markedly different from Lyndon Johnson's during the *Pueblo* crisis.

Structural explanations can explain the general importance accorded to the area of the Middle East by decision-makers. We have already noted in chapter 3, however, that such explanations generally come out rather poorly in the hostage crisis case. The distribution of power in the international system provides a rather weak predictor of even the general outcome in the Iran hostage situation. As Rose McDermott suggests, the United States was simply unwilling or unable to bring its massive nuclear and conventional superiority to bear, and structural realism has great difficulty explaining why this might have been the case.[1] Put succinctly, *actual* power did not translate into *usable* power. Iran's ability to hold the hostages for so long is hard to square with structural theory, for if power is what determines outcomes, why did Iran prevail over the United States for so long?

Kenneth Waltz's neo-realism has in recent years become the most popular version of systemic theory. Yet the theory cannot, by the author's own admission, explain a particular decision such as that of Khomeini to throw his political weight behind the hostage takers a few days into the crisis, or Carter's decision to authorize a rescue mission. Waltz draws a sharp distinction between theories of international relations and theories of foreign policy; external sources often only set the context for decision-making, he contends, but we require unit level theories to account for the particular policy choices made in any given situation.[2] This distinction is probably an essential one for Waltz to make; it allows him to rule unit level factors out of the analysis and thus preserves what is arguably neo-realism's major strength, its parsimony. Nevertheless, the validity of this distinction has increasingly been doubted by friends and foes alike. Colin Elman, for instance, argues that a neo-realist theory of foreign policy is in principle quite possible, though he does not attempt to develop one. Starting from an anti-realist position, Allison and Zelikow also refute the distinction, noting like Elman that Waltz often uses his theory to explain foreign policy choices.[3]

No published neo-realist analysis of the hostage crisis exists, and nor has there been a concerted effort to explain it in terms of any structural theory. How might we nevertheless construct such an explanation? Such an exercise, of course, carries with it the danger of setting up a straw man, but it is worth the risk if it allows us to derive a workable alternative explanation against which the one discussed in this book may be compared. Such a systemic account might go something like this. The international system during the entirety of the hostage crisis was, according to the vast majority of observers, bipolar. We can further

---

[1] McDermott, 'Prospect Theory in International Relations', p. 238.
[2] Kenneth Waltz, *Theory of International Politics* (Reading, Massachusetts: Addison-Wesley, 1979), especially pp. 102–28.
[3] Colin Elman, 'Horses For Courses: Why Not Neorealist Theories of Foreign Policy?', *Security Studies*, 6: 7–53, 1996; Allison and Zelikow, *Essence of Decision*, pp. 404–5.

propose that in a bipolar system a kind of inbuilt structural dynamic exists, whereby an advance or gain by one superpower necessarily leads to a counterreaction by the other. The power thus weakened seeks to re-establish the status quo, and this effort is a systemically derived imperative (that is, it occurs regardless of the internal characteristics of the states involved). Applied to US foreign policy during the Cuban missile crisis, for example, one can argue that the United States simply had to respond in some significant way to the Soviet placement of nuclear missiles in Cuba, since this altered the strategic balance of power in favour of one power at the expense of the other.

Applying this kind of framework to the hostage crisis is less straightforward, since only one of the parties to the conflict was a superpower. Nevertheless, we can argue that a fear of Soviet intervention – or, more generally, of creating a new Soviet power base in a strategically important area of the world – was what prevented the United States from acting more decisively in this instance. One could hence explain the decision to negotiate with the Iranians not as a result of the *Pueblo* and Angus Ward analogies or of Carter's own moralistic belief system, but as a consequence of American fear of either provoking the Soviets or providing them with a pretext to make a move on Iran.

This argument seems compelling when presented so simply. Moreover, there is also some empirical evidence that before the hostage crisis occurred – during the last days of the shah and the heated debates within the administration as to what, if anything, could or should be done to prop up his regime – President Carter was especially concerned about providing such a pretext. He states in his memoirs that if the shah fell, 'I was concerned that the Soviet leaders might be tempted to move in, a repetition of what they had already done three times in this century.'[4] This concern also seems to have carried over into the hostage crisis itself. At one key meeting held just before the implementation of the rescue mission, Carter told Cyrus Vance: 'my greatest fear all along is that this crisis could lead us into direct confrontation with the Soviets'.[5] According to Zbigniew Brzezinski, the Soviet move into Afghanistan made it less likely that America would take military action against Iran. 'Until the Soviet invasion of Afghanistan, the trend was toward more and more serious consideration of military action. The Soviet aggression against Afghanistan arrested this trend, and our strategy increasingly became that of saving the hostages' lives *and* of

---

[4] Carter, *Keeping Faith*, p. 449. [5] Jordan, *Crisis*, p. 237.

promoting our national interest by exercising military restraint', Brzezinski states.[6] Vance was also somewhat concerned after the events of December 1979 that the administration refrain from doing anything which might 'drive Iran into the arms of the Soviet Union'.[7]

Nevertheless, there are at least three notable difficulties with this approach. First, while concern about what the Soviets might do was still present after November 1979, it almost certainly took a back seat – in the minds of Carter and Vance at least – to the safe return of the hostages as the central motivation behind America's Iran policy. Although as the quote above illustrates, Carter did describe a conflict with the Soviets as his 'greatest fear', many of his other statements suggest that the lives of the hostages were his primary concern. He consistently rejected options he thought would jeopardize this objective.[8] Secondly, this version of the systemic argument also has difficulty accounting for the rescue mission, one of the central puzzles addressed in this book. After all, if fear of Soviet intervention was really the dominant concern, the military mission created the very pretext for the kind of intervention the Carter administration supposedly wished more than anything else to avoid. As Vance suggested in his argument against the mission, even if successful it might push Iran into the hands of the Soviets. 'We have to worry about the consequences of either a successful or unsuccessful rescue mission', Vance said. 'What will the Soviet Union do in response? . . . we call it a rescue mission, but it will be interpreted as a military action by others.'[9] Thirdly, the most important problem with this particular systemic explanation – highlighted in part by the second point – is that different decision-makers viewed or perceived the structural situation differently. For systemic forces or objective 'structure' to exercise the paramount effect upon decision-making, this effect should be more or less unambiguous; in other words, decision-makers should be inclined to view the nature of the situation in similar ways. However, the evidence suggests that Vance and Brzezinski, in particular, viewed the likely effects of various American actions upon Soviet behaviour differently. While all agreed that it was desirable to keep the Soviet Union out of Iran, they disagreed about the appropriate means of doing so. Though he used it as an argument against the rescue mission, Vance, in particular, thought the possibility of Iran turning to the Soviet Union remote. Khomeini disliked the Soviet Union as much as he did the United States, Vance notes, but Brzezinski seems to have considered

---

[6] Brzezinski, *Power and Principle*, p. 485.   [7] Vance, *Hard Choices*, p. 398.
[8] See for instance Carter, *Keeping Faith*, pp. 468–9 and 490.   [9] Jordan, *Crisis*, p. 236.

this outcome much more likely.[10] The perceptions of individuals, in the end, arguably mattered rather more than the existence of structural 'imperatives', since no one could agree what these were.

Perhaps more promising as an external-type explanation is Robert Jervis's reformulation of this kind of theory, especially his argument about domino theory effects.[11] Jervis contends that states are especially likely to resort to belligerent foreign policy acts when they have experienced recent losses abroad or at home. Powerful states, in other words, seek to restore their international reputation and prestige in the wake of defeats or losses of some sort, and he contends that one can at least partially explain Ford's *Mayaguez* operation or Reagan's Grenada invasion this way (the former being a reaction to the fall of Saigon, the latter to the Iran hostage situation).[12] This approach has an evident application to the Iranian rescue mission. The United States had suffered major losses in recent years – the loss of a client state in Iran, the invasion of Afghanistan and the seizure of the hostages – all of which made the United States look weak internationally. According to the theory, these recent losses made it increasingly likely that the United States would act in a belligerent way in order to re-establish its reputation and prestige in the world.

Again, this approach seems to have much to recommend it at first sight. In general, the invasion of Afghanistan may well, as briefly suggested in chapter 5, have tipped the advisory balance in favour of Brzezinski's world-view and away from Vance's. This factor certainly increased the pressure on Carter to 'look tougher' in relation to the Soviet Union, and perhaps may have caused him to 'act tougher' towards Iran. In other words, this external event may have had subtle effects on the decision-making environment that are hard to observe. Nevertheless, it is difficult to trace causal linkages between particular foreign policy losses and the decision to launch the rescue mission. For instance, there is a time lag of four months from the Afghanistan invasion to the launching of the rescue mission, of six months between the seizure of the embassy and the mission and of fifteen months from the fall of the shah to the mission. These lags perhaps cast doubt upon the primacy of such an effect, although there is nothing in Jervis's theory which fails to allow for such delays.

A more serious problem is that the rescue option was only one of *five* military options. This being so, why would this external pressure

---

[10] Vance, ibid.   [11] Jervis, *System Effects*, pp. 266–9.   [12] Ibid., p. 268.

– the need to re-establish America's reputation – compel a rescue operation rather than, say, a naval blockade or airstrike? The latter, after all, would have reinforced American prestige in a more telling way by sending an unambiguous message to Iran. One can of course respond that the rescue mission was selected because it was the least forcible of these options and because Carter was a humanitarian idealist, but as soon as one does this one has introduced non-external factors in order to bolster what would otherwise be a rather incomplete explanation.

The domino theory effects position is problematic as an explanation of the hostage crisis considered as a whole, and probably equally difficult to apply more narrowly to the rescue mission. One problem is that it cannot account for the decision to negotiate for so long, since the theory suggests that the reaction to losses will be belligerence, not patient attempts at constructing dialogue. Another notable problem is that already noted above: one cannot assume a unitary actor in this case. A few advisers placed the prestige of the United States first – making them particularly susceptible to the type of motivation discussed above – but for the majority the lives of the hostages were paramount. Thirdly, the member of that administration most given to advocating forceful military solutions to problems and most given to according America's reputation in the world priority over other goals – Zbigniew Brzezinski – has argued that the Soviet move into Afghanistan, though obviously a blow to American prestige, actually made it more important to tread carefully in Iran. Some of the most punitive measures considered by the administration early on, he argued, became inappropriate after Afghanistan, since these 'would be likely to drive Iran into the hands of the Soviets'.[13] Jimmy Carter also refused to see the hostage situation simply in terms of US reputation and prestige, and rejected the most forceful military solutions such as mining Iran's harbours or bombing Kharg Island, either or both of which would certainly have sent a powerful message of intent to Khomeini. As well as casting doubt upon the argument that the rescue mission was primarily designed to re-establish American prestige, Brzezinski's argument about the various military options available after the Soviet invasion suggests that the domino theory effects argument is too simplistic, in the sense that it focuses on only one external factor – international reputation – to the exclusion of others. It also

---

[13] Brzezinski, *Power and Principle*, p. 492.

ignores the effects of analogical reasoning, for if the loss previously incurred by the state involved the unsuccessful utilization of military measures – what one might term 'unsuccessful belligerence' – we would expect the state to *avoid* belligerence in the immediate future. The most obvious example of this in an American context is Vietnam, which has clearly led US policy-makers to exercise a good deal more caution when considering the use of force than was previously the case.[14]

The fact that different versions of the role external variables play are possible arguably highlights the indeterminacy of systemic level explanations as a whole. While one version of systemic theory might suggest that the Soviet invasion of Afghanistan had the effect of demilitarizing the American response to the hostage crisis, another version deems a military response more likely. Of course, *one* of the two theories discussed above may be correct and the other incorrect. But neither can account for both the initial decision to negotiate and the rescue mission. The first can potentially explain the decision to use non-forcible measures but not the rescue mission, while the reverse is true for the second theory. Both types of theory, moreover, suffer from an emphasis upon objective structures and situations, rather than the often competing ways in which those situations are perceived. The real problem with such explanations is not that they specify the existence of an international system involving constraints and pressures. This system is objectively 'there'. The difficulty is that they regularly downplay the ways in which these forces are open to interpretation, and the fact that they very often are interpreted in different ways by decision-makers. Systemic variables also do not generally predict the *content* of decisions. They constitute general forces propelling the decision-making process whose precise influence is hard to gauge, but they are also forces which are non-specific in terms of the particular policy options they encourage policy-makers to pursue. Such contextual forces create the need for a decision to be made, however, so we need to consider their general influence alongside content-predictive forces like analogies.

---

[14] The *Pueblo* hostage crisis provides a case in point. Unlike Carter, Lyndon Johnson appears to have deliberately downplayed the 1968 affair, fearful of escalating the situation militarily and of creating 'another Vietnam' in Korea. The swift use of military force in the *Mayaguez* example, in turn, seems to have been influenced by a desire not to repeat the errors which Ford and Kissinger thought Johnson had made in 1968.

Domestic politics

A second interpretation places more emphasis on what James Rosenau would call the 'societal' sources of the Iran decisions.[15] This approach opens up the black box of the state kept purposely closed by system level theorists, and stresses in particular the part played by domestic political considerations in the decisions of Khomeini and Carter. As we have seen already, there is broad agreement that the American hostages were useful to Khomeini as a domestic device to neutralize the appeal of other radical groupings in the wake of the Iranian revolution. While this account cannot explain why the students seized the embassy originally, most commentators would agree that the ayatollah's reasoning after this action took place was probably motivated by such considerations.

In his comprehensive review of the influence of domestic political forces on foreign policy decision-making, Joe Hagan suggests that Khomeini probably needed to utilize the embassy seizure, and more generally employed anti-Western rhetoric, in order to create a dominant or winning policy coalition. He thus imposed his will upon a situation plagued by hard-line and moderate factional infighting, where power was quite dispersed rather than centralized. The situation, he argues, was also characterized by a desperate search for political survival and a need for policy legitimization.[16] 'An atmosphere of political instability usually precludes bargaining with opposition that is to be distrusted and unlikely to be accommodated through mutual compromise', Hagan notes. 'Foreign policy is a correspondingly viable means for unifying the public and discrediting domestic adversaries.'[17] Hagan's analysis by implication also offers a convincing explanation as to why Iran might have challenged a much more powerful adversary and thus ignored systemic pressures. While he does not specifically make this point in relation to Khomeini, he notes that sustained efforts at political mobilization may 'result in an overreaction to foreign threats and/or an overextension of the nation's capabilities'.[18] Arguably, Iran's policies resulted not from its position in the international system but from domestic imperatives, the latter dictating an action entirely different to that suggested by the former.

---

[15] Rosenau, 'Pre-Theories and Theories of Foreign Policy', pp. 115–69.
[16] Joe Hagan, 'Domestic Political Explanations in the Analysis of Foreign Policy', in Laura Neack, Jeanne Hey and Patrick Haney (eds.), *Foreign Policy Analysis: Continuity and Change in its Second Generation* (Englewood Cliffs, New Jersey: Prentice Hall, 1995), especially pp. 124, 126 and 133.   [17] Ibid., p. 130.   [18] Ibid., p. 134–5.

On the American side also, there is some evidence that domestic political incentives played a role in the decision-making. In formulating American foreign policy decisions, no president can afford to ignore the effects on domestic political factors such as public opinion, his own popularity ratings, the pressure exerted by the mass media, the opinions and actions of members of Congress or internal societal developments in general. Of particular note under this heading is the fact that Jimmy Carter was due to face a presidential election in November 1980. The fact that the rescue operation occurred only seven months prior to this election seems to many observers to be of great significance. Carter was facing a strong challenge not only from Republican candidate Ronald Reagan but also from his own party in the form of Senator Ted Kennedy, in the Democratic presidential primaries. One also cannot discount the effects of intense pressure from the mass media, and from television in particular. On CBS, Walter Cronkite reprised his post-Tet Offensive Vietnam role during the hostage crisis, keeping up the pressure on Carter to ensure the safe return of the hostages from Tehran. Each night Cronkite would sign off by announcing the number of days the Americans had been held, and at least one of the decision-makers has admitted that this simple action did have some effect upon him.[19] On ABC, Ted Koppel began a nightly show updating the American people on the situation in Tehran, and emotive interviews with the hostages' families on this and other television programmes increased the pressure still further. Carter also faced mounting pressure to do something in Congress, although many feared being seen to oppose the president too strongly. For those running for a presidential party nomination in 1980, however, Carter's handling of Iran proved an almost irresistable issue. Some drew on the lessons of Munich and charged the president with Chamberlain-like 'coddling' of a dictator. Former Texas Governor John Connally, for instance, said not long after the hostages were seized that 'if appeasement were an art form, this Administration would be the Rembrandt of our time'. The United States, he argued, 'can't afford to be kicked around'.[20]

As noted in chapter 1, Carter's approval rating doubled from around 30 per cent to 60 per cent when the hostages were originally taken – almost certainly as a result of the familiar 'rally around the flag' effect – but as the crisis wore on from December to January and then beyond

---

[19] Zbigniew Brzezinski, interview with the author.
[20] Quoted in *Newsweek*, 19 November 1979, p. 10. Connally was at the time one of the contenders for the 1980 Republican presidential nomination.

voters clearly began to question the president's handling of the crisis. By April 1980 Carter's rating had dropped to just 40 per cent and falling, and only 30 per cent approved of his overall foreign policy performance. It is quite plausible, then, that any president would want to do something to stem the tide and to reverse his own flagging electoral fortunes. It is but a short inferential leap to conclude that the rescue mission must have been compelled by the political mathematics these figures imply. One might even make a case that the rescue mission would have gone ahead anyway, even if Entebbe had never happened, because of these potent domestic pressures.[21]

In subsequent years Carter and his key advisers have all argued in interviews and memoirs that this consideration had no influence upon the decision to mount the rescue mission. As Brzezinski notes, for instance, 'there was never any explicit discussion of the relationship between what we might have to do in Iran and domestic politics; neither the President nor his political advisers ever discussed with me the question of whether one or another of our Iranian options would have a better or a worse domestic political effect'.[22] Similarly, Stansfield Turner says that Carter's 'political standing . . . was something we never discussed in the SCC; our recommendations were based on what we considered best for the country, no matter what the domestic political implications might be'.[23] The former president has himself stated subsequently that 'if we could have rescued the hostages in April 1980, I have no doubt that I would have been a hero, that our country would have been gratified, that I would have been reelected President'.[24] Nevertheless, he has always denied that this mental scenario was what led him to launch the mission. At a press conference held shortly after the failure of the rescue attempt, for instance, Carter claimed that 'the political connotations of the holding of our hostages is not a factor for me . . . I see no relationship to this effort that I am continuing with the prospects or lack of prospects of political benefit to me.'[25] In similar vein, former Special Counsel Lloyd Cutler has argued that Carter was

---

[21] I am grateful to Phil Williams for pointing out this possibility to me.
[22] Brzezinski, *Power and Principle*, p. 490.   [23] Turner, *Terrorism and Democracy*, p. 82.
[24] Quoted in Rosenbaum and Ugrinsky, *Jimmy Carter*, p. 468. Interestingly, Hamilton Jordan disagrees with this assessment, arguing that the challenge from Ted Kennedy and the state of the economy would still have led to Carter's defeat, even if the rescue mission had been a great success. See Rosenbaum and Ugrinsky, p. 238.
[25] Quoted in Charles Cogan, 'Not to Offend: Observations on Iran, the Hostages and the Hostage Rescue Mission – Ten Years Later', *Comparative Strategy*, 9: 415–32, 1990, p. 427.

in fact willing to pay a substantial political price in order to free the hostages:

> it is very much to his credit, I think, that he did not do what other presidents might well have done, which would have been to take a very extreme, firm position, a declaration of war, an immediate naval blockade or some such thing. That could have won him the presidency in 1980. I don't have any question in my mind that had that been our response . . . it would have so dominated public attention that he would have won in 1980. And he didn't do that. He didn't do it. Recognize that by not doing it, he was imposing a political penalty on himself.[26]

Brzezinski agrees with this assessment. Interviewed in 1982, he argued that 'I think he would still be president if he was willing to take a position that at stake in the Iranian hostage issue is national honor, national security and not lives . . . and at some point bomb the hell out of Teheran and have the hostages killed.' This, however, is not something Carter was ever prepared to consider, even though he knew full well that by not doing so he would probably lose the White House. 'He wasn't in a curious way political enough' in foreign policy, Brzezinski claims.[27] A similar assurance has come from Turner, who notes that 'while the President and his political advisers must have been extremely conscious of the effect of the crisis on Jimmy Carter's prospects for re-election, I never saw any hint of his placing that consideration above what was in the best interests of the hostages'.[28]

What determined the timing of the rescue mission, these participants insist, was the weather and the time of year in Iran, combined with the exhaustion of Carter's patience. The president's military advisers pointed out that further delay would lessen the hours of darkness available in Iran, thus turning what was already a two-day operation in hostile territory into a three-day one. This, in turn, increased the risk of detection (an argument which is consistent with the obsession about operational security already discussed).

Nevertheless, despite these explicit disavowals, suspicion inevitably remains. It would obviously be unrealistic to claim that the domestic ramifications of various alternatives had no impact whatsoever on the administration's decision-making, and one can always choose to

---

[26] Lloyd Cutler, Miller Center Interviews, Carter Presidency Project, vol. XVIII, 23 October 1982, pp. 22–3, Jimmy Carter Library.
[27] Interview with Zbigniew Brzezinski, Miller Center Interviews, Carter Presidency Project, vol. XV, 18 February 1982, p. 90, Jimmy Carter Library.
[28] Turner, *Terrorism and Democracy*, p. 82.

disbelieve the exhortations of the decision-makers. There are, after all, social taboos on the discussion of domestic politics in foreign policy settings, and one would expect domestic politics to be discussed in places other than the NSC or SCC. In an effort to provide empirical evidence for the domestic motivation theory, Scott Sigmund Gartner has analysed trends in Carter's opinion poll ratings. Arguing that the 'presidential supporters' among the decision-making group – Jody Powell, Hamilton Jordan and Walter Mondale – were in the political ascendant within the administration by early 1980, Gartner finds that 'by looking at the rate of change of the dominant indicator set of the presidential supporters, we are able to explain the timing of the use of force as a domestic political decision. By the end of March, the President's popularity plummeted.'[29]

Gartner's argument that Powell and Jordan were becoming increasingly worried by these falling ratings is quite plausible. However, as usual, the data do not speak for themselves. To move from the undeniable fact that the pace of Carter's decline in popularity increased markedly at the end of March to the conclusion that this was the reason why the hostage rescue was initiated in April requires something of an inferential leap, a problem Gartner is clearly aware of.[30] More telling than the insistence of the Carter people that these sinister considerations were not central to the March and April 1980 decision-making, however, is the simple fact that domestic political considerations do not explain why *the rescue option* should have seemed so appealing to the decision-makers by the early part of 1980, as opposed to other military options that would have made the president 'look tough' and might conceivably have brought the hostages home before the presidential election. Even if one concedes the point that domestic politics may have led to the rescue mission going ahead, there is a further problem with this position from our own perspective. Gartner's argument, it should be noted, is really only about *timing*. He makes no effort to explain the content of the policies chosen. Thus, while various domestic pressures may have encouraged Carter to act in some way, they clearly did not dictate the particular decision reached. As with the external sources argument, the problem is that domestic explanations are usually non-content predictive; in this case, the domestic politics argument is compatible with five of the options discussed by the decision-makers, and fails to offer an account of why political

---

[29] Gartner, 'Predicting the Timing', p. 377.　　[30] Ibid., p. 383.

considerations would compel one choice as opposed to the others. Even if one were to subscribe to the argument that Carter attempted to rescue the hostages in order to save his electoral skin, then, we still lack an explanation of why the rescue operation looked to those around Carter most likely to achieve this end. The domestic politics argument also offers us no explanation as to why Carter waited so long before resorting to the use of force, if doing so would have boosted his chances of re-election. The analogical reasoning perspective, on the other hand, provides an explanation which accounts for both phenomena, without resorting to motivational inferences for which it is well-nigh impossible to find supporting evidence. Moreover, analogical reasoning explanations can in fact incorporate domestic political aspects. Recall that the Entebbe analogy has a domestic political component: it suggests that a rescue operation can not only rescue hostages but also restore the domestic political standing of those who planned and ordered the rescue. The *Pueblo* analogy, on the other hand, implied political *costs*, so there is clearly some sort of connection between the appeal of analogies and their domestic political impacts. We shall return to this point in the following chapter when discussing the relationship between analogizing and domestic politics, but for the moment it will be sufficient to note that domestic considerations are probably best thought of as a complementary, rather than rival, interpretation of what occurred. One should probably think of these domestic pressures as one of several contextual variables that changed the decision-making climate, perhaps changing the balance of power between the two options that had already been considered the 'feasible' ones – negotiation and a rescue mission – and thus helping Brzezinski and the Entebbe image prevail over Vance and his *Pueblo* image.

Bureaucratic politics

Graham Allison's theory of bureaucratic politics – first proposed in his path-breaking *Essence of Decision* and later refined in collaboration with Morton Halperin and then Philip Zelikow – has been widely discussed and commented upon in the literature on foreign policy decision-making.[31] This approach, however, is difficult to apply to Iranian

---

[31] Allison and Zelikow, *Essence of Decision* and Graham Allison and Morton Halperin, 'Bureaucratic Politics: A Paradigm and Some Policy Implications', *World Politics*, 24: 40–79, 1972. The criticisms of Allison's approach are too well known to require further elaboration here, but see, for instance, Stephen Krasner, 'Are Bureaucracies Important?

decision-making in 1979. Designed originally to explain American decision-making, the whole theoretical framework hinges crucially on the existence of well-developed institutions and bureaucratic loyalties. For Allison's Model II (Organizational Process) to account for decision-making, for instance, the state's institutions must have developed long-standing standard operating procedures (SOPs). Model III (Governmental Politics) similarly requires and assumes established organizations capable of socializing their members into their own parochial mind-sets. J. S. Migdal doubts whether one can apply this model to Third World states, which tend to lack these kind of developed bureaucratic structures.[32] Setting this broader question aside, however, it seems clear that the revolutionary conditions of Iran in 1979 do not lend themselves to the underlying preconditions of Allison's models, both of which require a measure of stability within the state that is noticeably absent on the Iranian side. To the extent that any system of authority existed in Iran in November 1979, it was fluid and contingent, and it stemmed from the initially fragile authority of one individual.

If one should not expect the bureaucratic politics model to tell us anything meaningful about Iranian decision-making in 1979, things look a good deal more promising on the American side. Steve Smith has offered an account of the decision to mount the rescue mission which follows the Allisonian model in attributing the policy preferences expressed by the leading players primarily to bureaucratic position. Although he admits to having some doubts about the perspective's applicability to the case, Smith argues that Don Price's famous but

(Or Allison Wonderland)', *Foreign Policy*, 7: 159–79, 1972; Robert Art, 'Bureaucratic Politics and American Foreign Policy: A Critique', *Policy Sciences*, 4: 467–90, 1972; Desmond Ball, 'The Blind Men and the Elephant: A Critique of Bureaucratic Politics', *Australian Outlook*, 28: 71–92, 1974; Amos Perlmutter, 'The Presidential Center and Foreign Policy: A Critique of the Revisionist and Bureaucratic Political Orientations', *World Politics*, 27: 87–106, 1974; Lawrence Freedman, 'Logic, Politics and Foreign Policy Processes: A Critique of the Bureaucratic Politics Model', *International Affairs*, 52: 434–49, 1976; Dan Caldwell, 'Bureaucratic Foreign Policy-Making', *American Behavioral Scientist*, 21: 87–110, 1977; James Nathan and James Oliver, 'Bureaucratic Politics: Academic Windfalls and Intellectual Pitfalls', *Journal of Political and Military Sociology*, 6: 81–91, 1978; David Welch, 'The Organizational Process and Bureaucratic Politics Paradigms', *International Security*, 17: 112–46, 1992; Jonathan Bendor and Thomas Hammond, 'Rethinking Allison's Models', *American Political Science Review*, 86: 301–22, 1992; and Edward Rhodes, 'Do Bureaucratic Politics Matter? Some Disconfirming Findings from the Case of the US Navy', *World Politics*, 47: 1–41, 1994. For summary of some of the classic criticisms that have been directed at Allison's approach, see Steve Smith, 'Allison and the Cuban Missile Crisis: A Review of the Bureaucratic Politics Model of Foreign Policy Decision-Making', *Millenium*, 9: 21–40, 1980.
[32] J. S. Migdal, 'External Structure and Internal Behavior: Explaining Foreign Policies of Third World States', *International Relations*, 4: 510–26, 1974.

rather weather-worn dictum – 'where you stand depends on where you sit'[33] – is able to account for the viewpoints taken by the various participants in the policy debate reasonably well. For instance, he argues that 'the positions adopted by those classified here as "hawks" could have been predicted in advance. What is striking about the evidence is the consistency with which these four men – Brown, Brzezinski, Jones and Turner – proposed policies that reflected their position in the bureaucratic network.'[34] The policy positions adopted by the presidential supporters – Mondale, Powell and Jordan – on the other hand, 'show that their concern was first and foremost with the effect of the crisis on the Carter presidency', and they tended to advocate whatever they saw as being in the president's domestic political interests.[35] Finally, Smith contends that 'the evidence that bureaucratic role determines policy stance is strongest of all in the case of the "doves": Cyrus Vance, the Secretary of State, and Warren Christopher, the Deputy Secretary of State'.[36]

Smith is careful to avoid the unduly restrictive 'hard version' of the bureaucratic politics model, however, recognizing that policy preferences are the result of the interaction between bureaucratic position and beliefs. Clearly, the more strident version gets rather mixed results when applied to the conduct of the crisis as a whole.[37] At first sight there appears to be a correlation between bureaucratic position and the policy preferences of US decision-makers on the hostage issue, particularly when one examines the immediate run-up to the rescue attempt. Yet aside from the undeniable fact that 'correlation is not necessarily causation', even this apparent relationship disappears for Harold Brown and David Jones when one examines their positions during the first months of the crisis. As defence secretary and chairman of the Joint Chiefs respectively, these were the very two men whom the bureaucratic politics model predicts would advocate military measures, and yet they were the *most* vociferous in ruling out such options at the outset. For the bureaucratic politics model to account for his policy preferences, Brown ought not to have been so sceptical about the prospect that military options might succeed in this case, as he was during the early meetings when he pointed out that this was 'no

---

[33] Smith, 'Policy Preferences and Bureaucratic Position'.
[34] Ibid., p. 16.   [35] Ibid., p. 17.   [36] Ibid., p. 18.
[37] For an in-depth examination of these issues, see Smith, 'Policy Preferences and Bureaucratic Position', and Hollis and Smith, 'Roles and Reasons'. Both articles adopt a 'soft' version of the bureaucratic politics approach, in which individual actors matter but where governmental role is a key factor in the shaping of policy attitudes.

Entebbe'. A similar point applies in the case of General Jones, whose hesitancy to mount a rescue operation is difficult to explain without knowing that he had planned a similar mission only four years earlier, which had been judged a monumental failure by many.

Moreover, Secretary Vance's advocacy of restraint and Brzezinski's argument for the use of force seem only tenuously related to their bureaucratic roles. Counterfactual reasoning suggests that where Cyrus Vance stood in this crisis, for instance, is unlikely to have been determined by where he sat. Let us imagine that Vance had been appointed to the post of secretary of defence when Jimmy Carter took office in 1977 instead of that of secretary of state. This is not altogether implausible, since Vance was once deputy secretary of defence under Johnson, and had Hubert Humphrey won the 1968 presidential election, Vance would probably have been offered the top post at the Pentagon. If bureaucratic politics theorists are correct about where policy preferences come from, Vance – if chosen for the defence post – would presumably have been an enthusiastic advocate of the rescue mission in 1980, not an irrevocably determined opponent. Yet it is difficult to imagine a change in Vance's location within the bureaucracy fundamentally altering his position on an issue he cared enough about to resign over. Vance himself cites the personal experiences to which he has been exposed – notably *Pueblo* and Vietnam – as the decisive factor influencing his position on the hostages.[38] Similarly, can one realistically imagine a Secretary of State Brzezinski arguing for negotiation and restraint in the face of provocation? As Smith notes of Brzezinski, 'it is arguable that whatever position he had occupied in Carter's administration, he would have adopted similar views'.[39]

If bureaucratic position does determine where one stands on a given issue, then historical analogies (and cognitions in general) are properly seen as *effects* rather than causes. Vance's pro-negotiation stance during the hostage crisis might have been determined by the fact that he headed the State Department and was consciously or unconsciously defending his own bureaucratic corner, in which case one would then expect him to search around for some analogy or other which would support the State Department's stance on this issue (and which might help impress upon other decision-makers the desirability of a non-belligerent approach to the problem). Decision-makers know that to be

[38] Cyrus Vance, interview with the author.
[39] Smith, 'Policy Preferences and Bureaucratic Position', p. 23; see also Hollis and Smith, 'Roles and Reasons', *passim*.

seen to defend the narrow, parochial interests of one's own organization over and above the 'national interest' – especially during a major
crisis, where such concerns are meant to be held in abeyance – will
delegitimize them in the eyes of their colleagues, so alternative justifications must be found that support the same conclusion, but reach it via
some more socially respectable route.

Conceivably, one could argue that Vance and Brzezinski were both
using their analogies in this manner. However – apart from the doubts
we have already cast upon this possibility – comparison with other case
studies tends to undermine the hard version of 'where you stand' upon
which this counter argument rests, for one can readily cite numerous
examples of cases where role players did not play their roles in the
manner which the axiom suggests. As chairman of the Joint Chiefs
before the Persian Gulf War, for instance, Colin Powell opposed the use
of military force and argued that economic sanctions needed to be given
more time; as secretary of defence, Robert McNamara opposed a surgical airstrike during the Cuban missile crisis and the bombing of North
Vietnam during his last couple of years at the Pentagon; Dean Rusk as
secretary of state consistently favoured the same bombing campaign;
Henry Kissinger as secretary of state favoured the *Mayaguez* rescue
mission; James Baker as secretary of state favoured US military involvement in the Persian Gulf; after the Beirut bombing of 1984, it was
Secretary of State Shultz who argued for military retaliation and Defence Secretary Weinberger who argued against; in 1988 Secretary
Shultz backed military action against Manuel Noriega in Panama,
while Defence Secretary Frank Carlucci and JCS chairman William
Crowe opposed it. Time and again, the deterministic approach fails to
predict or account for where the participants stand.

Recently, more systematic evidence has emerged which appears to
hammer the final nail in the coffin of this approach. Unlike most of the
critics – who have tended to focus on the theoretical shortcomings of the
bureaucratic politics approach – Edward Rhodes sets out to test 'where
you stand' empirically, and finds little support for it. What makes his
analysis so compelling and his findings of special interest, however, is
his choice of case study: Rhodes examines naval procurement and
budget issues – precisely the area where critics and advocates alike had
expected to find the model's insights most valid[40] – and finds very little

---

[40] See for instance Jervis, *Perception and Misperception in International Politics*, p. 26.
Analysts other than Allison have also posited that we are most likely to see bureaucratic politics at play on these kinds of issues; see, for example, Jerel Rosati, 'Develop-

relationship between parochial self-interests and policy preferences among the players involved in policy-making on these matters. He concludes that other factors – especially the belief systems of the deci-sion-makers – are probably more important than bureaucratic position, echoing the theoretical criticisms made by Stephen Krasner and Robert Art shortly after *Essence of Decision* was published. 'The findings from this case give us considerable reason for skepticism about any general-ized claims that bureaucratic politics are critical in shaping state behav-ior', he states.[41]

The evidence gleaned from this re-examination of the hostage crisis suggests that personal experiences stemming directly from the individ-ual play a much more potent role in decision-making than 'pure' versions of the organizational or bureaucratic politics perspectives would suggest. Moreover, once one loosens the assumption that posi-tion determines policy attitudes, the bureaucratic politics framework loses much of its explanatory and predictive value, and one is then forced to rely a great deal more upon individual, cognitive level vari-ables of the kind which have been emphasized here. Unlike the rational actor model, the bureaucratic politics approach at least offers us a theory of why given actors propose the policy positions they do and of who is likely to propose what position. However, both perspectives share a common failing, in the sense that, as Robert Axelrod has noted, neither provides any clear account of 'how the consequences of alterna-tives are estimated'.[42] And the analogical reasoning model, of course, provides just such an account, by linking perceived probabilities to past experiences.

If overall the argument that the positions of the doves and hawks were mainly attributable to bureaucratic position in the Iran case is open to question, one must take care to note those elements of the approach which *do* seem worth salvaging. Arguably, there is one element of the bureaucratic politics model that functions much better than the others: the notion that presidential supporters consistently look out for the president's interests. The evidence does suggest quite strongly that Hamilton Jordan and Jody Powell behaved throughout the crisis in the manner predicted by the bureaucratic politics approach, in the sense that they consistently appeared to put the interests and concerns of the White House first.

ing a Systematic Decision-Making Framework', *World Politics*, 33: 234–51, 1981.
[41] Rhodes, 'Do Bureaucratic Politics Matter?', p. 40.
[42] Axelrod, 'Argumentation in Foreign Policy Settings', p. 728.

Jordan always seems to have viewed his role in this way during his time in the Carter administration. He notes, for instance, that at foreign policy meetings 'I would try to raise political objections, problems and concerns with Vance, Brzezinksi and the President as they talked about how they were going to change the world', something he did of course when Vance suggested 'waiting it out' on the hostage issue.[43] Thus this kind of bureaucratic position may play a more significant part in shaping foreign policy decisions, since it involves a job description or role which is rather more simplified and sharply circumscribed than others. It is of course left to the presidential supporter to decide what is to constitute a defence of the president's interests, so that bureaucratic position may not exert as much predictive power in determining preferences as initial appearances might suggest. Yet being a presidential supporter does appear to exert great influence upon receptivity to the arguments of others. More needs to be said on this point, and we will expand upon it in the final chapter.

Victims of groupthink?

There is some evidence that the Carter decision-makers may well have been prey to 'groupthink' as they went about the process of deciding to launch the hostage rescue mission. Irving Janis (the originator of the theory), Steve Smith and Betty Glad have all suggested that the groupthink approach may have some relevance here.[44] Stated briefly, this approach suggests that we may divide most decision-making processes into one of two categories: *vigilant* decision-making (which corresponds rather closely to the rational actor model) and *groupthink*. The latter refers to a tendency which occurs in some groups to reach premature consensus without having fully thought through the complete range of available options or their implications. According to Janis, the groupthink effect typically occurs where opinionated leaders, the pressure to maintain unanimity and the exclusion of outside advice combine to ensure that options are not fully or rationally appraised. A number of symptoms, he argues, aid identification of, and are typically present in cases of, the groupthink syndrome. Chief among these are the exclusion of dissent, the emergence of 'mindguards' who police the decision-

[43] The quote is from Hamilton Jordan, Miller Center Interview, Jimmy Carter Library, p. 53.
[44] See Janis, *Groupthink*, pp. 180–2; Smith, 'Groupthink and the Hostage Rescue Mission'; Glad, 'Personality, Political and Group Process Variables', especially pp. 49–53.

making process, a belief in the inherent morality of the group and a belief in the group's invulnerability.[45] According to Steve Smith, there is a strong *prima facie* case to be made that the decision to launch the rescue mission derived, at least in part, from groupthink. First of all, he argues that 'those who made the decisions did not critically evaluate the probability of success. The mission was an extremely risky one, and because those who made the decisions wanted a rescue attempt to go ahead, they did not look at the very obvious weak points in the plan.'[46] There is evidence that the group shared an illusion of invulnerability which led it to take reckless risks, that it viewed itself as inherently moral and that dissent was internally suppressed. Smith also finds compelling evidence both that dissenters from the majority view were excluded from the group and that what Janis calls 'self-appointed mindguards' emerged to bolster the decision to go ahead with the military rescue. With respect to the exclusion of dissenting advice, Smith notes that this decision was initially taken while Cyrus Vance – known to disagree with the notion of launching the operation – was on vacation in Florida. He infers from this that Carter used Vance's absence as a kind of window of opportunity, as a chance to push ahead knowing that no one else would speak out against the decision. Given the opportunity to express his doubts about the decision upon his return, no one spoke up to support Vance. Moreover, once the secretary of state had tendered his resignation, it became easy for the other group members to write him off as 'someone who wanted to resign anyway', thus rationalizing and downplaying the substantive nature of his dissent. As Janis noted in a newspaper article published shortly after the failure of the rescue mission, 'one cannot help but wonder whether the way Cyrus R. Vance was treated was an instance of just such a symptom [of groupthink]'.[47] Smith also implies that Stansfield Turner acted as a 'mindguard' by suppressing a long-infamous March 1980 CIA report (alluded to in chapter 1), which suggested that 60 per cent of the hostages would lose their lives if the mission went ahead. Smith quite rightly notes that 'there is no record of Turner raising this report at any of the meetings'.[48]

The strongest part of the groupthink case as applied to Iran is unquestionably the exclusion of Vance, and the tendency to write him off

---

[45] These features are alluded to at various points in Janis's book, but see for instance *Groupthink*, pp. 174–5.   [46] Smith, ibid., p. 118.
[47] See Irving Janis, 'In Rescue Planning, How Did Carter Handle Stress?', *New York Times*, 18 May 1980.   [48] Smith, 'Group Think', p. 122.

is highly reminiscent of the way Lyndon Johnson is said to have treated Vance's former boss Robert McNamara over Vietnam. As Betty Glad has noted, highly consistent with the groupthink hypothesis in the Iran case is the fact that 'Vance's views were dealt with by deprecating Vance – a man most other observers would describe as unusually mature in his ability to hold firmly to positions he felt right. At this time, however, Jordan saw him as a pathetic figure – alone, isolated – his eyes begging for support. The President saw him as emotionally over-wrought.' Brzezinski, on the other hand, saw Vance as 'traumatized'.[49] Thus, two processes are argued to have gone on, which in combination had the effect of undermining Vance's message, one a presumably conscious attempt to take advantage of his physical absence, the other a presumably unconscious attempt to downplay his advice.

The evidence that other decision-makers 'deprecated' Vance is clear and unquestionable. The evidence that Vance was deliberately excluded, however, is more open to interpretation, for others have viewed Carter's behaviour in a less sinister way. James David Barber, for instance, implies that the fact that Vance was away on 11 April – the day Carter decided to launch the mission – was coincidental, since only the day before 'Carter noted in his diary that Iranian terrorists were threatening to kill the hostages if Iraq – in their eyes an American puppet – attacked Iran.'[50] It was the existence of this threat (whether real or imagined) which led Carter to decide in Vance's absence, Barber implies, rather than an attempt to keep the major dissenter out of the loop. One can counter, probably with some justification, that this was an instance of rationalizing after the fact on Carter's part. It is certainly astonishing that a president would make a decision of such import in the absence of his secretary of state, and it left Vance with little option but to resign. There are also, however, a number of problems with applying the groupthink approach here, aside from the various methodological and theoretical criticisms which have long been targeted at Janis's work. Among these is the fact that it took the Carter decision-makers five and a half months to reach the decision to launch the mission. Groupthink is typically associated with 'hasty' decision-making. It is difficult to make the case that the decision-making group reached a premature consensus in this case, given that they deliberated over the rescue option for so long before deciding that it was viable.

This quibble is far from decisive, since the evidence does suggest that

---

[49] Glad, 'Personality', p. 51. [50] Barber, *The Presidential Character*, p. 455.

the rescue operation was insufficiently thought out even after several months of consideration. Another problem of possibly more import is that the evidence that decision-makers engaged in self-censorship on the rescue mission, or that anyone acted as a mindguard, is rather patchy. Militating against the notion that Turner might have acted to insulate others from information they should have had access to is the fact that – operating in the shadow of Watergate and the revelations of past wrongdoing – the CIA did not play an advocacy role during the Carter years. It is therefore unlikely that Turner would have been able to strongly defend the wisdom of the rescue mission against dissenters in the way that Janis's mindguard function predicts. In its classic form, this role involves 'putting social pressure on any member who begins to express a view that deviates from the dominant beliefs of the group, to make sure that he will not disrupt the consensus of the group as a whole', according to Janis.[51] But if Turner exerted pressure on others to go along with the rescue plan, it must have been far more subtle than this.

As Smith suggests, there is a real possibility that in not passing on the March 1980 CIA report – allegedly critical of the rescue mission – Stansfield Turner might have been playing just this kind of subtle role. However, in recent years, Turner has defended his role in discounting the report and accounted for his decision not to draw it to the attention of the other decision-makers in a way that arguably makes sense, and which seems to rule out the possibility that he was consciously or unconsciously preventing the opinions of a doubting subordinate within the CIA from being heard. As noted in chapter 1, Turner said in an interview in 1994 that the still classified report examined 'a social scientific theory' which when applied to the hostage mission case suggested that the attempt had a high probability of failure. Turner recalls that the report concluded that 'this is not something on which you should make a decision', and he states that he therefore considered it of little significance.[52] Turner adds that 'the whole thing could be cleared up by having the report declassified', something which he favours.[53] Similarly, Frank Carlucci – at that time, Turner's deputy – says that he has 'a vague recollection of some report on potential

---

[51] Janis, *Groupthink*, p. 40.
[52] Stansfield Turner, interview with the author. It is not yet known to which 'social scientific theory' the report referred, but it sounds very much like a rational choice model. Some contemporaneous press reports around the same time mentioned mathematical predictions based on Martin Shubik's *The War Game*, so this may be the source used in the report.   [53] Ibid.

casualties based on assumptions that most people questioned'.[54] Just as Janis, Smith and Glad see evidence of groupthink in this instance, so Philip Tetlock and Rose McDermott see little or none. A study by Tetlock and his colleagues found scant evidence of groupthink in this case.[55] Using the GDQS method – designed to reach an intersubjective assessment of the nature of group characteristics by going beyond the case study method – Tetlock and his colleagues conclude that the Iran case comes closer to the characteristics of vigilance than of groupthink. For Janis, in a case of groupthink 'members' strivings for unanimity override their motivation to realistically appraise alternative courses of action', but McDermott argues that 'this clearly didn't happen in the Carter administration, as evidenced by the drastic differences in opinions espoused by Vance and Brzezinski, among others'.[56] She traces this to the differing world-views and personalities of the two men. While not necessarily definitive – one can always dispute the grounds on which they reached their conclusion, and McDermott's point is possibly moot since by March 1980 there was unanimity among Carter's advisers, with the exception again of Vance – the Tetlock analysis and McDermott's view about divisions within the Carter administration do show that the question of whether groupthink is present in the case is not as cut and dried as it might first appear. It is also unclear how many conditions or symptoms of the phenomenon need to be present before groupthink can be reliably diagnosed. This is a particular problem in this instance because the evidence suggests that some signs of groupthink (like the exclusion of dissent) are present, while other symptoms (presence of mindguards, opinionated leadership) do not appear to be.

It is also difficult to tell whether the mistakes that Smith alludes to resulted from what were specifically *group* processes, or whether these were merely the outcome of psychological misperceptions at the individual level. Drawing upon the findings of the Holloway report, Smith shows quite convincingly that Carter and his associates engaged in a strong element of wishful thinking on the rescue mission issue. But wishful thinking can also be induced by analogy – in this case, we have argued, by the tempting mental image of 'another Entebbe' – so the

[54] Carlucci, ibid.
[55] Philip Tetlock, Randall Peterson, Charles McGuire, Shi-jie Chang and Peter Feld, 'Assessing Political Group Dynamics: A Test of the Groupthink Model', *Journal of Personality and Social Psychology*, 63: 403–25, 1992.
[56] McDermott, 'Prospect Theory in International Relations', p. 252, fn.4.

question becomes: was this caused by group processes or by individual level processes?

Both were no doubt present to some degree. Again, however, one should not necessarily see groupthink and analogical reasoning as rival forms of explanation; analogical reasoning is a theory which aims to explain policy *content*, while groupthink is a theory of *process*. Thus each theory is strong where the other is weak. On balance, however, analogical reasoning is arguably more useful to us here because, again, it is the content of policy we are interested in. Groupthink has little or nothing to say about why one option is chosen rather than another, but examines rather what happens to the policy process once a given option has been arrived at. Moreover, relative to the analogical reasoning perspective this explanation suffers from a similar problem to the domestic politics account. It can probably only account for one (albeit very important) aspect of the decision-making, the decision to launch the ill-fated rescue mission.

A rational decison?

Another (apparently rival) approach is provided by the more traditional rational actor model favoured by many analysts of international relations. In the hostage case, supporters of that model might contend that the decisions to negotiate and then to mount a rescue mission were 'rational' in the sense that all feasible options were considered and the merits of each fully and comprehensively weighed. Negotiation, this approach might point out, was chosen initially because it was the only alternative that could conceivably release the hostages, or because it achieved the benefit sought at the least cost. The rescue mission option – the only other alternative judged likely to result in the release of the hostages – was chosen when, and only when, it actually became feasible, and when a reasonable 'cost-benefit' analysis suggested that it had more chance of gaining the hostages' release than did continued negotiation. One can also easily construct similar explanations for the ayatollah's decision to back the students' actions and for the embassy seizure itself.

This account contains a number of undeniable truths, but it tells the story in a way that glosses over the role played by the decision-makers' rival perceptions of their environment and how they came to have the preferences they did. Centring on these two options was a subjective process, in which the negotiation and rescue operation options became the only two alternatives viewed as likely to result in the hostages' release. Perceptual processes can be, and frequently are, incorporated within the rational choice perspective. What that approach fails to account for, however, is *why* the decision-makers came to view these two as the feasible options, and why the costs associated with these were considered relatively lower than those of the rival alternatives. Again, as noted above, of particular interest in this regard is the fact that these were the only two alternatives for which there were available historical analogies. By offering no answer to the question of what determined the content of the decisions reached, the rational actor approach in effect provides us with only a superficial account of what occurred as opposed to the analytical explanation we are looking for. In short, this approach is not really an *alternative* to the cognitive model proposed here, since it is concerned with different decision-making phenomena; while the former takes actors' preferences as given, the latter seeks to uncover the sources of these preferences. Debating whether the decisions to seize the embassy or to negotiate and then proceed with a rescue mission were 'rational' also seems like something of a philosophical dead end, since proponents on each side of the rationality/bounded rationality debate can make a reasoned case.

Personality

As a further 'rival' class of interpretations, one can ask whether *other* individual level variables can account as well or better for the decisions reached. One traditional (if long controversial) form of individual level explanation centres on personality traits.[57] In the Iran case, Betty Glad has proposed that Jimmy Carter's personality – and in particular what she terms his 'ego-defensive' traits – caused him to act rashly in proposing the hostage rescue mission. Though she does see positive aspects to his personality, Glad argues that Carter dramatically 'overplayed' the situation. His 'narcissistic, expansionist personality structure' led him to become obsessed by the hostage issue, elevating it to a point where it became self-defeating.[58] He launched the rescue mission, she suggests, in large part because he was a 'risk taker' who flirted with danger, arguing that 'expansionist types, with their seemingly boundless self-confidence, are apt to take risks, where others fear to tread'.

---

[57] For a classic example, see Alexander George and Juliette George, *Woodrow Wilson and Colonel House: A Personality Study* (New York: Dover, 1964).

[58] Glad, 'Personality, Political and Group Process Variables', p. 54.

Carter also exhibited a 'self-defeating self-centeredness'.[59] Where Smith traces the failure to fully consider the defects inherent in the rescue mission to groupthink, for Glad this failing derived rather more from flaws in Carter himself. 'The processes he set up for planning the rescue operation . . . almost guaranteed that vulnerabilities in the operation would not be seriously explored. Certain problems that might have been discovered were not corrected and the decision was made without a clear understanding of the risks it entailed . . . Carter's personal interests and distinctive style and personality led to these results', she concludes.[60]

Glad's analysis is not exclusively individual level – she looks at the part played by the external constraints of the situation itself and the domestic political and constitutional dynamics, as well as the role of group level factors – but at its root the argument strongly implies that the decision to mount the rescue mission was primarily related to Carter's personality, and that a different personality might have led to different policy choices and a different reaction to the external and domestic constraints identified. In a similar kind of analysis that reaches a rather different conclusion, James David Barber argues that Carter's handling of the hostage crisis issue was essentially a success, and attributes this to what he sees as the strength of the president's personality. 'The Carter character was, I think, severely tested by the Iranian hostage crisis and not found wanting . . . Unlike Wilson, Hoover, Johnson and Nixon, this President did not freeze onto some disastrous line of policy and ride it to the end. Rather he kept his head, kept his mind open, flexibly and energetically pursuing some way out of an apparently success-proof situation.' While Barber admits that Carter made mistakes, he argues that 'he could have done a great deal worse'. All in all, he claims, Carter had the best kind of personality for the job of president: he was an 'active-positive', someone who both works hard in the Oval Office and derives positive enjoyment from the role.[61]

The divergence between Barber and Glad on the essential nature of Carter's personality traits illustrates the obvious operationalization problems which these kind of explanations inevitably imply. Carter is a complex individual, and it is relatively easy to find sides of his personality which appear to explain a given policy outcome. Another diffi-

---

[59] Ibid., p. 55.   [60] Ibid., p. 58.
[61] Barber, *The Presidential Character*, pp. 456–7. Barber's objectivity in so describing Jimmy Carter might be called into question, since as a presidential candidate the latter had publicly praised and admired Barber's book.

culty relates to the same point made earlier about groupthink. Personality explanations arguably best account for policy processes, rather than policy content; they explain the 'how' but not the 'what'. While such factors obviously play some role in decision-making, it is difficult to show how one moves from a particular personality type to a particular policy decision, while it is a relatively easy matter to show the correlation between the lessons drawn from events and the policy positions proposed. Again, the problem is not that personality explanations are necessarily wrong, but that they throw relatively little light upon the puzzles we are interested in answering.

Belief system approaches

Probably more persuasive than the simple personality perspective is the notion that simple belief system approaches can explain the decisions taken during the hostage crisis, so that one presumably need not examine the historical analogies employed in order to arrive at a reasonable theoretical account of events.[62] As suggested in chapter 1, Jimmy Carter's moral idealist belief system proved a poor predictor of his decision to launch the rescue mission, which would almost certainly have led to more casualties than actually occurred had the mission not been aborted at an early stage. Nevertheless, Carter's actions early in the crisis – especially the decision to negotiate – are quite compatible with these beliefs. Furthermore, a strong argument can be made that Vance and Brzezinski would respectively have opposed and favoured the rescue mission, even in the absence of the *Pueblo* and Entebbe precedents, because their ideological world-views or belief systems predisposed them towards such positions. At the house of Shimon Peres, Brzezinski proposed that the Israelis 'storm the damn airport terminal' even before the Entebbe raid took place, and before the success of that operation became clear. His 'hawkish' world-view successfully predicts that he will adopt this position. And we know that Vance was opposed to *any* use of military force to resolve the crisis. His 'doveish' world view accurately predicts that he will take this position. Many of the Iran hostage decision-makers also describe Vance's

---

[62] For prominent efforts to use belief system explanations to account for foreign policy behaviour, see for instance, Holsti, 'The Belief System and National Images'; George, 'The "Operational Code"; and Stephen Walker, 'The Interface Between Beliefs and Behaviour: Henry Kissinger's Operational Code and the Vietnam War', *Journal of Conflict Resolution*, 21: 129–68, 1977.

opposition to the rescue mission in these terms; as several of them have pointed out in interviews, Vance was deeply opposed to the use of force, and knowledge of this perspective simply and accurately predicts that he will therefore oppose a military rescue mission (which implies at least the risk of the loss of human life). As Brzezinski put it, 'the key point about Vance's attitude, and this is what angered Carter, is that he was against it [the rescue mission] irrespective of whether we succeed or fail . . . he was against the use of force'.[63]

These propositions are undeniably true. Indeed, it can readily be conceded that *Pueblo* and Entebbe possibly only reinforced the views which Vance and Brzezinski already possessed, for a very simple reason: analogical and belief system variable explanations are probably highly complementary and interrelated forms of explanation. Return for a moment to our earlier discussion of schemas and their relationship to historical analogies, outlined in chapter 2. There, it will be recalled, it was noted that for many cognitive psychologists, analogies (and the lessons drawn from them) constitute the elemental 'building blocks' of more generalized beliefs and ideologies. Robert Abelson, for instance, has distinguished between what he calls 'episodic' and 'categorical' scripts. The former refers to a sequence of events specific to a particular experience, while the latter is composed of the general lesson derived from having gone through a number of similar experiences. To take one example, Vance's perceived histories of the *Pueblo* and Angus Ward crises might be stored in episodic form, and his perceived lesson – 'negotiate/wait it out in a hostage crisis' – in categorical form.[64] Analogies in this definitional scheme could be seen as a form of episodic script, while beliefs would represent a variant of the categorical type. Or, as some psychologists would prefer to put it, reasoning from a single case (or perhaps two) is analogical reasoning, whereas a generalized rule derived from a range of cases constitutes a 'schema'.[65]

Why not simply examine the ideological world-views of Vance and Brzezinski then, and employ this as our primary explanatory variable? This would have the advantage of parsimony on its side, and it would seem sufficient to explain what was going on in the Carter administration. For some limited purposes, such an approach probably is suffi-

---

[63] Zbigniew Brzezinski, interview with the author.
[64] Robert Abelson, 'Script Processing in Attitude Formation and Decision-Making', in John Carroll and John Payne (eds.), *Cognition and Social Behavior* (Hillsdale, New Jersey: Lawrence Erlbaum, 1976); Larson, *Origins of Containment*, pp. 50–7.
[65] On this point, see also Khong, *Analogies at War*, pp. 25–6.

cient. However, such an approach is hard to square with Carter's decision to use military force to get the hostages back, as we have seen. Moreover, while the belief systems variable can predict – and predict quite accurately – that Vance will oppose the use of military force and Brzezinski will support it, this is practically *all* that it can tell us. Only the analogies they draw upon, on the other hand, can provide the kind of detail which is necessary to explain how they define the nature of the hostage crisis, what kind of policy responses they will favour, how long they are prepared to wait until they see the desired results, and so on. Knowing that Brzezinski is a hawk, for instance, tells us that he will probably advocate a military solution of some sort, but it does not tell us which of the wide array of military options discussed within the Carter administration he is likely to favour; the Entebbe analogy, on the other hand, clearly can do this. In Vance's case, on the other hand, knowing that the secretary of state was opposed to the use of force to resolve international disputes merely tells us that he will oppose military solutions in this situation, but it cannot tell us what form his preferred response will take, why he was prepared to wait so long to get the hostages back, and so on. And since these are precisely the kind of details we require in order to understand why decision-makers spoke and acted as they did, the analogical reasoning approach is arguably quite justified in this context. In short, analogies and lessons are the elements of the belief system which provide definitions of situations, detailed policy recommendations and expectations of how events will turn out before they actually occur.

Closer examination, then, reveals that one should view analogies and belief systems not as rival forms of explanation, but as closely allied and related ways of understanding policy thinking. Because analogies play a key role in schema formation, they in effect provide the constituting elements of belief systems. Past experiences appear to retain a specific identity within belief systems, however, and seem to exercise an independent effect on the reasoning of policy-makers. What analogies do, in effect, is to provide the detail which overall ideological positions leave out; while these general positions determine the broad category of response which the policy-maker will advocate in a given instance – for example, 'use force' versus 'use pacific measures' – this is all they do. Analogical reasoning, on the other hand, tends to determine the specific option(s) selected by the policy-maker. It is therefore arguably essential to study analogies if one wishes to explain political thinking and eventual decisions. Of course, it can be argued that analogies just 'fill in the details' left out by world-views. My contention here, however, is that analogies *are* belief systems: events are used to form generalized schemas or rules – 'always negotiate with your enemies', 'use gunboat diplomacy' and so on – but those events are not forgotten. Instead, these specific experiences or analogies tend to be recalled along with the generalized rule, and the analogy which is recalled will depend on the situation it most closely resembles in the eyes of the decision-maker.

Prospect theory

As a final alternative explanation – albeit one which is partially related to the kind of analysis offered in this book – let us consider the application of what psychologists term 'prospect theory' to the Iran case. In essence, prospect theory – developed in the late 1970s by Kahneman and Tversky – suggests that the manner in which a problem is formulated and perceived can have a decisive impact on the attractiveness of various options.[66] As the authors of the theory put it, 'prospect theory distinguishes two phases in the choice process: an early phase of editing and a subsequent phase of evaluation. The editing phase consists of a preliminary analysis of the offered prospects . . . in the second phase, the edited prospects are evaluated and the prospect of highest value is chosen.'[67] The theory revolves around a dichotomy – risk *aversion* versus risk *acceptance* – and suggests that individuals will be risk averse (that is, will avoid risky options) when dealing with gains, but they will be risk accepting or seeking when dealing with losses. As Robert Jervis puts it, 'people are loss-averse in the sense that losses loom larger than the corresponding gains. Losing ten dollars, for example, annoys us more than gaining ten dollars gratifies us . . . more than the hope of gains, the specter of losses activates, energizes and drives actors, producing great (and often misguided) efforts that risk – and frequently lead to – greater losses.'[68]

Rose McDermott has applied prospect theory to the decision to mount the hostage rescue mission. She argues in essence that Carter was operating in a domain of loss by March 1980, which made him risk acceptant. His personal popularity was declining, he had just lost two presidential primaries to Senator Edward Kennedy and negotiations

---

[66] Daniel Kahneman and Amos Tversky, 'Prospect Theory: An Analysis of Decision Under Risk', *Econometrica*, 47: 263–91, 1979.   [67] Ibid., p. 274.

[68] Robert Jervis, 'Political Implications of Loss Aversion', *Political Psychology*, 13: 187–204, 1992, p. 187.

seemed to have run aground by early April. 'By the time of the rescue mission', she contends, 'Carter was a leader ready to take a gamble to return things to the status quo, with the hostages safely at home, national pride and international honor restored, and his political fortunes turned upward . . . in terms of prospect theory, he was a man operating in the domain of losses.'[69]

Prospect theory is obviously difficult to test in major foreign policy cases such as the one under discussion, because whether a decision-maker believes himself or herself to be operating in a domain of loss or gain is an entirely subjective process; as McDermott admits, we cannot know for sure in any given instance whether gain or loss was what was perceived, but must infer this from the available information. We must also infer from the information available in a given case how risky a decision-maker perceived the various choices to have been. McDermott argues that we can do both these things in this case, since it seems fairly apparent that Carter saw himself operating in a domain of loss by March 1980 and that he saw the rescue mission as the riskiest of the options available. Jack Levy, however, has cast doubt upon the validity of the latter claim, since he contends that it is not clear 'that Carter, given his high estimates of success of a rescue mission, perceived that a rescue mission involved more risks than did allowing the hostage crisis to continue, with all of its unpredictable consequences for his own upcoming reelection campaign as well as for the image and influence of the United States in the world'.[70] Alternatively, from Glad's perspective it was Carter's more or less permanent character or personality traits which led him to be a 'risk taker' during the hostage crisis, rather than the characteristics of the specific situation he faced.[71]

Even if one disputes these two points, the underlying theory itself may also be open to question as applied to political decision-making; while it might seem to be merely stating a truism – surely it is no more than common sense that leaders are more likely to act recklessly when they are incurring major losses – the real difficulty is probably just the opposite. It may be, in other words, that the perception of loss does *not* automatically lead to risk taking in complex, real world decision-making. If we apply the theory to the Cuban missile crisis, one can infer

[69] McDermott, 'Prospect Theory in International Relations', pp. 241–2.
[70] Jack Levy, 'Prospect Theory and International Relations: Theoretical Applications and Analytical Problems', *Political Psychology*, 13: 283–310, 1992, p. 302; see also Eldar Shafir, 'Prospect Theory and Political Analysis: A Psychological Perspective', *Political Psychology*, 13: 311–22, 1992, pp. 315–16.
[71] Glad, 'Personality, Political and Group Process Variables', p. 55.

that John Kennedy was almost certainly operating in the domain of loss by October 1962, both domestically and internationally. There was a congressional election coming up, Republicans like Kenneth Keating were hammering him on the missile issue, Kennedy had looked 'weak' in his confrontations with Khrushchev and needed a political victory, and the discovery of the missiles had been a slap in the face on the international stage (and might even, according to some of his advisers, have altered the overall military balance of power between the super-powers). And yet, out of the available options, Kennedy chose what was arguably the *least* risky: the naval blockade. The most risky option – which would also deliver the greatest payoffs if successful – was probably the airstrike. If it had worked it would at a stroke have removed the missiles, demonstrated international resolve and silenced Kennedy's Republican critics, but if it had failed it might have started World War III. This suggests at least the possibility that in political decision-making the notion that risk aversion equates with loss and risk acceptance with gain may be too simplistic. As Smyth *et al.* note, 'wider factors such as perceived desirability within the culture can remove both the standard preference for risk aversion with positive framing and risk seeking with negative framing',[72] and some research in cognitive psychology has suggested that prospect theory is in need of modification.[73] Cognitive and cultural factors may conceivably account in part for the rejection of the airstrike option – Robert Kennedy's argument that this would not be 'in America's traditions' and his use of the Pearl Harbor analogy come to mind here – but the Cuban case does seem to illustrate the complexity of decision processes and their resistance to simplifying theoretical constructs.

Nevertheless, there is a part of McDermott's argument which is logically separable from the rest. Although Kahneman and Teversky's original 1979 article makes no mention of analogical reasoning, McDermott also draws attention to a number of the historical analogies used by the Carter decision-makers, and argues that these had a critical effect upon the solutions which different advisers advocated. For instance, she notes that Cyrus Vance drew heavily upon the *Pueblo* and Angus

[72] See Mary Smyth *et al.*, *Cognition in Action* (Hillsdale, New Jersey: Lawrence Erlbaum, 1994), p. 379.
[73] See for example S. L. Schneider, 'Framing and Conflict: Aspiration Level Contingency, the Status Quo and Current Theories of Risky Choice', *Journal of Experimental Psychology: Learning, Memory and Cognition*, 18: 1040–57, 1992; J. G. March and Z. Shapiro, 'Variable Risk Preferences and the Focus of Attention', *Psychological Review*, 99: 172–83, 1992.

Ward analogies, and that for Zbigniew Brzezinski Entebbe and the Bay of Pigs analogies were more attractive. While there is no discussion of the other analogies which affected decision-making prior to the decision to go ahead with the mission – such as *Mayaguez*, Son Tay, the Perot rescue, the February analogy or the 1953 analogy among the Iranian students – this section of her analysis is similar to the one provided in this book. McDermott convincingly shows that the various participants offered competing analogies, and her discussion, again pre-empting this one, suggests that Entebbe had a particular effect on the decision-makers. In this respect, McDermott's argument is not a rival explanation at all, but a highly compatible – and, from the author's own perspective, perceptive – one. What it also suggests is that the Entebbe analogy itself, and the belief among the rescue planners that they had overcome the differences between Tehran and Entebbe, may offer sufficient explanation of the decision to go ahead with the rescue mission. Perhaps we do not really need to muddy the analytical waters by attempting to ascertain what a given decision-maker considered the 'status quo' to be at a given point, or to speculate on whether that individual perceived himself or herself to be operating in a domain of losses or gains, especially since prospect theory seems to work in some political decision-making cases and not others.[74] We also require some explanation as to why Carter and Brzezinksi overestimated the chances that the mission would succeed and underestimated the risks involved. The presence of Entebbe and Mogadishu as recent but statistically unrepresentative events can, as we have argued, account for these errors.

Analogical 'versus' other explanations

It is worth recalling that most if not all of the existing theories analysed here seek only to explain the Iran hostage rescue mission. As a result, it is not clear to what extent they can account for the decision-making in the almost six months which preceded this. In seeking to explain the decision-making *in toto*, we obviously require an account that can explain why the negotiation track was selected initially and why key

---

[74] For assessments of the strengths and shortcomings of prospect theory generally, see Jervis, 'Political Implications of Loss Aversion', Levy, 'Prospect Theory and International Relations' and Shafir, 'Prospect Theory and Political Analysis'. The McDermott, Jervis, Levy and Shafir articles are all part of a special edition of *Political Psychology* devoted to prospect theory.

decision-makers such as Vance were prepared to wait it out for so long before resorting to military action. We also need an explanation as to why the rescue operation was viewed as the only real alternative to negotiation, once the latter avenue had been closed off in the eyes of many of the decision-makers. Stated differently, in order to explain 'why choice X and not Y', we need a theory that explains and predicts policy content, rather than merely the pressures and circumstances which encouraged the Carter administration to change its policy in some way.

By the same token, there are aspects of the decision-making which an approach like the analogical reasoning one cannot account for. Moving through various other explanations for the hostage decision-making helps us refine our sense of where the analogical reasoning perspective stands in relation to other theoretical constructs. It also gives us a sense of what that perspective can and cannot do for us in terms of explanatory mileage. Part of the confusion in viewing the foregoing accounts as 'rival' explanations arguably lies in the fact that each is targeting a subtly different dependent variable, which is obscured if we think of the latter simply as 'the decision'. In practice, we can disaggregate that concept into at least four separate but related variables: *context, process, timing* and *content*. If we are interested in explaining the context which gives rise to decision-making rather than policy content, then structural and domestic politics explanations seem to provide a good account. The timing of the rescue mission seems to be especially well 'explained' by domestic political explanations, and the analogical reasoning, personality, bureaucratic politics and groupthink approaches have a corresponding difficulty accounting for this aspect. On the other hand, if we are interested in the process by which decisions get made rather than primarily the content of those decisions, the groupthink and personality theories look convincing. However, if we are interested in why X was chosen and not Y, then cognitive explanations like analogical reasoning and belief system approaches seem indispensable to the account. In short, then, the appropriateness of the choice of theoretical framework seems to vary according to which of the four aspects (or dependent variables) one is primarily interested in. What this also implies is that the analogical reasoning approach is not necessarily at all incompatible with other theoretical perspectives.

The hostage crisis has generated a wider range of theoretical explanations than perhaps any other case study in the analysis of American foreign policy, with the possible exception of the Cuban missile crisis.

One especially remarkable feature of these accounts is that several of them simultaneously incorporate explanations lying at different (and some might claim, competing) levels of analysis. Most explicitly, Betty Glad argues that structural, domestic and individual level factors all contributed actively to the decision to launch the rescue mission; Steve Smith has made a case for the relevance of *both* groupthink and bureaucratic politics in explaining that decision; and Scott Gartner accepts the validity of Smith's argument about the role of Carter's presidential supporters (in other words, of bureaucratic level forces) in making what is basically a domestic or societal level form of argument. Taken as a whole, this represents a recognition not just of the complexity of the case itself, but of the very real and simultaneous attraction of differing accounts and their contrasting ability to account for different features of the Iran decision-making. The concluding chapter expands upon this theme. Since there is clearly a relationship between the content of decisions and the context in which they are made, more needs to be said on this point.

8   Conclusion

Political argumentation, and presumably the art of persuasion also, plays a crucial role in the making of foreign policy. As Robert Axelrod has put it, 'argumentation is a vital part of the policy process when power is shared and when problems are so complex that the participants are not sure that their own initial positions are necessarily the best ones'.[1] What, then, does the Iran case tell us about the capacity of analogies to persuade others? This question really contains two matters of interest rolled into one: how persuasive are analogies in general, and what determines the persuasiveness of a particular analogy? Generally speaking, since analogies play such a powerful role in comprehension, the persuasiveness of arguments might be thought to be heavily influenced – and perhaps even fundamentally rooted – in analogy and metaphor. Since these devices govern the manner in which we learn and the way we understand the world around us, if we can get others to accept our analogies then we have gone a long way towards convincing them that the world is in fact as we see it. So analogizing seems vital both to the persuasion of the self, as well as to persuade others.

We can readily observe the persuasive power of analogical and metaphorical reasoning within political science itself. The general appeal and success of Antony Downs's *An Economic Theory of Democracy*, for instance, perhaps rests not on its ability to encapsulate empirical reality – arguably, it does so at best imperfectly – but in no small part upon its author's effective use of an analogy between politics and economics, which skilfully ties a theory of party competition to preexisting schemas and liberal images of how the market economy is

---

[1] See Axelrod, 'Argumentation in Foreign Policy Settings'; Paul Anderson, 'Justifications and Precedents as Constraints in Foreign Policy Decision-Making', *American Journal of Political Science*, 25: 738–61, 1981.

supposed to operate.[2] Similarly, the proposition that US hegemony within the international system is eroding draws its strength in part from an analogy between the decline of Great Britain in the late nineteenth and early twentieth centuries and the current relative economic decline of the United States,[3] while predictions of an imminent Republican realignment of the electoral and party system are based upon the historical experience of the Democratic Party in the New Deal era and the rule-based observation that a realignment normally occurs every fifty years or so.[4]

Aside from their applications within the study of political science, though, how inherently persuasive are such analogical tools in convincing policy-makers to view the world in a particular way? The persuasiveness of a given analogy cannot, of course, be considered apart from its merits as an accurate comparison and predictive device, although assessing these is of course a subjective process. The preceding analysis, however, suggests that an analogy will tend to be most persuasive and accepted as a blueprint for policy where it first of all seems to 'fit' cognitively, in the sense that the present situation can plausibly be mapped to the past event or episode with which it is being compared. Most obviously, the greater the degree of perceived overlap between two situations – overlap, that is, of features which are perceived to be causally relevant – the greater the attraction of the analogy between them. Moreover, the attractions of an analogy are probably greatly increased where the events on which it draws are both available and representative.

The persuasiveness of an analogy does not depend simply on its cognitive appeal, however, but on the extent to which it is compatible with the belief systems, political priorities and/or bureaucratic interests of the analogizer's colleagues. A major conclusion which can be drawn from this case study is that the process of analogizing and of applying the lessons drawn from history is distorted by political factors and requirements. Even if an analogy appears to fit the case in hand, it may prove unpalatable and ultimately unacceptable to certain audiences if it

---

[2] This demonstrates the use of metaphor 'to make the familiar unfamiliar', whereas in policy-making analogies and metaphors almost always serve the opposite purpose.
[3] See Robert Gilpin, *War and Change in World Politics* (New York: Cambridge University Press, 1981); Paul Kennedy, *The Rise and Fall of the Great Powers* (New York: Random House, 1987); see also Joseph Nye, 'The Analogy of National Decline: A Misleading Metaphor', *Current*, June 1990, pp. 10–17.
[4] Kevin Phillips, *The Emerging Republican Majority* (New Rochelle, New York: Arlington House, 1969).

implies courses of action which conflict with electoral or organizational interests. No one within the Carter administration seems to have seriously questioned the idea that the *Pueblo* strategy would eventually attain the release of the hostages during the Tehran crisis, but several key advisers questioned its applicability for reasons which had nothing to do with its cognitive appeal or relevance to the case. Cyrus Vance was unable to fully convince his colleagues of the worth of the *Pueblo* analogy because that comparison suggested that policy success could come only at the cost of political failure and humiliation.

The remainder of this book seeks to illuminate the relationship between analogical reasoning, domestic politics and bureaucratic politics. This triangular relationship has rarely been examined before in any depth, and so our comments must by necessity be of a rather limited and speculative nature. Nevertheless, we shall argue here that the degree to which a historical analogy proves 'persuasive' in a group context – that is, when it leaves the individual decision-maker's head and becomes part of a social process – is critically affected by domestic and bureaucratic level factors. As Brian Ripley has perceptively suggested, cognitive factors such as historical analogies need to be placed 'in context',[5] and factors lying at the structural, state and bureaucratic levels of analysis can provide this context, without necessarily being employed in a deterministic way. It is clear that analogies do not operate in a vacuum, outside the realm of the external and domestic contexts in which they are being proposed, although this is an observation which is at best left implicit in the existing literature on analogical reasoning.

In short, the argument presented here suggests that bureaucratic roles modify the impact of individual preferences and cognitions in at least two ways. First, in specialized roles for which clear and relatively unambiguous bureaucratic interests can be discerned, these interests may influence or determine the *receptivity* of actors to the arguments of others. While analogizing is essentially a cognitive operation, the reception of a decision-maker's analogies, we shall argue, is crucially affected by the contexts in which they are proposed. Less critically in the Iran case but still of importance, role variables, it will be proposed, can sometimes account for which cognitions are given vocal expression in a group context. Arguably, this adds something of importance to the

---

[5] Brian Ripley, 'Culture, Cognition and Bureaucratic Politics', in Neack *et al.*, *Foreign Policy Analysis: Continuity and Change in its Second Generation*.

foregoing analysis, since it adds a social dynamic to what thus far has been a largely individual level account.

Analogical reasoning, domestic politics and bureaucratic politics

We noted in chapter 7 that foreign policy analogies sometimes have a partially domestic political content. Indeed, on occasion they can be almost exclusively 'political' in the sense that the base event or situation being mapped onto the target may be drawn from the domestic political realm and may form the basis for drawing lessons about political strategy in foreign affairs. For instance, Dick Morris – a former counsellor to President Bill Clinton – has suggested that Clinton decided to intervene in Haiti in 1994 because it reminded him of a situation he faced in 1979 when he was governor of Arkansas. Morris relates a phone call between himself and the president in which Clinton sought Morris's advice about how best to deal with the situation in Haiti, which was then occupying a good deal of the former's time. According to Morris, the president 'ticked off' all the idealist or humanitarian reasons one might find for intervening militarily in Haiti in this discussion, but Morris suggests that this was just a smokescreen that obscured Clinton's true reasoning:

> I knew the real motivation. It was buried in our past together. In 1979, a young, anxious-to-please Governor Bill Clinton acceded to President Jimmy Carter's urgent request that Arkansas agree to take some Cuban refugees from Florida facilities and house them at Fort Chaffee. Carter couldn't afford to lose Florida. He needed to get the Cubans out. But then Carter had reneged on what Clinton believed was a promise to move them out of Arkansas before the 1980 election. 'He screwed me', Clinton had told me the following year over dinner . . . Clinton partially blamed the refugees for his defeat.[6]

Stated in the language of this book, Morris is suggesting that Clinton had reasoned analogically about the Haiti problem, mapping 'Arkansas 1979' onto the nationwide political situation he faced in 1994. More controversially, the journalist Christopher Hitchens has argued that in 1992 Bill Clinton personally attended the execution of a black prison inmate on death row so as not to lay himself open to another 'Willy Horton-style' allegation, making a special trip back to Arkansas in the

---

[6] Dick Morris, *Behind the Oval Office: Winning the Presidency in the Nineties* (New York: Random House, 1997), p. 5.

205

midst of the New Hampshire primary.[7] During the 1988 presidential election, Michael Dukakis's campaign had been scuppered in part by Republican campaign advertisements suggesting that he was soft on crime. Willy Horton was a convicted murderer who committed a rape while on furlough from a Massachusetts prison, and the case was used with great effect to damage Dukakis, who had previously been governor of Massachusetts. Clinton was clearly concerned that the same issue could be used against him in 1992, and this, according to Hitchens, was the source of his desire to be seen attending the execution of a convicted murderer. Again, the argument being made here is essentially that Clinton's actions derived from analogical reasoning.

Of course, these two claims may not have any real basis in fact. Both claims are, at this historical juncture, only allegations, though they seem to comport with other accounts of Clinton's decision-making style. Regardless of their truth value, however, the critical point to note is that it is quite *possible* to use an analogy which serves a domestic political purpose and which has a purely political content. More typical, however – and more relevant to the case study we have examined here – seem to be analogies which have *both* a policy content and a political content. For instance, the Entebbe analogy suggests that a well-executed raid can also be good politics, while the *Pueblo* analogy implies that getting hostages back safe and sound has political costs. Ultimately, of course, the most tempting and persuasive analogies appear to be those which promise both kinds of successful outcome.

The search for parsimonious explanation can easily degenerate into reductionism. We noted in chapter 2 that several studies of analogizing in policy-making contexts have drawn their inspiration from experimental studies conducted in the rarified atmosphere of the laboratory. We also suggested that we can extrapolate from the results these researchers have obtained, in the sense that political decision-making under conditions of uncertainty clearly often does provoke the use of analogical reasoning. Nevertheless, it should be noted that much of that literature arguably takes too much politics out of the mix, stemming perhaps from the fact that most (if not all) of these experiments usually fail to tap into the context in which *political* analogizing occurs. That this should be the case is less than surprising, since the studies referred to in chapter 2 were clearly not designed to serve this purpose. However, one potential problem with using this literature as a basis for extrapola-

---

[7] Christopher Hitchens, *No One Left To Lie To: The Triangulation of William Jefferson Clinton* (London: Verso, 1999).

tion is that in the vast majority of studies which have been conducted by cognitive psychologists thus far, the subjects have no vested interest one way or another in the outcome of the analogical process. Typically, the subject is confronted with a problem of some sort after various stories have been read to him or her which are designed to help the subject 'solve' the problem by analogy.[8] Frequently the subject has no stake whatsoever in the analogy employed. The reception of analogies is effectively a neutral process, whereby the analogist simply selects the best perceived 'fit' between a current problem and a past solution.

This condition clearly does not obtain in a policy-making context, or in any highly political context where vested bureaucratic interests and ideational agendas are at stake. It is easy to lose sight of the fact that the policy-making process is only partly a quasi-scientific attempt to understand the nature of the world. It is also a struggle for power, a process of competition for a resource which is both inherently satisfying in a proximate sense and instrumentally useful in the attainment of future objectives and desirable end-states. The making of policy is an enterprise engaged in by politicians with egos to preserve, careers to advance, elections to win and bureaucratic corners to defend. Accordingly, the FPDM scholar must reintroduce the political dimension if his or her model is to represent a faithful depiction of the policy-making process.

What effect does this have on decision-makers? Reasoning from a single case is, as many commentators have pointed out, dangerous. Nevertheless, we can at least reach a tentative conclusion based on the material presented in earlier chapters. Clearly, in this instance, several of the key decision-makers had one or two analogies in mind, which usually derived from their own experiences, and they suggested policy options which were consistent with those analogies. However, it is when these analogies enter a group process – that is, when they are placed upon the table for discussion and dissection by those whom the analogy is intended to persuade – that bureaucratic and domestic politics seems to exert a significant role. Again, the major example of this in the Iran case is the reaction of Hamilton Jordan to Vance's use of the *Pueblo* analogy. According to Brzezinski, Jordan said 'you can forget about a second term' if the Carter administration decided to follow a

---

[8] For some representative examples, see Gick and Holyoak, 'Analogical Problem-Solving'; Gentner and Toupin, 'Systematicity and Surface Similarity in the Development of Analogy'; Halpern *et al.*, 'Analogies as an Aid to Understanding and Memory'.

similar strategy to that followed in the *Pueblo* case.[9] The presidential supporters never seem to have truly accepted the *Pueblo* analogy, in the sense that they were not prepared to wait it out as long as that comparison suggested they ought to. When the crisis dragged on to the point where it challenged the prerogatives of those who were most concerned with the president's political prospects, 'pulling another *Pueblo*' became unacceptable as a strategy.

Differing backgrounds and beliefs, and to some extent the goals and objectives associated with particular governmental roles as well, ensure that policy-makers will tend to exhibit different value hierarchies, and the reception of a given analogy will be determined in part by what it implies about the fate of the policy-maker's most treasured goals and values. Analogizing may be vital to the persuasion of the self, but what happens to an analogy which implies policy directions which conflict with political priorities, or which runs into opposition from a rival analogy proposed by a superior? Even if an analogy appears to fit the case in hand, it may prove unpalatable and ultimately unacceptable to certain audiences if it implies courses of action which conflict with electoral politics, as Cyrus Vance found to his cost. It is noticeable also that Vance could afford to follow principle – he was not subject to election and had intended to leave office after the 1980 presidential contest no matter what the outcome – whereas Carter and his staff were compelled to weigh principle against political interest.

Chapter 7 suggests that 'where you stand . . .' powerfully shapes 'where you sit' for *presidential supporters* in this case study, but that the positions of foreign policy professionals, such as the secretaries of state and defence and the national security adviser, are generally not determined this way. Why might this be the case? Again, our answer must be speculative at this point, but to assert that the utility of the 'where you stand' axiom depends on the kind of actor in question logically implies that there is something different about being a presidential supporter as opposed to a foreign policy professional that leads to differences in behaviour. What is that difference?

The blanket application of the 'where you stand' notion across different government roles has probably failed to differentiate between role occupants in at least one significant respect: different positions involve different degrees of role complexity and ambiguity, so that the space or opportunity for individual characteristics to 'matter' differs according

[9] Brzezinski, interview with the author.

to the role in question. Individuals occupying complex roles probably do not have a single interest, making it difficult if not impossible to predict preferences or behaviour from a knowledge of the position occupied by the actor. On the other hand, those placed in more circumscribed positions are able to target a single objective or interest, making it easier for the analyst to predict behaviour once one knows the position the decision-maker occupies. This distinction between simple and complex roles can best be illustrated by comparing the demands placed upon the secretary of state and the national security adviser, on the one hand, and those typically faced by the White House press secretary on the other.

Role complexity and policy behaviour

As Bruce Biddle notes, 'roles vary in terms of complexity', from positions involving simple and well-defined tasks to those which impose multiple tasks and competing goals.[10] As we move up the foreign policy hierarchy the degree of complexity tends to increase, for the top positions tend to involve the decision-maker in several roles that compete for his or her time. The secretary of state's job is a case study in role complexity, for it is in fact not one role but many. Cyrus Vance has noted that the secretary is the president's adviser, the chief defender of the administration's foreign policies on Capitol Hill, a major representative of the country overseas, the president's chief spokesman on international affairs and the head of a major department and a massive bureaucracy; in addition to this, he has responsibility for meeting with visiting dignitaries.[11]

Although it frequently proves physically exhausting and a source of psychological stress, the role complexity of the secretary's job is a source of strength in one sense, for he is both the head of a powerful organization which offers 'professional' advice about foreign policy and a close political adviser to the president. Under such conditions the occupant is permitted to offer both technical advice and political advice. It is essentially up to him or her which aspects of the job take precedence, although all must be fulfilled to some extent. This role complexity is probably what makes it so difficult to go beyond this

---

[10] Bruce Biddle, *Role Theory: Expectations, Identities and Behaviors* (New York: Academic Press, 1979), p. 73. On role complexity, see also Vertzberger, *The World in their Minds*, pp. 226–8, 251–2, 263–4 and James Naylor et al., *A Theory of Behavior in Organizations* (New York: Academic Press, 1980), pp. 142–56.   [11] Vance, *Hard Choices*, pp. 13–15.

position to a rigid 'where you stand' perspective, and what makes the occupant's preferences so unpredictable by reference to this factor alone. Cyrus Vance clearly did not feel it was his role to offer political advice to President Carter. Indeed, he appears to have believed that it was his job to hold out against those pressing such considerations, and to adhere to principled policy goals. James Baker, on the other hand, seems to have been much more attuned to the politics of foreign policy, having previously occupied the role of White House chief of staff. 'At its core', Baker says, 'the Secretary of State's job is political.' Although he stresses that he did not reason solely in such terms, he notes that as secretary of state he always thought about how a given policy would 'play' both at home and abroad.[12]

The national security adviser's role is similarly complex. As Colin Powell puts it, he or she must simultaneously perform the roles of 'judge, traffic cop, truant officer, arbitrator, fireman, chaplain, psychiatrist and occasional hit man'.[13] Still a relatively new position, the national security adviser's 'proper' role is unclear and its boundaries poorly specified, and consequently the behavioural range of its occupants has varied greatly, even within single administrations.[14] The role has frequently appeared to be what the president and the role occupier makes of it, for it has a built-in ambiguity and role complexity to it, a structural conflict which compels the role occupier to referee the foreign policy process, but which also tempts him to become a player in his own right. Writing in 1980, I. M. Destler noted that a consensus of sorts existed 'as to what the national security adviser should, and should not, be doing', the view held in many quarters being that he 'should concentrate on certain types of actions and avoid others'. Subsequent events, however, have shown that this consensus is so weak as to permit easy deviation from it. As Destler readily concedes, the NSA has in some administrations performed the role of a 'second secretary of State'.[15] One conception of the NSA's role stresses the view that he or she should be an 'honest broker' or facilitator, but 'one can infer from recent practice an alternative role conception, far less confining than that of a facilitator – that of a senior freewheeling aide and *ad hoc* operator, serving the president personally and flexibly as the institutionally encumbered

[12] James Baker, *The Politics of Diplomacy: Revolution, War and Peace, 1989–1992* (New York: G. P. Putnam's, 1995), pp. 38–9. [13] Colin Powell, *My American Journey*, p. 352.
[14] Consider the roles of Richard Allen and William Clark in the Reagan administration, for instance, when compared with those of Robert McFarlane and John Poindexter.
[15] I. M. Destler, 'National Security Management: What Presidents Have Wrought', *Political Science Quarterly*, 95: 573–88, 1980–1, p. 576.

secretary of state no longer can'.[16] The first, more limited role – associated principally with McGeorge Bundy, Walt Rostow and Brent Scowcroft – is positively tempting to exceed, often giving way to the second modal type, commonly identified with Henry Kissinger and Zbigniew Brzezinski.

We have observed even wider variations in the role of the NSA in the years since Destler wrote, with role occupants like McFarlane and Poindexter during the Iran–Contra affair effectively (and with apparent ease) appropriating policy functions that properly belonged to several of the departments. As Colin Powell puts it, during the Iran–Contra operations the NSC 'had filled a power vacuum and had become its own Defense Department, running little wars, its own State Department, carrying out its own secret diplomacy, and its own CIA, carrying out clandestine operations'.[17] This last point is especially significant, because Destler at the dawn of the 1980s had highlighted covert operations as one of the absolute 'don'ts' of the consensus on what the NSA ought and ought not to be doing.[18]

Just as role complexity both enhances the scope for individual actions and makes those actions less predictable, role simplicity or specificity seems to have the opposite effect. Conventionally, presidential supporters are limited in their capacity to break out of their roles in foreign policy contexts by their relatively lowly position in the foreign policy hierarchy. But the strength of role variables probably increases with specificity or clarity of job description, and the presidential supporter role is so sharply defined – 'look out for the President's interests' – that behaviour in that role acquires a measure of predictability. While recent events have thrown the roles of many policy actors into confusion, the job of the presidential supporter remains crystal clear, and occupants of that role are still especially predisposed to view foreign policy proposals in terms of how these will impact upon the president's political prospects. As Michael Deaver, Reagan's deputy chief of staff, put it 'I was not there to enforce a philosophy. I had one criterion: was it in the best interest of the President? I did not confuse Ronald Reagan with America, but I often felt that what was good for the one had to be good for the other.'[19] White House aides do not stand at the top of any established organization, and their only client or interest is the president and his political health. While it is up to the presidential supporter

---

[16] Ibid., p. 577.   [17] Powell, *My American Journey*, p. 333.
[18] Destler, 'National Security Management', p. 577.
[19] Michael Deaver, *Behind the Scenes* (New York: William Morrow, 1987), p. 131.

to decide *what* is in the best interest of the president in a particular instance, it is almost true by definition that his or her primary concern will be for the chief executive.

Perhaps this difference in role specificity accounts for the differential performance of the 'where you stand' axiom. Much has been made of the philosophical division of opinion between the hawkish Brzezinski and the doveish Vance during the Carter years, but in many ways the divide between the foreign policy professionals and the political advisers in the White House was just as significant. Steve Smith, we may recall, has suggested that Carter's political advisers consistently took positions during the hostage crisis which seemed designed to maximize the president's chances of re-election in the forthcoming presidential race of 1980, and we have argued here that Carter's presidential supporters were unreceptive to the doveish arguments of Secretary Vance for domestic political reasons. To foreign policy professionals such as the secretary of state and national security adviser, it often appears that the president's men do not appreciate the geopolitical consequences of the actions they propose. Moreover, this tendency does not seem to have been unique to the Carter administration. Former Reagan Secretary of State Alexander Haig complains that the issue of lifting the Soviet grain embargo in 1981 was viewed by the president's political advisers 'almost exclusively as a domestic issue',[20] for instance, and Zbigniew Brzezinski has complained that Vice-President Walter Mondale was too inclined to see foreign policy solely in terms of its domestic ramifications.[21]

It is perhaps unfortunate that so much attention has been focused on the 'where you stand' notion in explaining state behaviour, since psychologists have long argued that role performance is a rather complex matter. Relatively little attention has been devoted to how 'turf wars' might affect decision-making, for instance. Again, role complexity and position within the bureaucratic hierarchy seem to have an effect here. Those occupying highly specified and unambiguous roles have little leeway for going beyond those roles without defying the consensual expectations associated with the position. Those in complex positions involving a multiplicity of roles, on the other hand, enjoy more leeway of this sort. This implies that roles in general probably affect decisions not by shaping the core beliefs or arguments of decision-makers, but by

---

[20] Alexander Haig, *Caveat: Realism, Reagan and Foreign Policy* (New York: Macmillan, 1984), p. 83.   [21] Brzezinski, *Power and Principle*, p. 35.

the more indirect route of influencing their conduct in ways that may affect the substance of decisions.

Role specificity and the willingness to 'speak out'

Modern government depends to a large extent on compartmentaliz-ation and the parcelling out of tasks and functions to different organiz-ations. Not unnaturally, the occupants of these compartments come to see themselves as protectors of their own piece of turf in a general sense, even though they may not necessarily become mouthpieces for their organization's interests. Since those who occupy other roles are not privy to the information and expertise located in one's own depart-ment, it is easy to assume that one ought to defer to 'the expert' and correspondingly difficult to offer advice outside one's own domain. Many decision-makers in bureaucratic settings are consequently zeal-ous guardians of their own turf, and most are sensitive to the turf claims of others. As Dan Quayle puts it, whenever large interdepartmental groups of policy-makers assemble 'turf ends up getting more sharply staked out by the individual secretaries'.[22]

Role expectations change in every administration to some extent. Nevertheless, at least some roles carry expectations that are intersubjec-tive in character, in the sense that the participants tend to agree on the extent to which boundaries exist which delimit behaviour, and also on roughly where those boundaries lie. For some positions, bureaucratic role is probably one of the most important social constraints on 'speak-ing your mind' in a group context. As Brian Ripley has suggested, there is some evidence that the major impact of role is not to magically transform the policy-maker's core beliefs, but to shape and constrain the decision-maker's own perception of what he ought to be doing and saying, as well as the expectations of his colleagues in that regard. 'The concept of "bureaucratic role" ', he notes, 'could be expanded to cap-ture what Allison refers to as a bureaucrat's "style of play" and a "code of conformity", based, among other things, on career tenure and long-term expectations.' Well-understood roles constrain both the substance and the style of the advice the president's men feel able to give.[23]

---

[22] Dan Quayle, *Standing Firm: A Vice Presidential Memoir* (New York: HarperCollins, 1994), p. 102.
[23] See Brian Ripley, 'Cognition in Context: Revitalizing Bureaucratic Politics in Foreign Policy Analysis', paper presented at the Annual Meeting of the American Political Science Association, Washington DC, September 1993. A shortened version of this paper appears as 'Culture, Cognition and Bureaucratic Politics' in Neack *et al., Foreign*

According to this perspective, there are unwritten rules or tendencies which constrain accepted behaviour, and roles influence decisions by affecting the kind of arguments that get heard and those that do not. Presidents rarely hear the full range of advice that a policy-maker is capable of offering. They hear only that advice which is consistent with a particular role, since a decision-maker will feel constrained by his or her position not to give certain types of advice, and in some cases not to give advice at all.

The unwritten rules associated with some roles are quite vague and flexible for some positions, and the scope for individual action is therefore substantial. This is especially true for relatively new positions and, as James Rosenau suggests, 'the leeway for individual discretion is probably greater the higher a position is located in the system'.[24] In the top positions, 'variations in individual role-definition are tolerated or even encouraged within relatively wide limits'.[25] Some roles, on the other hand, are quite specific in the unwritten rules that apply to them, and consensual norms and tacit understandings exist which limit the scope for individuality quite considerably. In this type of role, Daniel Levinson notes, 'the role-requirements are so narrowly defined, and the mechanisms of social control so powerful, that only one form of role-performance can be sustained for any given position'.[26] It is when we are dealing with this latter form of role classification, of course, that we can expect to observe most conformity and regularities in the behaviour of those who occupy such roles. The influence of role will be at its strongest at this well-specified end of the spectrum, for decision-makers are especially constrained here in what they may say and do. They are likely to feel the urge to say something out loud, for instance, but then to decide against it for fear of 'going beyond' their role or stepping on the toes of others. Equally, those at the other end of the spectrum are likely to exhibit less regularized and therefore less predictable behaviour, so that the analyst must inevitably pay greater attention to individual or cognitive characteristics in explaining where he or she 'stands'.

Policy Analysis: Continuity and Change in its Second Generation. This aspect of my argument builds upon, and owes a great deal to, Ripley's piece, but it differs in the sense that the general conception of bureaucratic position offered here explicitly differentiates between roles according to role specificity.
24 James Rosenau, 'Private Preferences and Political Responsibilities: The Relative Potency of Individual and Role Variables in the Behavior of US Senators', in Rosenau, *The Scientific Study of Foreign Policy*, p. 184.
25 Daniel Levinson, 'Role, Personality and Social Structure in the Organizational Setting', *Journal of Abnormal and Social Psychology*, 58: 170–80, 1959, p. 179.   26 Ibid., p. 178.

While, as already noted, the key foreign policy professionals perform complex roles that involve a diversity of sometimes competing interests, this is not true for all the actors. For instance, by statute and convention CIA directors generally confine themselves to providing relatively neutral intelligence information rather than explicit policy advice. 'The Director of Central Intelligence is not supposed to play a policy role. His job is to provide objective analysis of the situation in various parts of the world', Robert McFarlane notes.[27] Former occupants of the role seem to agree. Stansfield Turner, for instance, states that 'my responsibility to the President was to provide the information he needed to make decisions, not to be an advocate for a specific course. A DCI's major contribution is his unbiased and disinterested stance in the President's councils. Without that, he brings only one more opinion to the table.'[28] Turner felt constrained by his role, both during the Iran hostage crisis and before, not to offer direct policy advice to the president: 'once an intelligence chief begins to recommend policy, it becomes very difficult for him not to want his intelligence to support that policy. However honest a DCI may be, advocacy creates a mental filter that tends to give less credence to intelligence that does not support his policy choice.'[29]

On foreign policy questions, presidential supporters are similarly circumscribed in noticeable ways, although the constraints here seem to be predominantly informal and unwritten rather than formal-legal. Nevertheless, a president's chief of staff or press secretary may have strong beliefs about the conduct of foreign policy. As Jody Powell points out, 'press secretaries . . . are human beings too. Your judgments may be superficial, but they are there nevertheless. On occasion, they may be every bit as good as those of the experts, who sometimes miss large issues in their fascination with nuances.'[30] Yet the occupants of the press secretary role are rarely seen as qualified to offer foreign policy advice by *other* decision-makers – particularly by those on whose 'turf' the president's spokesman will inevitably be stepping – and they thus conventionally hold back from doing so explicitly.[31] Memoir accounts of presidential supporters reveal that they are usually uneasy when dealing with foreign policy issues. Part of this uneasiness undoubtedly

---

[27] Robert McFarlane, *Special Trust* (New York: Cadell and Davies, 1994), p. 174.
[28] Turner, *Terrorism and Democracy*, p. 35.   [29] Ibid., pp. 50–1.
[30] Powell, *The Other Side of the Story*, p. 303.
[31] As Powell notes in *The Other Side of the Story*, there are also practical reasons why a press secretary would want to 'duck' an overt policy role, p. 301.

relates to an absence of expertise in this area, but, as Powell's statement makes clear, on at least some foreign policy issues presidential supporters do feel as qualified as the experts to give advice, even though they feel unable to express this directly. Former Johnson administration press secretaries George Reedy and Bill Moyers both had very strong feelings about Vietnam, but only Reedy tried to convey these directly to the president. Moyers' approach was more subtle. As David Halberstam reports, the latter's technique was to encourage those who occupied more accepted foreign policy roles and who doubted the wisdom of Johnson's Vietnam policies to speak for him, rather than attempting to persuade the president directly. Moyers 'showed his own doubts on Vietnam largely by encouraging other doubters to speak and by trying to put doubters in touch with one another',[32] and according to Clark Clifford he did so because he 'felt he could not play an open role in policy-making because his job as Press Secretary constrained him from active policy formulation'.[33]

How often do substantively important thoughts go without being voiced in policy forums because of role factors? It is obviously difficult to measure this, or to say what the impact of such thoughts would have been if they *had* been expressed. Nevertheless, we do know that on occasion role consciousness can have at least some concrete policy effects. Sometimes no one speaks up for an important option, even the experts whose turf the question or consideration covers, and there is at least some evidence to suggest that norms within decision-making groups do actively impact on the decisional outputs, some of the time. Is there any evidence of such an effect in the Iran hostage case?

Though he offers no specific examples of this, Warren Christopher contends that there is. Jimmy Carter dealt with the hostage crisis mainly through formal mechanisms such as the National Security Council, but Christopher argues that this had an unfortunate side-effect:

> The formal NSC structure tended to cast each Cabinet secretary in his role as a spokesman for his department. On some of the subsets of issues (for example sanctions, visa cancellations), this sometimes could result in a form of bargaining or in attempts to reach compromises. The compartmentalized approach almost inevitably led each participant to protect the area of his expertise. Some participants tended to be diffident in expressing views outside their own area,

[32] David Halberstam, *The Best and the Brightest* (New York: Random House, 1969), p. 497.
[33] Clark Clifford, *Counsel to the President* (New York: Random House, 1991), p. 416; also quoted in Ripley, 'Cognition in Context'.

and probing questions outside one's own area sometimes were
answered by a welter of bureaucratic jargon that there was no time to
penetrate.[34]

That members of the administration felt constrained by their roles
and expertise not to tread on the toes of others is also suggested by
Stansfield Turner. As mentioned earlier, Carter's SCC considered the
possibility of placing the USS *Midway* off the coast of Iran. Turner
believed that doing so would send a threatening message to the hostage
takers, and that the carrier 'would be in place to launch an attack on
short notice should the President decide that was necessary'.[35] The ship
was currently in the Indian ocean and was scheduled to dock at Mom-
basa, Kenya, but at an NSC meeting held the same day President Carter
decided to allow the *Midway* to continue on its present course. Turner, a
former admiral who was no stranger to naval questions, states that 'I
wanted to speak up, but I was silenced by two conflicting principles.'
On the one hand, he believed that placing the *Midway* close to the
Persian Gulf could do no harm and might well do some positive good.
'As a professional military officer, I wanted the President to have this
advice.' But what kept Turner quiet was his conception of the DCI's
role. 'It was inappropriate for me to raise such a matter', he maintains.
'My responsibility to the President was to provide the information he
needed to make decisions, not to be an advocate for any specific course
. . . further, as a military officer I understood that this issue was in the
domain of the Secretary of Defense and the Chairman of the Joint
Chiefs, not the DCI . . . despite my strongly held professional view, I
did not speak up.' No one else spoke up for Turner's internally held
view either, and the decision stood.[36] There was at least one member of
the administration who did 'step outside' the agreed limits of his role.
White House Chief of Staff Hamilton Jordan during the French connection negotiations took on a direct foreign policy role. However, it
should be noted that he did so under emergency conditions, on the
explicit instructions of the president and with the acquiescence of
Vance. Ordinarily, it seems unlikely in the extreme that a political
operative would intrude in such an obvious way upon what could
certainly be regarded as the secretary of state's 'turf', and Jordan makes
his unease with doing so clear in his memoirs.

What is the relationship of all of this to analogical reasoning? The
major effect of bureaucratic forces, again, seems to be their influence on

[34] Christopher, *American Hostages in Iran*, p. 31.
[35] Turner, *Terrorism and Democracy*, p. 32.   [36] Ibid., p. 35.

how 'persuasive' a given analogy appears to those occupying a particular role. Just as an analogy which conflicts with domestic political imperatives is unlikely to receive a receptive hearing from a presidential supporter, so an analogy which appears solely to serve such imperatives is unlikely to appeal to those occupying professional policy roles, such as the chairman of the Joint Chiefs. Stated differently, what makes an analogy persuasive or unpersuasive to other decision-makers is not just the degree to which it appears representative of the case at hand, but the degree to which its perceived lessons and precepts comport with the existing beliefs and bureaucratic priorities of the group members. Thus a theory of cognitive preferences must always be considered alongside the contexts, at various levels of analysis, within which the cognitive construct is being applied.

The Iran hostage crisis as analogy

In the years since the hostage crisis ended, the whole event has itself been used as an historical analogy by members of subsequent US administrations. Prior to the invasion of Grenada in 1983, for instance, members of the Reagan administration drew the lesson from the Iran raid that the rescue force had been too small – in particular, that an insufficient number of helicopters had been employed in the raid – and that a larger force ought to be used on the next occasion where the need arose. In the administration's invasion of the island that year, which included (but was clearly not confined to) a rescue operation of American students, a much larger military force was employed. In his study of the decision-making behind the Grenada invasion, Gary Williams notes the effect that Iran had upon Ronald Reagan as a presidential candidate in 1980. The fact that Reagan had been forced to consider the Iran case extensively during his campaign for the presidency, Williams argues, 'made the analogy very available as a base: it was dramatic, recent, a failure and first-hand for most decisionmakers. As well as the potentially disastrous domestic political repercussions of such a crisis, Iran represented US humiliation, helplessness and loss of credibility on the world stage. The taking of Americans as hostages was Reagan's greatest concern.'[37]

The US ambassador to Grenada feared that the situation he faced there could become 'another Iran',[38] and both Secretary of State George

[37] Gary Williams, 'Analogical Reasoning and Foreign Policy Decisionmaking', p. 363.
[38] Ibid., p. 364.

Shultz and his assistant Tony Motley felt that in Grenada 'conditions were ripe . . . for hostage taking. We both had the searing memory of Tehran and the sixty-six Americans seized from our embassy on November 4, 1979, and held hostage for over a year.'[39] Moreover, Shultz and former Defence Secretary Caspar Weinberger both later wrote in their memoirs that the more substantial force used in the Grenada case had been employed as a result of the 'learning experience' of the Tehran raid.[40] While the two men often disagreed on the issues, both employed the Tehran analogy in arguing for a large invasion and rescue force. 'Double whatever force the military proposes' was the lesson both seemed to have derived. While many analysts have doubted the administration's claim that the invasion of Grenada was solely a rescue operation, it is beyond doubt that the military operation did include a rescue component. There is also scant reason to suppose that either decision-maker was not sincere in his use of the Iranian analogy in relation to this component. After all, policy-makers have a strong, vested political interest in learning what they can from the failures of previous administrations.

Given the centrality of the experience of negotiating the hostages' release for Warren Christopher, it would be unusual indeed if he had failed to use the Tehran experience as an analogy during his time as secretary of state under President Clinton. Indeed, so far, we know of at least one instance where he did so. During the 1995 diplomatic initiative which ended the war in Bosnia, Christopher drew on the lessons of Iran when deciding how much leeway to give Richard Holbrooke, the American chief negotiator, in dealing with the situation in the Balkans. Christopher recalls:

> To maximize US negotiating flexibility, I felt that Holbrooke and his team had to be allowed to shape the specifics of an agreement. I remembered my efforts 15 years before in Algiers to secure release of the American hostages in Iran, when President Carter and Secretary of State Edmund Muskie allowed me wide bargaining flexibility. From this experience, I knew how essential such latitude would be in Bosnia.[41]

Just as the Angus Ward, *Pueblo*, *Mayaguez*, Mogadishu, Entebbe and

---

[39] George Shultz, *Turmoil and Triumph: My Years as Secretary of State* (New York: Scribner's, 1993), p. 328.
[40] See ibid., p. 331, and Caspar Weinberger, *Fighting for Peace: Seven Critical Years in the Pentagon* (New York: Warner Books, 1990), p. 111.
[41] Warren Christopher, *In The Stream Of History: Shaping Foreign Policy For A New Era* (Stanford, California: Stanford University Press, 1998), p. 349.

various other hostage crises would affect the deliberations of the Iran crisis decision-makers, so Iran has itself formed a base situation which can be mapped onto new target situations. Since the future by definition cannot be known in advance, our only cognitive guide will be the belief that the future is likely to resemble the past and that things will turn out as they did before. Such an assumption, of course, is inherently flawed. And therein lies the dilemma.

Policy implications and future research

Prudent men are wont to say – and this not rashly or without good ground – that he who would foresee what has to be, should reflect on what has been, for everything that happens in the world at any time has a genuine resemblance to what happened in ancient times.
Niccolo Machiavelli, *The Discourses*, Book III, Chapter 43.

This study has assumed that decision-makers use analogies for genuinely cognitive purposes and has examined the extent to which these devices influenced key decisions taken during the Iran hostage crisis. Approaching this whole area more normatively, however, it seems reasonable to ask how reliable analogies are as tools for making sense of a complex reality. Was Machiavelli correct? Are analogies in fact a useful guide for policy-makers in most situations, or do they represent inherently dangerous and misleading devices which frequently lead to perceptual error? Should decision-makers rely upon them at all?

One may conclude that analogies are in a real sense both misleading and necessary. First of all, we have seen from the preceding case study that analogizing can lead to misperceptions, overreactions and even policy disaster. This is so because the contingency of the political endeavour – while it forces the analyst to impose order on the world, to try to make it predictable by discerning cause and effect patterns – also renders his or her efforts to comprehend reality inherently flawed and unreliable. Yet if the analysis suggests that there are inherent dangers in analogical reasoning, and that the reception of analogies is in part determined by values, bureaucratic roles and domestic political pressures, it also illustrates the inherent necessity of drawing lessons from the past. The paradox of analogical reasoning is that such reasoning is both essential in politics *and* inherently dangerous. As human beings possessed of only limited cognitive capabilities, policy-makers require a means of coping with structural uncertainty, especially in the domain of international politics but also in the domestic arena, where states must predict the likely movements of economic markets in order to make policy effectively.

The learning process is best viewed as one in which analogies are both cause *and* effect of policy outputs. In this respect, it is possible with hindsight to trace the existence of what might be termed 'analogical trees', whereby an analogy leads to a policy output, the outcome of this output is then judged a failure or success, this leads to the drawing of an analogy in another (related) policy situation, and so to another policy output. One can, for instance, trace a pattern from Entebbe to Tehran to Grenada, where the features and perceived lessons of a strategy are translated to an ostensibly similar situation, the strategy fails to repeat the same outcome in the new situation, and an opposite kind of lesson is drawn for use the next time.

Yet our ability to trace such patterns after the fact ought not to obscure the fact that learning from events is a difficult – and perhaps inherently flawed – mechanism for understanding the social and political world; indeed, the 'lesson' which might be drawn from these patterns is that analogies rarely provide a reliable guide to the future. As Paul Sabatier has noted, it is difficult to learn in a world where, amongst other things, 'opponents are doing everything possible to muddle the situation and otherwise impede one from learning, and even allies' motives are often suspect because of personal and organizational rivalries'.[42]

Even if these political inhibitors were not present, learning would still be exceptionally difficult for the intuitive scientist, for he or she must work under the structural uncertainty already alluded to. In a complex and ever-changing environment, cause and effect patterns are hard to discern with any accuracy. For instance, what the decision-maker views as a cause and effect relationship may sometimes turn out to represent what the political scientist would call a spurious correlation. Accurate analogizing is also intimately dependent upon policy evaluation, and it therefore carries all the well-known difficulties which attend the latter.[43] Evaluation is necessary to draw lessons effectively, but the complications of such exercises are particularly pronounced in a federal system such as that of the United States, where a whole host of

---

[42] Paul Sabatier, 'Knowledge, Policy-oriented Learning, and Policy Change: An Advocacy Coalition Framework', *Knowledge*, 8: 649–92, 1987, p. 675.

[43] B. Guy Peters, *American Public Policy: Promise and Performance* (Chatham, New Jersey: Chatham House, 1993), pp. 150–1.

different programmes designed to address a single problem are running simultaneously. This is the case in US drug policy, for instance. As Elaine Sharp has noted:

> virtually every jurisdiction in America is the site of a variety of drug-related 'programs,' including prevention programs in the schools, law enforcement efforts of one or more agencies, national media campaigns against drugs, publicly funded drug treatment, and private drug rehabilitation programs. Attributing aggregate changes in the incidence of drug use or trafficking to any one of these is impossible because the relative impact of each cannot be determined.[44]

The evaluation of anti-crime measures appears to face a similar obstacle, and seems to constitute one of those unfortunate cases where the policy-maker experiences difficulty in measuring the dependent variable, let alone in determining the relative weight to be ascribed to the various independent variables. AIDS policy is even more problematic in this respect, since proposals to discover the precise extent of the disease's spread are complicated by concerns over civil rights and worries about the uses to which the data obtained might be put.

Distinguishing between structural and superficial commonalities is also exceptionally difficult in practice, which makes analogizing – based, of course, upon judgements such as these – a truly hazardous activity. When domestic policy-makers examine other countries for successful policy programmes to take home in their suitcases, they are entering the cognitive universe populated by foreign policy decision-makers, since they often possess a limited knowledge of the institutions and culture of the society being borrowed from. Inevitably, we will almost always be misled by analogy; nevertheless, we are compelled to use history and experience as our guide.

Just as reasoning from a single analogy is dangerous, so it would be ill-advised to read too much into the Iran hostage crisis as a single case study. The finding that analogical reasoning played a key role at various stages of the decision-making in this instance may stand on its own. Clearly, however, further research is necessary before we can conclude definitively that factors such as the level of novelty and structural uncertainty engendered by the dynamics of the situation are what causes decision-makers to analogize. More research is also needed into the role played by the availability and representativeness heuristics in

---

[44] Elaine B. Sharp, *The Dilemma of Drug Policy in the United States* (New York: Harper-Collins, 1994), p. 66.

naturalistic political settings, something which has been suggested in this and other studies but which is in need of further investigation and verification across a broader range of cases and evidence. The next step for research of the kind presented in this book is to generate larger *n* comparisons of cases. Such research might attempt to identify more rigorously than it has been possible to do here where decision-makers generally do and do not use analogical reasoning in their deliberations. Apart from attempting to verify the conclusions offered here, through careful comparisons of cases where analogizing is found to play a prominent role, future research might concentrate on developing our understanding of where and when *spatial* analogies – analogies drawn across the dimension of space rather than time – are used in policy-making. We also need to more sharply delineate the stages of the policy-making process at which analogizing is used, since as a preliminary observation it seems clear that analogical reasoning is more often used (as noted earlier) at the early stages of a novel event as opposed to the latter phases. Furthermore, we need to generate studies of the circumstances under which individual decision-makers utilize analogies in domestic policy situations. While there have been some preliminary attempts to do this, investigating this question properly will in the future require comparisons of the kind already alluded to.[45]

[45] See for instance David Patrick Houghton, 'The Role of Analogical Reasoning in Foreign and Domestic Policy Contexts', unpublished Ph.D. Dissertation, Department of Political Science, University of Pittsburgh and Houghton, 'Analogical Reasoning and Policymaking'.

Appendix 1
Dramatis personae
(In alphabetical order)

David Aaron   Deputy National Security Adviser (1977–81)
Abbas Abdi   Student leader and hostage taker
Ibrahim Asgharzadeh   Student leader, spokesman and hostage taker
Abol Hassan Bani-Sadr   Iranian Foreign Minister (November 1979),
   Iranian President (1980–81)
Mehdi Bazargan   Prime Minister of Iran (February–November 1979)
Charles Beckwith   Commander of Delta Force
Christian Bourguet   French lawyer and negotiation channel to Iran
Harold Brown   Secretary of Defence (1977–81)
Zbigniew Brzezinski   National Security Adviser (1977–81)
Frank Carlucci   Deputy CIA Director (1978–81)
Jimmy Carter   President of the United States (1977–81)
Warren Christopher   Deputy Secretary of State (1977–81)
Ramsay Clark   Former Attorney General and presidential envoy to
   Iran, November 1979
W. Graham Claytor   Deputy Secretary of Defence (1979–81)
Richard Cottam   Former CIA member, sometime informal channel to
   the Iranians and Professor of Political Science, University of
   Pittsburgh
Lloyd Cutler   Special Counsel to President (1979–81)
Massoumeh Ebtekar   Student and hostage taker
Sadegh Ghotbzadeh   Iranian Foreign Minister (1979–81)
Joe Hall   Warrant Officer, US Embassy and hostage
Charles Jones   Communications Officer, US Embassy and hostage
General David Jones   Chairman, Joint Chiefs of Staff (1978–82)

224

Hamilton Jordan   Assistant to the President (1977–79), White House Chief of Staff (1979–80)

Malcolm Kalp   Economics Officer, US Embassy and hostage

Ayatollah Musavi Khoieniha   Aide to Ayatollah Khomeini and confidant of the hostage planners

Ayatollah Khomeini   Spiritual leader of Iran (1979–89)

Bruce Laingen   Chargé d'Affaires, US Embassy (1979–81)

Michael Metrinko   Political Officer, US Embassy, and hostage

William Miller   Senate Intelligence Committee staff director and presidential envoy to Iran, November 1979

Mohsen Mirdammadi   Student and hostage taker

Walter Mondale   Vice President of the United States (1977–81)

Mohammed Mossadegh   Prime Minister of Iran (1951–53)

Edmund Muskie   Secretary of State (1980–81)

Mohammed Reza Pahlavi   Shah of Iran (1941–79)

Reza Shah Pahlavi   Shah of Iran (1925–41)

Jody Powell   Press Secretary (1977–81)

Barry Rosen   Press Officer, US Embassy, and hostage

Harold Saunders   Assistant Secretary of State, Near Eastern Affairs (1978–81)

Lee Schatz   Agricultural Attaché, US Embassy, and hostage

Colonel Charles Scott   US Military Officer, US embassy, and hostage

Gary Sick   Adviser on Iran, Chief Assistant to National Security Adviser Brzezinski and notetaker at many NSC meetings (1977–81)

William Sullivan   US Ambassador to Iran (1977–79)

Sadegh Tabatabai   Relative of Ayatollah Khomeini, former member of the revolutionary government and Khomeini's negotiator at the end of the hostage crisis

Victor Tomseth   Chief Political Officer, US embassy, and hostage

Stansfield Turner   CIA Director (1977–81)

Cyrus Vance   Secretary of State (1977–80)

Hector Villalon   Argentine businessman and negotiation channel to Iran

Ibrahim Yazdi   Iranian Foreign Minister (February–November 1979)

Appendix 2
The major historical analogies used
(In chronological order)

Angus Ward hostage incident
A relatively minor but troubling hostage crisis in which a US consul, Angus Ward, was taken captive along with his staff by pro-government forces in Mukden, China. Ward and his family remained in captivity for a year, from November 1948 to November 1949. A rescue mission was ruled out due to the strategic and political problems it would entail, and the Truman administration negotiated Ward's release instead. The analogy was used by Cyrus Vance and Jimmy Carter during the Iran hostage crisis.

Tehran coup
In August 1953 the CIA and British intelligence led a coup in which the Iranian prime minister, Mohammed Mossadegh, was overthrown and replaced by the pro-American candidate General Zahedi. At first the coup seemed destined to fail, and the shah of Iran – who had been persuaded by the CIA to go along with the plan – fled to Baghdad and then Rome, returning only when Zahedi was safely in place. The analogy was in widespread use in Iran throughout 1979, and was drawn upon by the students who seized the American embassy in November 1979.

Bay of Pigs invasion
In April 1961 Cuban exiles trained in secret by the CIA attempted and failed to invade Cuba (and depose Fidel Castro) at the Bay of Pigs. The hand of the United States in the disasterous afffair was quickly exposed, and new President Kennedy was forced to admit this. Kennedy had called off American air support for the invasion in order to try to

disguise US involvement in the attempt. The analogy was used in 1980 by Jimmy Carter and Zbigniew Brzezinski.

Pueblo *hostage crisis*

In January 1968 a Navy spy ship called the USS *Pueblo* was captured by the North Koreans, and its crew were taken hostage. The crisis lasted 11 months, and the crew's release was achieved only after extensive negotiations. Preoccupied in part by the war in Vietnam, the Johnson administration ruled out the use of military force in this instance. This analogy was used most heavily by Cyrus Vance.

Son Tay *rescue*

An otherwise perfectly planned and executed military rescue mission which failed when the rescue team arrived to find that the hostages had been transported to another location. The raid was ordered by Richard Nixon, and involved a daring incursion behind enemy lines in North Vietnam. The analogy was used in 1980 in the military planning group, probably most of all by Stansfield Turner.

Tehran embassy mock raid

Periodically, the security of American embassies abroad is tested as a matter of routine. In 1974 a group of US Army Special Forces personnel conducted four mock raids on the American embassy in Tehran, and were successful on all four occasions. The analogy was probably used in the military planning group in 1980.

Mayaguez *rescue*

In May 1975 a US merchant ship called the SS *Mayaguez* was seized by Cambodia, evoking memories of the *Pueblo*. The crew were taken hostage but released just as a rescue team of US Marines arrived. Though a political success, the raid was hurriedly planned and led to more casualties than there were hostages. The analogy was used by David Jones at the outset of the hostage crisis in November 1979, by Jimmy Carter in 1980 and possibly by others.

Entebbe rescue

Probably the most famous – and most successful – military rescue mission of recent times. The rescue was conducted at Entebbe Airport in Uganda in July 1976 by Israeli forces, having been ordered by Yitzhak Rabin and the Israeli cabinet. The raid was planned over the course of a week, and the safe return of the hostages brought the government huge national and international acclaim. The analogy was used by Zbigniew Brzezinski over the course of the hostage crisis.

Mogadishu rescue

In October 1977 Palestinian terrorists hijacked a German Lufthansa plane bound for Frankfurt. Eventually the plane was diverted to Mogadishu in Somalia. Four days into the hostage crisis Germany's GSG-9 stormed the aircraft. The raid was even more successful than the Entebbe raid a year earlier, since none of the hostages were killed. The event had a major impact upon the development of America's own Delta Force, which initially trained to confront a Mogadishu-type situation.

USS Midway *incident*

In 1978 Jimmy Carter ordered an aircraft carrier to the Indian ocean, close to the coast of Iran, in the event that it might be needed if the shah of Iran (by then in the last months of his reign) fell from power. The move backfired, since when made public it suggested to Iranians and the rest of the world that the shah was indeed in deep trouble. The analogy was used by President Carter in 1979.

Perot rescue

A celebrated, though much questioned, small-scale rescue operation which took place in Iran in February 1979. Billionaire businessman Ross Perot ordered the rescue of his employees from an Iranian prison. They escaped when local Iranians, apparently paid by the rescue team to create a diversion, stormed the prison and released the employees. The analogy was used by Stansfield Turner and possibly others as well.

Valentine's Day ('Open House') incident

In February 1979 the American embassy in Tehran was seized for the first time that year, on this occasion by a radical Fedayeen group. The incident never developed into a full-scale crisis in the way the November seizure did, since in the former case the moderate government was still sufficiently strong to expel the invaders. Attempts by then Foreign Minister Ibrahim Yazdi to expel the students, which had worked the first time around, came to naught on the second occasion. The analogy was used – or at least implicit in the thinking of – practically all of Carter's foreign policy advisers.

Bibliography

Abelson, Robert, 'Script Processing in Attitude Formation and Decision-Making', in John Carroll and John Payne (eds.), *Cognition and Social Behavior* (Hillsdale, New Jersey: Lawrence Erlbaum, 1976).

Allison, Graham and Morton Halperin, 'Bureaucratic Politics: A Paradigm and Some Policy Implications', *World Politics*, 24: 40–79, 1972.

Allison, Graham and Philip Zelikow, *Essence of Decision: Explaining the Cuban Missile Crisis*, 2nd edn (New York: Longman, 1999).

Abernathy, Glen (ed.), *The Carter Years: The President and Policy Making* (London: Pinter, 1994).

Anderson, Paul, 'Justifications and Precedents as Constraints in Foreign Policy Decision-Making', *American Journal of Political Science*, 25: 738–61, 1981.

Armstrong, Scott, George Wilson and Bob Woodward, 'Debate Rekindles on Failed Iran Raid', *Washington Post*, 25 April 1982.

Art, Robert, 'Bureaucratic Politics and American Foreign Policy: A Critique', *Policy Sciences*, 4: 467–90, 1972.

Axelrod, Robert, 'Argumentation in Foreign Policy Settings: Britain in 1918, Munich in 1938 and Japan in 1970', *Journal of Conflict Resolution*, 21: 727–56, 1977.

Baars, Bernard, *The Cognitive Revolution in Psychology* (New York: Guilford Press, 1986).

Baker, James, *The Politics of Diplomacy: Revolution, War and Peace, 1989–1992* (New York: G. P. Putnam's, 1995).

Baldwin, David, 'Power Analysis and World Politics: New Trends Versus Old Tendencies', *World Politics*, 31: 161–94, 1979.

Ball, Desmond, 'The Blind Men and the Elephant: A Critique of Bureaucratic Politics', *Australian Outlook*, 28: 71–92, 1974.

Barber, James David, The *Presidential Character: Predicting Performance in the White House*, 3rd edn (Englewood Cliffs, New Jersey: Prentice Hall, 1985).

Barnet, Richard, 'The Failure of a Raid – and of a Policy', *Los Angeles Times*, 29 April 1980.

Bibliography

Beckwith, Charlie, and Donald Knox, *Delta Force* (London: Harcourt Brace Jovanovich, 1983).

Bendor, Jonathan and Thomas Hammond, 'Rethinking Allison's Models', *American Political Science Review*, 86: 301–22, 1992.

Beschloss, Michael (ed.), *Taking Charge: The Johnson White House Tapes, 1963–1964* (New York: Simon and Schuster, 1997).

Biddle, Bruce, *Role Theory: Expectations, Identities and Behaviors* (New York: Academic Press, 1979).

Bill, James, *The Eagle and the Lion: The Tragedy of American–Iranian Relations* (London: Yale University Press, 1988).

Bourne, Peter, *Jimmy Carter: A Comprehensive Biography from Plains to Post-Presidency* (New York: Scribner, 1997).

Brinkley, Douglas, *The Unfinished Presidency: Jimmy Carter's Journey Beyond the White House* (New York: Viking, 1998).

Brooks, Lloyd, 'Non-Analytic Concept Formation and Memory for Instances', in E. Rosch and B. Lloyd (eds.), *Cognition and Categorization* (Hillsdale, New Jersey: Lawrence Erlbaum, 1978).

'Decentralized Control of Categorization: The Role of Prior Processing Episodes', in U. Neisser (ed.), *Concepts and Conceptual Development* (New York: Cambridge University Press, 1987).

Brzezinski, Zbigniew, 'The Failed Mission: The Inside Account of the Attempt to Free the Hostages in Iran', *New York Times Magazine*, 18 April 1982.

Power and Principle: Memoirs of the National Security Adviser, 1977–1981 (New York: Farrar, Strauss and Giroux, 1983).

Buhite, Russell, *Lives at Risk: Hostages and Victims in American Foreign Policy* (Wilmington, Delaware: Scholarly Resources, 1995).

Caldwell, Dan, 'Bureaucratic Foreign Policy-Making', *American Behavioral Scientist*, 21: 87–110, 1977.

Carter, Jimmy, *Keeping Faith: Memoirs of a President* (Fayetteville, Arkansas: University of Arkansas Press, 1995).

Christopher, Warren, *In the Stream of History: Shaping Foreign Policy for a New Era* (Stanford, California: Stanford University Press, 1998).

Christopher, Warren *et al.*, *American Hostages in Iran: The Conduct of a Crisis* (New Haven, Connecticut: Yale University Press, 1985).

Clement, Catherine and Dedre Gentner, 'Systematicity as a Selection Constraint in Analogical Mapping', *Cognitive Science*, 15: 89–132, 1991.

Clifford, Clark, *Counsel to the President* (New York: Random House, 1991).

Cogan, Charles, 'Not to Offend: Observations on Iran, the Hostages and the Hostage Rescue Mission – Ten Years Later', *Comparative Strategy*, 9: 415–32, 1990.

Combs, Barbara and Paul Slovic, 'Causes of Death: Biased Newspaper Coverage and Biased Judgments', *Journalism Quarterly*, 56: 837–43, 1979.

Cottam, Richard, *Iran and the United States: A Cold War Case Study* (Pittsburgh, Pennsylvania: University of Pittsburgh Press, 1988).

D'Andrade, Roy, 'Cultural Cognition', in Michael Posner (ed.), *Foundations of Cognitive Science* (Cambridge, Massachusetts: MIT Press, 1989).

Daniszewski, John, 'Twenty Years After Hostages, Iran Reflects on Costs', *Los Angeles Times*, 4 November 1979.

'Twenty Years After Revolution, Iran Has Hope', *Los Angeles Times*, 11 February 1999.

Daugherty, William, 'A First Tour Like No Other', *Studies In Intelligence*, 41: 1–45, 1998.

Dawisha, Adeed, 'The Middle East', in Christopher Clapham (ed.), *Foreign Policy Making in Developing States: A Comparative Approach* (Farnborough: Saxon House, 1977).

Deaver, Michael, *Behind the Scenes* (New York: William Morrow, 1987).

Destler, I. M., 'National Security Management: What Presidents Have Wrought', *Political Science Quarterly*, 95: 573–88, 1980–1.

Destler, I. M., Leslie Gelb and Anthony Lake, *Our Own Worst Enemy: the Unmaking of American Foreign Policy* (New York: Simon & Schuster, 1984).

Dreistadt, Roy, 'The Use of Analogies and Incubation in Obtaining Insights in Creative Problem Solving', *Journal of Psychology*, 71: 159–75, 1969.

Dumbrell, John, *The Carter Presidency* (Manchester: Manchester University Press, 1995).

The Economist, 'Shrunken America', 3 May 1980.

The Economist, 'A Rescue That Worked', 19 May 1980.

Eisenhower, Dwight D., *The White House Years: Mandate for Change, 1953–1956* (London: Heinemann, 1963).

Elman, Colin, 'Horses for Courses: Why Not Neorealist Theories of Foreign Policy?', *Security Studies*, 6: 7–53, 1996.

Emerson, Steven, *Secret Warriors: Inside the Covert Military Operations of the Reagan Era* (New York: Putnam, 1988).

Eysenck, Michael and Mark Keane, *Cognitive Psychology: A Student's Handbook* (Hove: Lawrence Erlbaum, 1990).

Fallows, James, 'The Passionless Presidency', *The Atlantic Monthly*, 243: 33–48, May 1979.

Fiske, Susan and Shelley Taylor, *Social Cognition* (Reading, Massachusetts: Addison-Wesley, 1984).

Freedman, Lawrence, 'Logic, Politics and Foreign Policy Processes: A Critique of the Bureaucratic Politics Model', *International Affairs*, 52: 434–49, 1976.

Gabriel, Richard, *Military Incompetence: Why the American Military Doesn't Win* (New York: Hill and Wang, 1985).

Gartner, Scott, 'Predicting the Timing of Carter's Decision to Initiate a Hostage Rescue Attempt: Modelling a Dynamic Information Environment', *International Interactions* 18: 365–86, 1993.

Gasiorowski, Mark, 'The 1953 *Coup D'Etat* in Iran', *International Journal of Middle East Studies*, 19: 261–86, 1987.

Gazit, Shlomo, 'Risk, Glory and the Rescue Operation', *International Security*, 6: 111–35, 1981.

Bibliography

Gentner, Dedre, 'Structure Mapping: A Theoretical Framework for Analogy', *Cognitive Science*, 7: 155–70, 1983.

'The Mechanism of Analogical Learning', in Stella Vosniadou and Andrew Ortony (eds.), *Similarity and Analogical Reasoning* (Cambridge: Cambridge University Press, 1989).

Gentner, Dedre and Cecile Toupin, 'Systematicity and Surface Similarity in the Development of Analogy', *Cognitive Science*, 10: 277–300, 1986.

George, Alexander, 'The "Operational Code": A Neglected Approach to the Study of Political Leaders and Decision-Making', *International Studies Quarterly*, 23: 190–222, 1969.

'The Causal Nexus between Cognitive Beliefs and Decision-Making Behavior: The "Operational Code" Belief System', in Lawrence Falkowski (ed.), *Psychological Models and International Politics* (Epping: Bowker, 1979).

George, Alexander and Juliette George, *Woodrow Wilson and Colonel House: A Personality Study* (New York: Dover, 1964).

Gick, Mary and Keith Holyoak, 'Analogical Problem Solving', *Cognitive Psychology*, 12: 306–55, 1980.

'Schema Induction and Analogical Transfer', *Cognitive Psychology*, 115: 1–38, 1983.

Gilovich, Thomas, 'Seeing the Past in the Present: The Effect of Associations to Familiar Events on Judgements and Decisions', *Journal of Personality and Social Psychology*, 40: 797–808, 1981.

Gilpin, Robert, *War and Change in World Politics* (New York: Cambridge University Press, 1981).

Glad, Betty, *Jimmy Carter: In Search of the Great White House* (New York: W. W. Norton, 1980).

'Personality, Political and Group Process Variables in Foreign Policy Decision-Making: Jimmy Carter's Handling of the Iranian Hostage Crisis', *International Political Science Review* 10: 35–61, 1989.

Gleitman, Henry, *Psychology*, 4th edn (London: W. W. Norton, 1995).

Greenberg, Daniel, 'Mission Improbable', *Washington Post*, 29 April 1980.

Greenstein, Fred, 'The Impact of Personality on Politics: An Attempt to Clear Away the Underbrush', *American Political Science Review*, 61: 629–41, 1967.

Guthman, Edwin O. and Jeffrey Shulman (eds.), *Robert Kennedy: In His Own Words* (New York: Bantam Books, 1988).

Haas, Garland, *Jimmy Carter and the Politics of Frustration* (Jefferson, North Carolina: McFarland, 1992).

Hagan, Joe, 'Domestic Political Explanations in the Analysis of Foreign Policy, in Laura Neack, Jeanne Hey and Patrick Haney (eds.), *Foreign Policy Analysis: Continuity and Change in its Second Generation* (Englewood Cliffs, New Jersey: Prentice Hall, 1995).

Haig, Alexander, *Caveat: Realism, Reagan and Foreign Policy* (New York: Macmillan, 1984).

Halberstam, David, *The Best and the Brightest* (New York: Random House, 1969).

Halpern, Diane, Carol Hansen and David Riefer, 'Analogies as an Aid to

Understanding and Memory', *Journal of Educational Psychology*, 82: 298–305, 1990.

Hargrove, Erwin, *Jimmy Carter As President: Leadership and the Politics of the Public Good* (Baton Rouge, Louisiana: Louisiana State University Press, 1988).

Haskell, Robert, *Cognitive and Symbolic Structures: The Psychology of Metaphoric Transformation* (Norwood, New Jersey: Ablex, 1987).

Head, Richard, Frisco Short and Robert McFarlane, *Crisis Resolution: Presidential Decision Making in the Mayaguez and Korean Confrontations* (Boulder, Colorado: Westview Press, 1978).

Helman, David, *Analogical Reasoning: Perspectives on Artificial Intelligence, Cognitive Science and Philosophy* (Boston, Massachusetts: Kluwer Books, 1988).

Hemmer, Christopher, 'Historical Analogies and the Definition of Interests: The Iran Hostage Crisis and Ronald Reagan's Policy Toward the Hostages in Lebanon', *Political Psychology*, 20: 267–89, 1999.

Henderson, John, 'Leadership Personality and War: The Case of Richard Nixon and Anthony Eden', *Political Science*, 28: 141–64, 1976.

Hersh, Seymour, *The Price of Power: Kissinger in the Nixon White House* (New York: Summit Books, 1983).

Hitchens, Christopher, *No One Left To Lie To: The Triangulation of William Jefferson Clinton* (London: Verso, 1999).

Hollis, Martin and Steve Smith, 'Roles and Reasons in Foreign Policy Decision Making', *British Journal of Political Science* 16: 269–86, 1986.

Holsti, Ole, 'The Belief System and National Images: A Case Study', *Journal of Conflict Resolution*, 6: 244–52, 1962.

Holyoak, Keith, 'The Pragmatics of Analogical Transfer', in Gordon Bower (ed.), *The Psychology of Learning and Motivation, Vol. I* (New York: Academic Press, 1985).

Holyoak, Keith and Paul Thagard, 'Rule-Based Spreading Activation and Analogical Transfer', in Stella Vosniadou and Andrew Ortony (eds.), *Similarity and Analogical Reasoning* (Cambridge: Cambridge University Press, 1989).

Houghton, David Patrick, 'The Role of Analogical Reasoning in Foreign and Domestic Policy Contexts', unpublished Ph.D. dissertation, University of Pittsburgh, USA, 1996.

'The Role of Analogical Reasoning in Novel Foreign Policy Situations', *British Journal of Political Science*, 26: 523–52, 1996.

'Analogical Reasoning and Policymaking: Where and When Is It Used?', *Policy Sciences*, 31: 151–76, 1998.

'Historical Analogies and the Cognitive Dimension of Domestic Policymaking', *Political Psychology*, 19: 279–303, 1998.

Hoveyda, Fereydoun, *The Fall of the Shah* (London: Weidenfeld and Nicolson, 1980).

Hybel, Alex, *How Leaders Reason: US Intervention in the Caribbean Basin and Latin America* (Cambridge, Massachusetts: Basil Blackwell, 1990).

233

Bibliography

'Learning and Reasoning by Analogy', in Michael Fry (ed.), *History, the White House and the Kremlin: Statesmen as Historians* (New York: Pinter, 1991).

Indurkhya, Bipin, *Metaphor and Cognition* (Boston, Massachusetts: Kluwer Books, 1992).

Ioannides, Christos, 'The Hostages of Iran: A Discussion with the Militants', *Washington Quarterly*, 3: 12–35, 1980.

America's Iran: Injury and Catharsis (Lanham, Maryland: University Press of America, 1984).

Isaacson, Walter, *Kissinger: A Biography* (New York: Simon and Schuster, 1992).

Jane's Defence Weekly, 'The Impossible Mission of Credible Sport', 5 March 1997.

Janis, Irving, 'In Rescue Planning, How Did Carter Handle Stress?', *New York Times*, 18 May 1980.

Groupthink: Psychological Studies of Policy Decisions and Fiascos (London: Houghton Mifflin, 1982).

Crucial Decisions (New York: Free Press, 1989).

Jervis, Robert, *Perception and Misperception in International Politics* (Princeton, New Jersey: Princeton University Press, 1976).

'Political Implications of Loss Aversion', *Political Psychology*, 13: 187–204, 1992.

System Effects: Complexity in Social and Political Life (Princeton, New Jersey: Princeton University Press, 1997).

Johnson-Laird, P. N., 'Mental Models', in Michael Posner (ed.), *Foundations of Cognitive Science* (Cambridge, Massachusetts: MIT Press, 1989).

Jones, Charles, *The Trusteeship Presidency: Jimmy Carter and the United States Congress* (Baton Rouge, Louisiana: Louisiana State University Press, 1988).

Jordan, Hamilton, *Crisis: The Last Year of the Carter Presidency* (New York: Berkley, 1983).

Kahneman, Daniel and Amos Tversky, 'Prospect Theory: An Analysis of Decision Under Risk', *Econometrica*, 47: 263–91, 1979.

Kahneman, Daniel, Paul Slovic and Amos Tversky (eds.), *Judgment Under Uncertainty: Heuristics and Biases* (London: Cambridge University Press, 1982).

Keane, Mark, *Analogical Problem-Solving* (New York: Wiley, 1988).

Kegley, Charles, 'Is Access Influence? Measuring Adviser–Presidential Interactions in the Light of the Iranian Hostage Crisis', *International Interactions* 18: 343–64, 1993.

Kegley, Charles and Eugene Wittkopf, *American Foreign Policy: Pattern and Process* (New York: St. Martin's Press, 1996).

Keisling, Philip, 'The Wrong Man and the Wrong Plan', *The Washington Monthly*, December 1983.

Kennedy, Paul, *The Rise and Fall of the Great Powers* (New York: Random House, 1987).

Khong, Yuen Foong, 'The Lessons of Korea and the Vietnam Decisions of 1965', in George Breslauer and Philip Tetlock (eds.), *Learning in US and Soviet Foreign Policy* (Boulder, Colorado: Westview Press, 1991).

Analogies at War: Korea, Munich, Dien Bien Phu and the Vietnam Decisions of 1965 (Princeton, New Jersey: Princeton University Press, 1992).

'Vietnam, the Gulf, and US Choices: A Comparison', *Security Studies* 2: 74–95, 1992.

Kifner, John, 'Bitter Hatred – of the Shah and the US – Reunites Iran', *New York Times*, 18 November 1979.

Klunk, Brian, *Consensus and the American Mission* (Lanham, Massachusetts: University Press of America, 1986).

Korany, Bahgat, 'The Take-Off of Third World Studies? The Case of Foreign Policy', *World Politics*, 35: 464–87, 1983.

Krasner, Stephen, 'Are Bureaucracies Important? (Or Allison Wonderland)', *Foreign Policy*, 7: 159–79, 1972.

Kucharsky, David, *The Man From Plains* (London: Collins, 1977).

Laingen, Bruce, *Yellow Ribbon: The Secret Journal of Bruce Laingen* (Washington, DC: Brassey's, 1992).

Larson, David, 'The American Response to the Iranian Hostage Crisis: 444 Days of Decision', *International Social Science Review*, 57: 195–209, 1982.

Larson, Deborah Welch, *Origins of Containment: A Psychological Explanation* (Princeton, New Jersey: Princeton University Press, 1985).

Leary, David, 'William James and the Art of Human Understanding', *American Psychologist*, 47: 152–60, 1992.

Lebow, Richard Ned, 'Miscalculation in the South Atlantic: The Origins of the Falklands War', in Robert Jervis *et al.*, *Psychology and Deterrence* (London: Johns Hopkins University Press, 1985).

Ledeen, Michael and William Lewis, *Debacle: The American Failure in Iran* (New York: Alfred Knopf, 1981).

Levinson, Daniel, 'Role, Personality and Social Structure in the Organizational Setting', *Journal of Abnormal and Social Psychology*, 58: 170–80, 1959.

Levy, Jack, 'Prospect Theory and International Relations: Theoretical Applications and Analytical Problems', *Political Psychology*, 13: 283–310, 1992.

Los Angeles Times, 'US Patience Not Endless, Kissinger Says of Effort', 16 April 1980.

'Israel Blames Poor Planning for Iran Raid Failure', 27 April 1980.

'Bucher Compares Pueblo, Iran Plights', 8 May 1980.

Love, Kenneth, 'Shah Flees Iran After Move to Dismiss Mossadegh Fails', *New York Times*, 17 August 1953.

Luttwak, Edward, *The Pentagon and the Art of War: The Question of Military Reform* (New York: Simon and Schuster, 1984).

Macleod, Scott, 'Can Iran Be Forgiven?', *Time*, 3 August 1998.

'Radicals Reborn', *Time*, 15 November 1999.

McDermott, Rose, 'Prospect Theory in International Relations: The Iranian Hostage Rescue Mission', *Political Psychology*, 13: 237–63, 1992.

McFarlane, Robert, *Special Trust* (New York: Cadell and Davies, 1994).

McNamara, Robert, *In Retrospect: The Tragedy and Lessons of Vietnam* (New York: Times Books, 1995).

Maoz, Zeev, 'The Decision To Raid Entebbe: Decision Analysis Applied to Crisis Behavior', *Journal of Conflict Resolution*, 25: 677–707, 1981.

March, James G. and Z. Shapiro, 'Variable Risk Preferences and the Focus of Attention', *Psychological Review*, 99: 172–83, 1992.

Martin, David and John Walcott, *Best Laid Plans: The Inside Story of America's War Against Terrorism* (New York: Harper & Row, 1988).

May, Ernest, *Lessons of the Past* (New York: Oxford University Press, 1973).

May, Ernest and Philip Zelikow (eds.), *The Kennedy Tapes: Inside the White House During the Cuban Missile Crisis* (London: The Belknap Press, 1997).

Mefford, Dwain, 'Analogical Reasoning and the Definition of the Situation: Back to Snyder for Concepts and Forward to Artificial Intelligence for Method', in Charles Hermann, Charles Kegley and James Rosenau, *New Directions in the Study of Foreign Policy* (Boston, Massachusetts: Allen and Unwin, 1987).

'The Power of Historical Analogies: Soviet Interventions in Eastern Europe and US Interventions in Central America', in Michael Fry (ed.), *History, the White House and the Kremlin: Statesmen as Historians* (New York: Pinter, 1991).

Migdal, J. S., 'External Structure and Internal Behavior: Explaining Foreign Policies of Third World States', *International Relations*, 4: 510–26, 1974.

Moin, Baqer, *Khomeini: Life of the Ayatollah* (London: I. B. Tauris, 1999).

Morris, Dick, *Behind the Oval Office: Winning the Presidency in the Nineties* (New York: Random House, 1997).

Morris, Kenneth, *Jimmy Carter: American Moralist* (Athens, Georgia: University of Georgia Press, 1996).

Moses, Russell, *Freeing the Hostages: Re-Examining the US–Iranian Negotiations and Soviet Policy, 1979–1981* (Pittsburgh, Pennsylvania: University of Pittsburgh Press, 1985).

Nathan, James and James Oliver, 'Bureaucratic Politics: Academic Windfalls and Intellectual Pitfalls', *Journal of Political and Military Sociology*, 6: 81–91, 1978.

Naylor, James, Robert Pritchard and Daniel Ilgen, *A Theory of Behavior in Organizations* (New York: Academic Press, 1980).

Neustadt, Richard and Ernest May, *Thinking in Time: The Uses of History for Decision-Makers* (New York: Free Press, 1986).

Nisbett, Richard and Lee Ross, *Human Inference: Strategies and Shortcomings of Social Judgment* (Englewood Cliffs, New Jersey: Prentice Hall, 1980).

Nye, Joseph, 'The Analogy of National Decline: A Misleading Metaphor', *Current*, June 1990.

Ortony, Andrew, *Metaphor and Thought* (New York: Cambridge University Press, 1979).

Perlmutter, Amos, 'The Presidential Center and Foreign Policy: A Critique of the Revisionist and Bureaucratic Political Orientations', *World Politics*, 27: 87–106, 1974.

Peters, B. Guy, *American Public Policy: Promise and Performance* (Chatham, New Jersey: Chatham House, 1993).

Peterson, M. J., 'The Use of Analogies in Outer Space Law', *International Organization*, 51: 245–74, 1997.

Phillips, Kevin, *The Emerging Republican Majority* (New Rochelle, New York: Arlington House, 1969).

Powell, Colin with Joseph Persico, *My American Journey* (New York: Random House, 1995).

Powell, Jody, *The Other Side of The Story* (New York: William Morrow, 1984).

Quayle, Dan, *Standing Firm: A Vice Presidential Memoir* (New York: Harper-Collins, 1994).

Reber, Arthur, 'Transfer of Syntactic Structure in Synthetic Languages', *Journal of Experimental Psychology*, 81: 115–19, 1969.

'Implicit Learning and Tacit Knowledge', *Journal of Experimental Psychology*, 118: 219–35, 1989.

Reyes, R. M., W. C. Thompson and G. H. Bower, 'Judgmental Biases Resulting from Differing Availabilities of Arguments', *Journal of Personality and Social Psychology*, 39: 2–12, 1980.

Rhodes, Edward, 'Do Bureaucratic Politics Matter? Some Disconfirming Findings from the Case of the US Navy', *World Politics*, 47: 1–41, 1994.

Ribicoff, Abraham, 'Lessons and Conclusions', in Warren Christopher (ed.), *American Hostages in Iran* (New Haven, Connecticut: Yale University Press, 1985).

Ripley, Brian, 'Cognition in Context: Revitalizing Bureaucratic Politics in Foreign Policy Analysis', paper presented at the Annual Meeting of the American Political Science Association, Washington DC, September 1993.

'Culture, Cognition and Bureaucratic Politics', in Laura Neack, Jeanne Hey and Paul Kreisberg, *Foreign Policy Analysis: Continuity and Change in its Second Generation* (Englewood Cliffs, New Jersey: Prentice Hall, 1995).

Risen, James, 'Secrets of History: The CIA in Iran', *New York Times*, 16 April 2000.

Roosevelt, Kermit, *Countercoup: The Struggle for the Control of Iran* (New York: McGraw-Hill, 1979).

Rosati, Jerel, 'Developing a Systematic Decision-Making Framework', *World Politics*, 33: 234–51, 1981.

The Carter Administration's Quest for Global Community: Beliefs and their Impact on Behavior (Columbia, South Carolina: University of South Carolina Press, 1987).

Rosenau, James, 'Pre-Theories and Theories of Foreign Policy', in Rosenau, *The Scientific Study of Foreign Policy* (New York: Nichols, 1980).

'Private Preferences and Political Responsibilities: The Relative Potency of Individual and Role Variables in the Behavior of US Senators', in Rosenau, *The Scientific Study of Foreign Policy* (New York: Nichols, 1980).

Rosenbaum, Herbert and Alexej Ugrinsky (eds.), *Jimmy Carter: Foreign Policy and the Post-Presidential Years* (Westport, Connecticut: Greenwood Press, 1994).

Bibliography

The Presidency and Domestic Policies of Jimmy Carter (Westport, Connecticut: Greenwood Press, 1994).

Rubin, Barry, *Paved with Good Intentions: The American Experience and Iran* (New York: Penguin, 1981).

Rumelhart, David and A. A. Abrahamson, 'A Model for Analogical Reasoning', *Cognitive Psychology*, 5: 1–28, 1973.

Ryan, Paul, *The Iran Hostage Rescue Mission: Why It Failed* (Annapolis, Maryland: Naval Institute Press, 1985).

Sabatier, Paul, 'Knowledge, Policy-Oriented Learning, and Policy Change: An Advocacy Coalition Framework', *Knowledge*, 8: 649–92, 1987.

Salinger, Pierre, *America Held Hostage: The Secret Negotiations* (Garden City, New York: Doubleday, 1981).

Saunders, Harold, 'The Crisis Begins', in Warren Christopher (ed.), *American Hostages in Iran* (New Haven, Connecticut: Yale University Press, 1985).

Schelling, Thomas, *Arms and Influence* (New Haven, Connecticut: Yale University Press, 1966).

Schemmer, Benjamin, 'Presidential Courage – And the April 1980 Iranian Rescue Mission', *Armed Forces Journal International*, May 1981.

Schlesinger, Arthur, *Robert Kennedy and His Times* (Boston, Massachusetts: Houghton Mifflin, 1978).

Schlesinger, James, 'Some Lessons of Iran', *New York Times*, 6 May 1980.

Schneider, S. L., 'Framing and Conflict: Aspiration Level Contingency, the Status Quo and Current Theories of Risky Choice', *Journal of Experimental Psychology: Learning, Memory and Cognition*, 18: 1040–57, 1992.

Scott, Alexander, 'The Lessons of the Iranian Raid for American Military Policy', *Armed Forces Journal International*, June 1980.

Shafir, Eldar, 'Prospect Theory and Political Analysis: A Psychological Perspective', *Political Psychology*, 13: 311–22, 1992.

Sharp, Elaine B., *The Dilemma of Drug Policy in the United States* (New York: HarperCollins, 1994).

Shawcross, William, *The Shah's Last Ride* (London: Chatto and Windus, 1989).

Shultz, George, *Turmoil and Triumph: My Years as Secretary of State* (New York: Scribner's, 1993).

Sick, Gary, 'Military Options and Constraints', in Warren Christopher and Paul Kreisberg, *American Hostages in Iran: The Conduct of a Crisis* (New Haven, Connecticut: Yale University Press, 1985).

All Fall Down: America's Tragic Encounter With Iran (New York: Random House, 1985).

October Surprise: America's Hostages in Iran and the Election of Ronald Reagan (New York: Times Books/Random House 1991).

Simon, Herbert, 'The Information-Processing Theory of Human Problem Solving', in William Estes (ed.), *Handbook of Learning and Cognitive Processes*, vol. V (Hillsdale, New Jersey: Lawrence Erlbaum, 1978).

Skowronek, Stephen, *The Politics Presidents Make: Leadership from John Adams to Bill Clinton* (Cambridge, Massachusetts: Belknap Press, 1997).

Smelser, Neil, *Comparative Methods in the Social Sciences* (Englewood Cliffs, New Jersey: Prentice Hall, 1976).

Smith, Reginald Ross, 'A Comparative Case Analysis of Presidential Decision-Making: The *Pueblo*, the *Mayaguez* and the Iranian Hostage Crisis', unpublished MA dissertation, Emory University, Atlanta, 1984.

Smith, Steve, 'Allison and the Cuban Missile Crisis: A Review of the Bureaucratic Politics Model of Foreign Policy Decision-Making', *Millenium*, 9: 21–40, 1980.

'Policy Preferences and Bureaucratic Position: The Case of the American Hostage Rescue Mission', *International Affairs* 61: 9–25, 1984/85.

'Groupthink and the Hostage Rescue Mission', *British Journal of Political Science* 15: 117–23, 1985.

Smith, Terence, 'Putting the Hostages' Lives First', *New York Times Magazine*, 17 May 1981.

Smyth, Mary *et al.*, *Cognition in Action* (Hillsdale, New Jersey: Lawrence Erlbaum, 1994).

Snyder, Glenn and Paul Diesing, *Conflict Among Nations: Bargaining, Decision Making and System Structure in International Crises* (Princeton, New Jersey: Princeton University Press, 1977).

Sorensen, Theodore, *Kennedy* (New York: Harper and Row, 1965).

Spellman, Barbara and Keith Holyoak, 'If Saddam is Hitler then Who is George Bush? Analogical Mapping Between Systems of Social Roles', *Journal of Personality and Social Psychology*, 62: 913–33, 1992.

Spencer, Donald, *The Carter Implosion: Jimmy Carter and the Amateur Style of Diplomacy* (New York: Praeger, 1988).

Stein, Janice Gross and Raymond Tanter, *Rational Decision-Making: Israel's Security Choices, 1967* (Columbus, Ohio: Ohio University Press, 1980).

Stempel, John, *Inside the Iranian Revolution* (Bloomington, Indiana: University of Indiana Press, 1981).

Stevenson, William, *90 Minutes at Entebbe* (New York: Bantam, 1976).

Sullivan, William, *Mission to Iran* (New York: Morton, 1981).

Taheri, Amir, *Nest of Spies: America's Journey to Disaster in Iran* (London: Hutchison, 1988).

The Unknown Life of the Shah (London: Hutchison, 1991).

Taylor, Andrew and John Rourke, 'Historical Analogies in the Congressional Foreign Policy Process', *Journal of Politics*, 57: 460–68, 1995.

Taylor, Maxwell D., 'Analogies (II): Was Desert One Another Bay of Pigs?', *Washington Post*, 12 May 1980.

Tetlock, Philip, 'Psychological Research on Foreign Policy: A Methodological Overview', in Ladd Wheeler (ed.), *Review of Personality and Social Psychology*, vol. IV (Beverly Hills, California: Sage, 1983).

Tetlock, Philip, Randall Peterson, Charles McGuire, Shi-jie Chang and Peter Feld, 'Assessing Political Group Dynamics: A Test of the Groupthink Model', *Journal of Personality and Social Psychology*, 63: 403–25, 1992.

Bibliography

Thomas, Clarke, 'Pitt Professor Tells of Role in Hostage Talks', *Pittsburgh Post-Gazette*, 25 July 1984.

Torgerson, Dial, 'US Blundered in Iran Mission, Israeli Military Experts Claim', *Los Angeles Times*, 2 May 1980.

Turner, Stansfield, *Terrorism and Democracy* (Boston, Massachusetts: Houghton Mifflin, 1991).

Tversky, Amos and Daniel Kahneman, 'Judgment under Uncertainty: Heuristics and Biases', *Science*, 185: 1124–31, 1974.

Valliere, John, 'Disaster at Desert One: Catalyst for Change', *Parameters*, 22: 69–95, 1992.

Vance, Cyrus, *Hard Choices: Four Critical Years in Managing America's Foreign Policy* (New York: Simon and Schuster, 1983).

Vandenbroucke, Lucien, *Perilous Options: Special Operations as an Instrument of US Foreign Policy* (Oxford: Oxford University Press, 1993).

VanLehn, Kurt, 'Problem Solving and Cognitive Skill Acquisition', in Michael Posner (ed.), *Foundations of Cognitive Science* (Cambridge, Massachusetts: MIT Press, 1989).

VanLehn, Kurt and J. S. Brown, 'Planning Nets: A Representation for Formalizing Analogies and Semantic Models of Procedural Skills', in R. E. Snow *et al.* (eds.), *Aptitude, Learning and Instruction* (Hillsdale, New Jersey: Lawrence Erlbaum, 1980).

Vertzberger, Yaacov, 'Bureaucratic-Organizational Politics and Information Processing in a Developing State', *International Studies Quarterly*, 28: 69–95, 1984.

    The World in their Minds: Information Processing, Cognition and Perception in Foreign Policy Decisionmaking (Stanford, California: Stanford University Press, 1990).

Vosniadou, Stella and Andrew Ortony, *Similarity and Analogical Reasoning* (Cambridge: Cambridge University Press, 1989).

Voss, James and Ellen Dorsey, 'Perception and International Relations: An Overview', in Eric Singer and Valerie Hudson (eds.), *Political Psychology and Foreign Policy* (Boulder, Colorado: Westview Press, 1990).

Walker, Stephen, 'The Interface Between Beliefs and Behaviour: Henry Kissinger's Operational Code and the Vietnam War', *Journal of Conflict Resolution*, 21: 129–68, 1977.

Waltz, Kenneth, *Theory of International Politics* (Reading, Massachusetts: Addison-Wesley, 1979).

Weinberger, Caspar, *Fighting for Peace: Seven Critical Years in the Pentagon* (New York: Warner Books, 1990).

Weinstein, Franklin, 'The Uses of Foreign Policy in Indonesia: An Approach to the Analysis of Foreign Policy in the Less Developed Countries', *World Politics*, 24: 356–81, 1972.

Welch, David, 'The Organizational Process and Bureaucratic Politics Paradigms', *International Security*, 17: 112–46, 1992.

Wells, Tim, *444 Days: The Hostages Remember* (San Diego, California: Harcourt Brace, 1985).

Williams, Gary, 'Analogical Reasoning and Foreign Policy Decisionmaking: US Intervention in the Caribbean Basin with Particular Reference to Grenada 1983', unpublished dissertation, University of Hull, England, 1996.

Wilson, James Q., *American Government: Institutions and Policies*, 5th edn (Lexing-ton, Massachusetts: DC Heath, 1992).

Woodhouse, Christopher, *Something Ventured* (London: Granada, 1982).

Woodward, Bob, *Veil: The Secret Wars of the CIA 1981–1987* (New York: Simon and Schuster, 1987).

Woolsey, R. James, 'Sometimes the Long Shots Pay Off', *Washington Post*, 28 April 1980.

Zonis, Marvin, *Majestic Failure: The Fall of the Shah* (Chicago, Illinois: Chicago University Press, 1991).

Index

Aaron, David, 124, 224
Abelson, Robert, 194
Abdi, Abbas, 65, 224
 as student planner of US embassy
 seizure, 54
 reasons for seizing embassy, 64
Acheson, Dean, 164
'action indispensability', 73, 142
'actor indispensability', 73
Afghanistan, invasion of, 110
 effect on Iran hostage crisis, 169–70,
 171
'ahistorical' thinkers, 145–46
Allison, Graham, 47, 168, 179–80, 213
Amin, Idi, 82, 115
analogical reasoning,
 1953 coup in Iran and, 57–70
 'analogical explanation' model and, 18,
 147
 as bureaucratic 'weaponry', 158
 as a cognitive, *ex-ante* or diagnostic
 device, 22–3, 34, 159–65
 as an *ex-post* justification device, 32, 34,
 156–65
 as a form of cognitive bias, 23
 as a process, 25–8, 147–51
 as a theory of policy content, 190
 contemporary international conflicts
 and, 30
 domestic politics and, 36, 203–8
 electoral realignment theory and, 203
 Entebbe raid and, 82–7
 February 1979 embassy incident and,
 76–9
 inherent flaws within, 220–2
 limits of as a form of explanation, 155,
 200
 Mayaguez rescue operation and, 87–9

personal experience and, 18, 144, 146,
 157–62
persuasiveness of, 162–4, 202–8
political science literature on
 summarized, 31–5
prevalence in early stages of US
 decision-making, 155–6
provision of detailed explanation in,
 195
psychological literature on
 summarized, 24–31
relationship to belief systems, 158,
 193–6
relationship to schema theory, 26–28,
 194–5
structural and superficial similarity in,
 150, 222
US hegemony and, 203
wishful thinking and, 189
Angus Ward affair, 151, 219, 226
 cognitive availability of, 154
 described, 92–3
 doubts about the influence of as
 analogy, 99
 influence on Cyrus Vance, 91, 92–3,
 95–101
 influence on Jimmy Carter, 100–1
Arbenz, Jacobo, 33
Art, Robert, 184
Asgharzadeh, Ibrahim, 64, 65, 224
 admission of Shah to United States and,
 60–1
 as student planner of embassy seizure,
 54–5
attribution theory, 23, 144
availability heuristic, 17, 29–30, 33, 222–3
 1953 analogy and, 65–6
 US decision-making during the Iran

242

Index

CAMBRIDGE STUDIES IN INTERNATIONAL RELATIONS